The Easy Mediterranean Diet Cookbook

Easy Mediterranean Recipes for Beginners and Advanced Users

Marcie Janes

Table of Contents

Introduction

The **MEDITERRANEAN DIET** is an eating plan based on the traditional cuisines of different countries such as Turkey, Greece, Italy, Spain, France, and many more. The Mediterranean diet is one of the healthiest diets you can adopt. It is essentially a plant-based diet that consists of fruits, vegetables, legumes, nuts, whole grains, heart-healthy fats, cereals, seeds, spices, herbs, seafood, etc. Olive oil is the main ingredient in this diet. Fish, seafood, and poultry are included in moderate amounts.

The Mediterranean diet may promote weight loss and help prevent heart attacks, type-2 diabetes, strokes, and premature death. It also improves health and lowers the risk of chronic diseases. This diet encourages you to eat healthy food. It is quite a simple diet. It is incredibly easy to follow and suit your lifestyle.

The Mediterranean diet is magical because of its lack of restriction and abundance of healthy and delicious foods. It has endless health benefits, and it is a satisfying and rewarding diet. In this cookbook, you will get tasty and healthy Mediterranean diet recipes. These are rich in veggies, beans, legumes, olive oil, herbs, and spices, often seafood, fish, and chicken.

Principles of the Mediterranean Diet:

- Drink plenty of water
- Use olive oil in each dish
- Eat fish at least twice a week
- Eat a lot of fruits and vegetables
- Serve fresh fruit in dessert
- Do exercise

Eat well and stay healthy!

What Is Mediterranean Diet?

A Mediterranean diet is a type of diet that people in the region around the Mediterranean Sea eat. It consists of vegetables, fruits, whole grain, seeds, nuts, olive oil, spices, herbs, and legumes. You should use olive oil to make Mediterranean diet meals. This diet focused on only healthy foods. This diet is pretty easy-to-follow and straightforward because it has a lot of health benefits. However, it is essential to use olive oil to make recipes. The main drink included in this diet is water. It would be best if you drink plenty of water in this diet. You can consume healthy smoothies like avocado, strawberries, or mango smoothies – this is a good option for a break from the water.

Eight Main Steps to Getting Started With Mediterranean Diet

The Mediterranean is a super easy diet if you follow these steps:

Eat A Lot Of Veggies

In this diet, you should eat many veggies such as broccoli, asparagus, leeks, Brussels sprouts, pumpkins, green beans, green onions, chilies, cauliflower, zucchini, and many more. Make these dishes with olive oil.

Use Some Dairy Products

This diet does not restrict dairy products. You can eat Greek or plain yogurt in this diet. Try to use a small amount of cheeses.

Change Your Mind About Meat

You should eat a small amount of meat such as chicken and poultry, beef, and lamb.

Eat Fish Twice A Week

You can eat fish twice a week. Fish such as sardines, salmon, tuna, herring are good sources of omega-3 fatty acids. Seafood such as oysters, clams, and mussels are good for heart and brain health.

Use Healthy Fats

This diet focused on healthy fats such as nuts, peanuts, extra-virgin olive oil, avocados, olives, sunflower seeds, and almonds. It would be best if you ate these fats daily in your meal.

Cook Vegetarian Meal Two Nights Per Week

This diet promotes whole grains, legumes, beans, veggies, herbs, and spices. Try to make a veggie meal two nights per week. Make these meals with olive oil.

Use A Large Amount Of Whole Grain

Whole grains are rich in nutrients. It keeps you satisfied for many hours. It has a nutty and delicious taste. Cook Mediterranean grains such as barley, red, brown, black, or farro rice (made with whole-grain flour), and legumes!

For Dessert, Eat Fresh Fruits Only

Eat fresh fruits such as peach, pomegranate, grapes, oranges, kiwi, figs, apples, and dates instead of cookies, cakes, ice creams, and sweet treats. Choose fresh fruits only!

Health Benefits of Mediterranean Diet

There are many health benefits of the Mediterranean diet. Some of the following:

Protect against Asthma

In both Mediterranean and non-Mediterranean countries, scientist suggests the Mediterranean diet because this diet protects you from asthma.

Minimize Stroke in Women

The researcher has shown that the risk of stroke could be lower if people followed a Mediterranean diet. It is true especially in women.

Strong Heart Health

A study of 7000 people in Spain showed that the people who followed the Mediterranean diet were less likely to have a heart attack. The study proves that this diet is healthy. It lowers the risk of heart diseases. Most health professionals agree that the Mediterranean diet lowers the risk of heart diseases.

Lower Risk of Cancer Diseases and Diabetes

According to the study, the Mediterranean diet lowers the risk of cancer diseases.
As you know, the Mediterranean diet focuses on healthy foods only. Researchers compared a low-fat diet to a higher-fat Mediterranean diet and found that diabetes rates were lower in people who followed the Mediterranean diet.

Lower LDL Cholesterol Level

The Mediterranean diet lowers the risk of heart diseases because people eating this way have a lower level of LDL blood cholesterol. LDLs are bad cholesterol, which is more apt to build up deposits in arteries. The researcher reviewed 40 diets in 2018 in the US. The experts high-ranked the Mediterranean diet as the best diet overall.

Lower Blood Pressure

Healthy fats are present in the Mediterranean diet. It is the main key to lowering blood pressure. Healthy fats are present in olive oil, nuts, and omega-3 fats are found in fish.

Good for Cognition

Health experts say that the Mediterranean diet can protect against brain health problems. It also lowers the risk of cognitive diseases.

Reduce Inflammation

Omega-3 fatty acids have decreased inflammation and many other diseases such as joint pain, cardiovascular disease, digestive disorders, etc. The Mediterranean diet is full of omega-3 fatty acids such as chia seeds, walnuts, salmon, tuna, etc. The researcher found that eating this type of food improves cholesterol levels; decrease the risk of diabetes, control weight loss and multiple types of cancer.

What Foods Are Allowed On Mediterranean Diet?

Fresh Fruits and Vegetables

Fresh vegetables such as tomatoes, broccoli, turnips, kale, cauliflower, sweet potatoes, potatoes, cucumber, yellow squash, Brussels sprouts, carrot, onions, spinach, asparagus, green beans, etc. The plant consists of essential phytonutrients that ward off diseases and insects. When we eat plants, these phytonutrients can help us ward off different diseases. Fresh fruits such as peaches, grapes, melons, dates, figs, strawberries, blueberries, oranges, pears, apples, bananas, etc., are fiber-rich and lower the risk of chronic diseases. There are a lot of nutrients present in fresh vegetables and fruits, such as fiber, vitamins, carbohydrates, and it can help reduce the risk of cancer and cardiovascular diseases.

Nuts and Seeds

Nuts and seeds such as almonds, almond butter, peanut butter, sunflower seeds, hazelnuts, macadamia, walnuts, cashews, pumpkin seeds, pistachios, etc. Nuts and seeds contain protein, monounsaturated, and polyunsaturated fats, and these healthy fats can decrease the risk of different diseases. Also, nuts and seeds have fiber, protein, phytonutrients, etc.

Beans, Legumes, and Whole Grains

Legumes such as beans, peas, lentils, pulses, chickpeas, and peanuts are used in the Mediterranean diet. These are rich in vitamin B, fiber, and protein. Whole grains such as pasta, oats, whole wheat bread, buckwheat, corn, barley, rye, and brown rice may lower the risk of many diseases.

Olives and Olive Oil
Olive oil is a main ingredient in the Mediterranean diet. Following the Mediterranean diet means eating olives and olive oil daily. Olives are rich in heart-healthy monounsaturated fatty acids and antioxidants. Moreover, olive fruit contains a healthy amount of iron and fiber.

Herbs and Spices
Herbs and spices such as garlic, sage, parsley, chives, rosemary, nutmeg, pepper, cinnamon, mint, and basil consist of powerful phytonutrients. It gives unique flavor in the Mediterranean diet recipes. Using herbs and spices increases the nutrition, color, and fresh flavors in the meals.

Oily Fish and Seafood
Seafood such as salmon, sardine, tuna, trout, mackerel, clams, oyster, crab, mussels, herring, etc., is rich in omega-3 fat nutrients. These are important for good health. Eat fish twice a week. It is essential during pregnancy and helps children develop healthy brains and eyes. It improves memory in adults.

Poultry, Egg, Cheese, and Yogurt
According to a Mediterranean diet, you should eat chicken in significantly fewer amounts. Poultry is consumed in smaller portions than seafood. Eggs are rich in protein, immune-strengthening vitamin D, and brain-boosting choline. Yogurt and cheese contain calcium and potassium, good for bone health.

Red Meat
You should eat red meat in very less amount. You can eat it on special occasions.

What Foods Should Be Limited On Mediterranean Diet?

However, there are several foods that you should avoid when consuming Mediterranean diet meals.

Butter

Butter should be avoided if you are following the Mediterranean diet. You should use olive oil and avocado oil, which have a lot of heart-healthy nutrients.

Processed Meat

Processed meat such as bacon and the hot dog should be avoided if you follow the Mediterranean diet. According to the study, consuming a large amount of processed meat increases mortality risk.

Refined Grains

Whole grains, including millet, farro, couscous, and brown rice, are staples in the Mediterranean diet. Refined grains such as white pasta and white bread should be avoided if you follow the Mediterranean diet.

Alcohol

Wine should be avoided if you are following the Mediterranean diet. It is necessary to avoid alcohol.

Added Sugar

You should avoid candies, cookies, ice creams, table sugar, syrup, soda, and baked goods following the Mediterranean diet.

Refined Oils

Refined oils such as canola oil, soybean oil, grapeseed oil, and cottonseed oil should be avoided following the Mediterranean diet.

Trans Fat

Trans fat is present in fried foods, and margarine should be avoided.

Refined Grains

Refined grains such as tortillas, crackers, chips, white bread, and white pasta should be avoided following the Mediterranean diet.

Common Foods and Flavors of Mediterranean Diet

Vegetables and Tubers

Zucchini, turnips, Sweet potatoes, spinach, shallots, scallions, rutabaga, radishes, purslane, potatoes, peppers, peas, onion, okra, nettles, mustard greens, mushrooms, mache, lettuce, leeks, kale, fennel, eggplant, dandelion greens, collard, cucumber, chicory, celeriac, celery, cabbage, carrots, Brussels sprouts, beets, broccoli, artichoke, and arugula

Fruits

Tomatoes, tangerines, strawberries, pumpkin, pears, olives, pomegranate, oranges, peaches, nectarines, melons, lemons, grapes, grapefruit, dates, figs, clementines, cherries, apricots, avocados, and apples

Grain

Wheat berries, rice, polenta, oats, millets, freekeh, farro, durum, couscous, bulgur, buckwheat, barley, breads

Poultry and Eggs

Quail eggs, chicken eggs, duck eggs, chicken, duck, guinea fowl, quail

Sweets

Treats made with fruits, nuts, whole grains, minimal sugars, biscotti, baklava, chocolate, gelato, crème caramel, mousse, kunefe, and sorbet

Fish and Seafood

Yellow tail, whelk, tuna, tilapia, squid, shrimp, sea bass, sardines, salmons, oyster, octopus, mussels, mackerels, lobster, flounder, crab, eel, clams, cockles, and abalone

Legumes, Nuts, and Seeds

Walnuts, split peas, tahini, sesame seeds, pistachios, pine nuts, lentils, hazelnuts, cashews, green kidney beans, fava, chickpeas, cannellini, beans, and almonds

Herbs and Spices

Za'atar, thyme, tarragon, sumac, savory, sage, rosemary, Aleppo pepper, pepper, oregano, parsley, mint, marjoram, lanvender, garlic, fennel, cumin, cloves, chilies, bay leaf, basil, and star anise

Cheese and Yogurt

Greek yogurt, ricotta, pecorino, Parmigiano-reggiano, manchego, halloumi, feta, corvo, chevre, and brie

Meats

Pork, mutton, lamb, beef, goat

Avocado Toast

Prep Time: 10 Minutes
Cook Time: 0 Minutes
Serves: 2
Ingredients:
- 1 tablespoon goat's cheese, crumbled
- 1 avocado, peeled, pitted, and mashed
- A pinch of salt and black pepper
- 2 whole-wheat bread slices, toasted
- ½ teaspoon lime juice
- 1 persimmon, thinly sliced
- 1 fennel bulb, thinly sliced
- 2 teaspoons honey
- 2 tablespoons pomegranate seeds

Preparation:
1. Combine the avocado flesh with salt, pepper, lime juice, and the cheese and whisk in a bowl.
2. Spread this mixture onto toasted bread slices, top each slice with the remaining ingredients and serve for breakfast.
Serving Suggestion: Serve with scrambled eggs.
Variation Tip: Choose perfectly ripe avocados; unripe avocados become hard to mash and aren't flavorful.
Nutritional Information per Serving:
Calories 348 | Fat 20.8g | Sodium 249mg | Carbs 38.7g | Fiber 12.3g | Sugar 37.4g | Protein 7.1g

Strawberry Smoothie Bowl

Prep Time: 10 minutes
Serves: 2
Ingredients:

- 1 banana, peeled and cut into chunks
- 2 cups frozen strawberries
- ⅓ cup whey protein powder
- 2 cups unsweetened almond milk
- 2 tablespoons organic acai powder

Preparation:
1. Place all the ingredients in a high-speed blender and pulse until well combined.
2. Transfer the mixture into two serving bowls.
Serving Suggestion: Top it with granola, chia seeds, and banana slices before serving.
Variation Tip: Cinnamon can be replaced with cardamom.
Nutritional Information per Serving:
Calories: 693 | Fat: 59.2g | Sat Fat: 52g | Carbohydrates: 41.4g | Fiber: 9.8g | Sugar: 24.3g | Protein: 9.8g

Blueberry Pancakes

Prep Time: 10 Minutes
Cook Time: 15 Minutes
Serves: 6
Ingredients:
- 15 ounces blueberries
- ¼ teaspoon salt
- 3 tablespoons oil
- 3 eggs
- 1 teaspoon vanilla extract
- ⅔ cup sugar
- 1 cup milk
- ½ teaspoon baking powder
- 1½ cups unbleached all-purpose flour

Preparation:
1. In a bowl, mix the flour, salt, baking powder, and sugar.
2. In another bowl, beat the eggs and milk.
3. Add the milk and egg mixture into the flour mixture. Mix it and fold in the blueberries. Set the mixture aside for one hour.
4. Heat a pan over medium-high heat.
5. Pour enough batter onto the griddle for one pancake. Cook on both sides.
6. Repeat until all the batter is used.
Serving Suggestion: Top with some blueberries.
Variation Tip: For a better taste, use aluminum-free baking powder.
Nutritional Information per Serving:
Calories 301 | Fat 13.9g | Sodium 140mg | Carbs 16g | Fiber 1.4g | Sugar 36.8g | Protein 3g

Almond Chia Porridge

Prep Time: 10 Minutes
Cook Time: 30 Minutes
Serves: 4
Ingredients:
• 3 cups organic almond milk
• ⅓ cup chia seeds, dried
• 1 teaspoon vanilla extract
• 1 tablespoon honey
• ¼ teaspoon ground cardamom
Preparation:
1. Pour the almond milk into a saucepan and bring it to a boil.
2. Remove from the heat and chill the almond milk to room temperature for 15 minutes.
3. Add the vanilla extract, honey, and ground cardamom. Stir well.
4. Add chia seeds and stir again.
5. Close the lid and let the chia seeds soak in the liquid for 20–25 minutes.
6. Transfer the cooked porridge into serving ramekins.
Serving Suggestion: Serve with fresh raspberries.
Variation Tip: Stir the chia seeds well to avoid lumps from forming.
Nutritional Information per Serving:
Calories 444 | Fat 43.6g | Sodium 28mg | Carbs 15.4g | Fiber 4.7g | Sugar 10.5g | Protein 4.5g

Avocado Milkshake

Prep Time: 5 Minutes
Cook Time: 0 Minutes
Serves: 3
Ingredients:
• 1 avocado, peeled and pitted
• 2 tablespoons liquid honey
• ½ teaspoon vanilla extract
• ½ cup heavy cream
• 1 cup milk
• ⅓ cup ice cubes

Preparation:
1. Chop the avocado and put it in a food processor.
2. Add the liquid honey, vanilla extract, heavy cream, milk, and ice cubes.
3. Blend the mixture until smooth.
4. Pour the milkshake into tall serving glasses.
Serving Suggestion: Serve with pancakes or waffles.
Variation Tip: Use almond or coconut milk for a vegan milkshake.
Nutritional Information per Serving:
Calories 291 | Fat 22.1g | Sodium 51mg | Carbs 22g | Fiber 4.5g | Sugar 15.6g | Protein 4.4g

Couscous with Dried Fruit

Prep Time: 15 minutes
Cook Time: 13 minutes
Serves: 4
Ingredients:
• 1 cup uncooked whole-wheat couscous
• 3 cups low-fat milk
• ¼ cup dried currants
• 6 teaspoons dark brown sugar, divided
• Salt, to taste
• ⅓ cup dried apricots, chopped
• ¼ teaspoon ground cinnamon
• 2 teaspoons unsalted butter, melted
Preparation:
1. In a saucepan placed over medium-high heat, add the milk and cook for about 3 minutes or until heated through.
2. Remove from the heat and immediately stir in the couscous, 4 teaspoons of brown sugar, the dried fruit, salt, and cinnamon.
3. Cover the saucepan and set it aside for about 10 minutes.
4. Divide the couscous mixture evenly between four bowls.
5. Top each with the remaining brown sugar and melted butter evenly.
6. Serve immediately.
Serving Suggestion: Serve with some toasted almonds on the top.
Variation Tip: Nutmeg can also be added.
Nutritional Information per Serving:
Calories: 284 | Fat: 4.1g | Sat Fat: 2.4g | Carbohydrates: 49.5g | Fiber: 2.8g | Sugar: 15.6g | Protein: 12g

Yogurt Bowl with Caramelized Figs

Prep Time: 10 minutes
Cook Time: 7 minutes
Serves: 4
Ingredients:
- 8 ounces fresh figs, halved
- 3 tablespoons honey, divided
- 2 cups plain Greek yogurt
- Pinch of ground cinnamon
- ¼ cup pistachios, chopped

Preparation:
1. In a preheated skillet over medium heat, add 1 tablespoon of the honey and cook for about 2 minutes.
2. In the skillet, place the figs, cut sides down, and cook for about 5 minutes or until caramelized.
3. Remove from the heat and set aside for about 2–3 minutes.
4. Divide the yogurt into serving bowls and top each with the caramelized fig halves.
5. Sprinkle with the pistachios and cinnamon.
6. Drizzle each bowl with the remaining honey and serve.

Serving Suggestion: Serve with blueberries on top.
Variation Tip: You can add some orange zest.
Nutritional Information per Serving:
Calories: 276 | Fat: 2.3g | Sat Fat: 0.3g | Carbohydrates: 53.6g | Fiber: 6g | Sugar: 43.7g | Protein: 14.7g

Overnight Oatmeal with Figs

Prep Time: 10 minutes (plus overnight for chilling)
Serves: 2
Ingredients:
- 2 tablespoons almonds, chopped
- ½ cup quick oats
- 1 tablespoon chia seeds
- 1 tablespoon honey
- 1 cup unsweetened soy milk
- 2–3 fresh figs, sliced

Preparation:
1. In a large bowl, mix the oats, soy milk, almonds, and chia seeds until well combined.
2. Cover the bowl and refrigerate overnight.
3. Divide the oatmeal into serving bowls evenly and drizzle with the honey.
4. Serve with the topping of fig slices.
Serving Suggestion: Serve with a topping of crushed walnuts.
Variation Tip: You can use almond milk instead of soy milk.
Nutritional Information per Serving:
Calories: 298 | Fat: 7.8g | Sat Fat: 0.9g | Carbohydrates: 51.1g | Fiber: 7.6g | Sugar: 27.6g | Protein: 9.5g

Potato Hash

Prep Time: 10 Minutes
Cook Time: 15 Minutes
Serves: 4
Ingredients:
- A drizzle of olive oil
- 2 Yukon Gold potatoes, cubed
- 2 garlic cloves, minced
- 1 yellow onion, chopped
- 1 cup canned chickpeas, drained
- Salt and black pepper, to taste
- 1½ teaspoons ground allspice
- 1 pound baby asparagus, trimmed and chopped
- 1 teaspoon sweet paprika
- 1 teaspoon dried oregano
- 1 teaspoon dried cilantro
- 2 tomatoes, cubed
- 1 cup fresh parsley, chopped
- ½ cup feta cheese, crumbled

Preparation:
1. Heat a pan with a drizzle of oil over medium-high heat, add the potatoes, onion, garlic, salt, and pepper and cook for 7 minutes.
2. Add the rest of the ingredients except the tomatoes, parsley, and cheese. Toss together and then cook for seven more minutes. Transfer to a bowl.
3. Add the remaining ingredients, toss and serve for breakfast.

Serving Suggestion: Serve with a dollop of sour cream.
Variation Tip: Add cayenne pepper for a spicier flavor.
Nutritional Information per Serving:
Calories 535 | Fat 20.8g | Sodium 337mg | Carbs 34.5g | Fiber 6.6g | Sugar 13.5g | Protein 26.6g

Tahini Banana Breakfast Shake

Prep Time: 5 Minutes
Cook Time: 0 Minutes
Serves: 3
Ingredients:
- ¼ cup ice, crushed
- 1½ cup almond milk
- ¼ cup tahini
- 4 Medjool dates
- 2 bananas, sliced
- A pinch of ground cinnamon

Preparation:
1. Blend all the ingredients in the blender to obtain a creamy and smooth mixture.
2. Pour the mixture into cups and serve.
Serving Suggestion: Serve with a dash of cinnamon sprinkled over the top.
Variation Tip: Use 2 tablespoons of lime juice to change up the flavor.
Nutritional Information per Serving:
Calories 469 | Fat 39.6g | Sodium 42mg | Carbs 29.9g | Fiber 6.7g | Sugar 14.6g | Protein 5.7g

Tomato Omelet

Prep Time: 10 minutes
Cook Time: 5 minutes
Serves: 2
Ingredients:
- ¼ cup water
- 4 large eggs
- Salt and black pepper, to taste
- ¼ cup goat's cheese, crumbled
- 1 scallion, chopped
- 1 tablespoon olive oil
- ¼ cup tomato, chopped

Preparation:
1. Put the eggs, water, salt, and black pepper in a small bowl, and beat well.
2. Heat the olive oil over medium-high heat in a non-stick skillet until melted.
3. Whisk in the egg mixture and cook for about 2 minutes.
4. Carefully flip the omelet and cook for another 2 minutes or until completely set.
5. Place the cheese, scallions, and tomato over one side of the omelet.
6. Carefully fold the omelet in half and remove it from the heat.
7. Cut into two equal-sized portions and serve.
Serving Suggestion: Serve with toasted whole-wheat bread slices.
Variation Tip: Goat's cheese can be replaced with feta cheese.
Nutritional Information per Serving:
Calories: 216 | Fat: 17g | Sat Fat: 7.6g | Carbohydrates: 2.3g | Fiber: 0.5g | Sugar: 1.6g | Protein: 14.1g

Raspberry Oats

Prep Time: 10 minutes
Cook Time: 5 minutes
Serves: 1
Ingredients:
- ½ cup fresh raspberries
- ¼ teaspoon vanilla
- ¾ cup unsweetened almond milk
- 1 teaspoon honey
- 2 teaspoon chia seeds
- ⅓ cup rolled oats
- Pinch of salt

Directions:
1. Add raspberries into the bowl and mash using the fork.
2. Transfer mash raspberries and remaining ingredients into the glass jar and stir everything well.
3. Cover jar with lid and place in refrigerator for overnight.
Serving Suggestion: Add little drizzle of milk and serve.
Variation Tip: Add one to two drops of almond extracts.
Nutritional Information per Serving:
Calories 289 | Fat 11.1g | Sodium 296mg | Carbs 41.8g | Fiber 14.2g | Sugar 8.9g | Protein 8.5g

Eggs with Avocado

Prep Time: 20 minutes
Cook Time: 25 minutes
Serves: 6
Ingredients:
- Olive oil cooking spray
- 1 large avocado, peeled, halved, and pitted
- 3 tablespoons feta cheese, crumbled
- Salt and black pepper, to taste
- 4 eggs, at room temperature

Preparation:
1. Preheat the oven to 400°F.
2. Place two gratin dishes onto a baking pan. Transfer to the oven to heat up for about 10 minutes.
3. Cut each avocado half into 6 slices.
4. Take the dishes out of the oven and grease with the cooking spray.
5. Arrange the avocado slices in each dish and carefully crack two eggs in each dish.
6. Sprinkle with the feta cheese, salt, and black pepper.
7. Bake for 15 minutes until the eggs are cooked to the desired doneness.
8. Take out from the oven and serve hot.

Serving Suggestion: Serve alongside hot coffee or tea.
Variation Tip: You can replace the feta with cottage cheese.
Nutritional Information per Serving:
Calories: 123 | Fat: 10.5g | Sat Fat: 3g | Carbohydrates: 3.3g | Fiber: 2.3g | Sugar: 0.6g | Protein: 5g

Breakfast Quinoa

Prep Time: 10 minutes

Cook Time: 16 minutes
Serves: 4
Ingredients:
- 1 cup quinoa, rinsed
- ½ teaspoon nutmeg
- 1 teaspoon cinnamon
- ⅓ cup flax seeds
- ½ cup slivered almonds
- ½ cup dried apricots, chopped
- 2 cups water

Directions:
1. Add quinoa and water in a saucepan and bring to boil over medium heat.
2. Turn heat to low and simmer for 8-12 minutes or until liquid is absorbed.
3. Stir in nutmeg, cinnamon, flax seeds, almonds and apricots and cook for 2-3 minutes.

Serving Suggestion: Drizzle with little milk and serve.
Variation Tip: If sweetness is desired, add splash of honey.
Nutritional Information per Serving:
Calories 287 | Fat 11.7g | Sodium 9mg | Carbs 35.2g | Fiber 7.8g | Sugar 2.5g | Protein 10.5g

Egg Breakfast Bowl

Prep Time: 10 minutes
Cook Time: 5 minutes
Serves: 1
Ingredients:
- 2 eggs
- 1 teaspoon olive oil
- ½ bell pepper, chopped
- ½ scallion, chopped
- ¼ cup Feta cheese, crumbled
- ¼ cup olives, pitted
- Pepper
- Salt

Directions:
1. In a bowl, whisk eggs with pepper and salt. Add olives, scallion, bell pepper and cheese and stir well.
2. Heat oil in a pan over medium-high heat.
3. Add egg mixture to the pan and let it cook for 2 minutes, then start scrambling the egg mixture.
4. Stir for 3 minutes more.

Serving Suggestion: Garnish with parsley and serve.
Variation Tip: You can also use goat cheese instead of feta cheese.
Nutritional Information per Serving:
Calories 325 | Fat 25.2g | Sodium 992mg | Carbs 9.4g | Fiber 2.1g | Sugar 5.4g | Protein 17.4g

Vegetable Egg Cups

Prep Time: 10 minutes
Cook Time: 20 minutes
Serves: 12
Ingredients:
- 6 eggs
- 2.7 ounces goat cheese, crumbled
- 1 ½ cups spinach, sliced
- 1 red bell pepper, chopped
- ¼ cup unsweetened almond milk
- Salt

Directions:
1. Preheat the oven to 350° F.
2. In a bowl, whisk eggs with milk.
3. Add remaining ingredients and stir well.
4. Pour egg mixture into the greased muffin pan and bake in preheated oven for 20 minutes.
Serving Suggestion: Allow to cool completely then serve.
Variation Tip: You can also use coconut milk.
Nutritional Information per Serving:
Calories 76 | Fat 5.7g | Sodium 68mg | Carbs 1.5g | Fiber 0.3g | Sugar 1g | Protein 5g

Yogurt and Date Smoothie

Prep Time: 10 minutes
Serves: 2
Ingredients:
- 1 cup plain Greek yogurt
- 4 Medjool dates, pitted and chopped roughly
- 2 tablespoons almond butter

- 1 cup ice cubes, crushed
- 1 cup fresh apple juice
Preparation:
1. Place all the ingredients in a blender and pulse until smooth and creamy.
2. Transfer the smoothie into two serving glasses and serve immediately.
Serving Suggestion: Top with berries before serving.
Variation Tip: Almond butter can be replaced with cashew butter.
Nutritional Information per Serving:
Calories: 364 | Fat: 9.2g | Sat Fat: 0.8g | Carbohydrates: 62.5g | Fiber: 5.9g | Sugar: 52.2g | Protein: 14.5g

Mushroom and Spinach Omelets

Prep Time: 10 Minutes
Cook Time: 15 Minutes
Serves: 2
Ingredients:
- 1 egg
- 1 cup spinach
- 1 tablespoon parmesan cheese, shredded
- 3 egg whites
- 1 tablespoon cheddar cheese, grated
- ⅛ teaspoon red pepper flakes
- ¼ teaspoon salt
- ⅛ teaspoon garlic powder
- ⅛ teaspoon black pepper
- ⅛ teaspoon nutmeg
- ½ teaspoon olive oil
- ¼ cup green onion, sliced
- ½ cup mushrooms, sliced
- 2 tablespoons red bell pepper, sliced
- ½ cup tomato, sliced
Preparation:
1. Beat the egg and egg whites in a bowl. Mix in the cheeses, salt, red pepper flakes, garlic, nutmeg, and black pepper.
2. Heat the oil in a skillet. Add the mushrooms, onion, and bell pepper. Stir and cook for 5 minutes.
3. Add the spinach to the skillet and cook until it wilts.
4. Add the egg mixture and tomatoes to the skillet and keep cooking until it sets on top.
5. Once done, cut into pieces, and serve immediately.
Serving Suggestion: Serve with some sliced tomatoes.
Variation Tip: Add cayenne or smoked paprika for a spicier taste.
Nutritional Information per Serving:
Calories 114.4 | Fat 5.1g | Sodium 88mg | Carbs 5.7g | Fiber 1.8g | Sugar 10.1g | Protein 12.5g

Delicious Cauliflower Soup

Prep Time: 10 minutes
Cook Time: 4 hours
Serves: 4
Ingredients:
- 6 cups cauliflower florets
- ¼ teaspoon mustard powder
- 3 cups vegetable stock
- 1 teaspoon garlic, minced
- 4 ounces Mascarpone cheese
- 1 ½ cup Cheddar cheese, shredded
- Pepper
- Salt

Directions:
1. Add cauliflower, mustard powder, stock, and garlic into the slow cooker and stir well.
2. Cover and cook on low for 4 hours.
3. Stir in Mascarpone cheese and Cheddar cheese.
4. Puree the soup using a blender until smooth. Season with pepper and salt.
Serving Suggestion: Garnish with parsley and serve.
Variation Tip: Add your choice of seasonings.
Nutritional Information per Serving:
Calories 96 | Fat 6.6g | Sodium 150mg | Carbs 3.8g | Fiber 1.5g | Sugar 1.6g | Protein 6.2g

Apple Oat Breakfast Cake

Prep Time: 10 minutes
Cook Time: 25 minutes
Serves: 8
Ingredients:
- 2 eggs
- 1 apple, peeled & chopped
- 1 cup oats
- 1 tablespoon olive oil
- 3 tablespoons yogurt
- ½ teaspoon baking powder
- ½ teaspoon baking soda
- 1 teaspoon cinnamon
- 1 teaspoon vanilla
- 3 tablespoons honey

Directions:
1. Preheat the oven to 350° F.
2. Add ¾ cup oats and remaining ingredients into the blender and blend until smooth.
3. Add remaining oats and stir well. Pour batter into the parchment-lined baking pan.
4. Bake in preheated oven for 20-30 minutes.
Serving Suggestion: Allow to cool completely then slice and serve.
Variation Tip: Add melted coconut oil instead of olive oil.
Nutritional Information per Serving:
Calories 115 | Fat 3.6g | Sodium 100mg | Carbs 18.2g | Fiber 1.9g | Sugar 10g | Protein 3.2g

Salsa Chicken Soup

Prep Time: 10 minutes
Cook Time: 25 minutes
Serves: 6
Ingredients:
- 1 pound chicken breasts, boneless and cut into chunks
- 1 ½ cups salsa
- 1 teaspoon Italian seasoning
- 2 tablespoons fresh parsley, chopped
- 3 cups chicken stock
- 8 ounces cream cheese
- Pepper
- Salt

Directions:
1. Add all ingredients except parsley and cream cheese into the instant pot and stir well.
2. Cover and cook on high pressure for 25 minutes.
3. Once done, release pressure manually. Remove lid.
4. Remove chicken from pot and shred using a fork.
5. Return shredded chicken to the pot along with cream cheese and stir well.
6. Cook on sauté mode until cheese is melted.
Serving Suggestion: Garnish with parsley and serve.
Variation Tip: Add your choice of seasonings.
Nutritional Information per Serving:
Calories 301 | Fat 19.4g | Sodium 977mg | Carbs 5.6g | Fiber 1.1g | Sugar 2.5g | Protein 26.1g

Chicken Spinach Soup

Prep Time: 10 minutes
Cook Time: 10 minutes
Serves: 6
Ingredients:
- 3 cups cooked chicken, shredded
- 8 ounces cream cheese
- ¼ cup olive oil
- 4 cup baby spinach, chopped
- ⅛ teaspoon nutmeg
- 4 cup chicken stock
- ½ cup Parmesan cheese, shredded
- 1 teaspoon garlic, minced
- Pepper
- Salt

Directions:
1. Heat oil in a saucepan over medium heat.
2. Add garlic and spinach and cook until spinach is wilted.
3. Add cream cheese and parmesan cheese and stir until cheese is melted.
4. Add remaining ingredients and stir well and cook for 5 minutes. Season with pepper and salt.
Serving Suggestion: Stir well and serve warm.
Variation Tip: You can also use vegetable stock instead of chicken stock.
Nutritional Information per Serving:
Calories 346 | Fat 25.8g | Sodium 778mg | Carbs 2.7g | Fiber 0.5g | Sugar 0.6g | Protein 26.6g

Greek Scrambled Eggs

Prep Time: 10 minutes
Cook Time: 10 minutes
Serves: 2
Ingredients:
- 4 eggs
- ¼ teaspoon dried oregano
- 1 tablespoon capers

- 2 tablespoons olives, sliced
- 8 grape tomatoes, quartered
- 1 tablespoon olive oil
- 2 spring onions, sliced
- 1 bell pepper, diced
- 2 tablespoons fresh parsley, chopped
- Pepper
- Salt

Directions:
1. Heat oil in a pan over medium heat.
2. Add spring onions and bell pepper and sauté until vegetables are softened.
3. Add tomatoes, capers, and olives and sauté for a minute.
4. Add eggs into the pan and scramble with a spoon.
5. Add oregano, pepper and salt and stir until the eggs are cooked.
Serving Suggestion: Garnish with parsley and serve.
Variation Tip: Once done then add some crumbled Feta cheese.
Nutritional Information per Serving:
Calories 311 | Fat 17.9g | Sodium 327mg | Carbs 26.6g | Fiber 7.7g | Sugar 17g | Protein 16.6g

Tuna Breakfast Quiche

Prep Time: 10 minutes
Cook Time: 20 minutes
Serves: 4
Ingredients:
- 3 eggs
- 3 tablespoons oats
- 3 tablespoons cream cheese
- 1 tablespoon dill
- 1 tablespoon basil
- 1 cup can tuna, drained
- ½ onion, chopped
- ½ carrot, grated
- ½ zucchini, grated
- Pepper
- Salt

Directions:
1. Preheat the oven to 350° F.
2. In a bowl, whisk eggs with cream cheese, pepper, and salt.
3. Add remaining ingredients and stir until well combined.
4. Pour egg mixture into the greased quiche pan and bake in preheated oven for 20 minutes.
Serving Suggestion: Allow to cool completely then slice and serve.
Variation Tip: Add your choice of seasonings.
Nutritional Information per Serving:
Calories 151 | Fat 6.6g | Sodium 138mg | Carbs 6.4g | Fiber 1.3g | Sugar1.7g | Protein 16.4g

Omelet Casserole

Prep Time: 10 minutes
Cook Time: 35 minutes
Serves: 12
Ingredients:
- 12 eggs
- 1 tablespoon olive oil
- 1 teaspoon lemon pepper
- 1 teaspoon dried oregano
- 1 tablespoon dill, chopped
- 5 ounces sun-dried tomato, crumbled
- 12 ounces artichoke, drained & chopped
- 1 teaspoon garlic, minced
- 8 ounces spinach, chopped
- 2 cups almond milk
- 1 teaspoon salt

Directions:
1. Preheat the oven to 375° F.
2. Heat oil in a pan over medium heat.
3. Add garlic and spinach and sauté for 3 minutes.
4. In a bowl, whisk eggs with milk and salt. Add sun-dried tomato, dill, oregano, lemon pepper and sautéed spinach.
5. Pour egg mixture into the greased baking dish and bake for 35 minutes.
Serving Suggestion: Allow to cool completely then slice and serve.
Variation Tip: You can also use coconut milk instead of almond milk.
Nutritional Information per Serving:
Calories 210| Fat 16.9g | Sodium 335mg | Carbs 9.4g | Fiber 3.7g | Sugar 2.1g | Protein 8.6g

Coconut Pumpkin Soup

Prep Time: 10 minutes
Cook Time: 30 minutes
Serves: 6
Ingredients:
- 2 cups pumpkin puree

- 1 teaspoon curry powder
- 2 shallots, chopped
- ½ onion, chopped
- 4 tablespoon olive oil
- 1 cup coconut cream
- 4 cups vegetable broth
- ½ teaspoon ground ginger
- Pepper
- Salt

Directions:
1. Heat oil in a saucepan over medium heat.
2. Add onion and shallots and sauté until softened.
3. Add ginger and curry powder and stir well.
4. Add broth, coconut cream, and pumpkin puree and stir well. Simmer for 10 minutes.
5. Puree the soup using a blender until smooth. Season with pepper and salt.
Serving Suggestion: Stir well and serve warm.
Variation Tip: You can also use vegetable stock instead of broth.
Nutritional Information per Serving:
Calories 351 | Fat 20.3g | Sodium 567mg | Carbs 38.6g | Fiber 3.6g | Sugar 4.9g | Protein 9.4g

Veggies and Egg Scramble

Prep Time: 15 minutes
Cook Time: 8 minutes
Serves: 2
Ingredients:
- 1 cup fresh baby spinach
- 1 tablespoon olive oil
- ⅓ cup fresh tomato, chopped
- 2 tablespoons feta cheese, cubed
- 3 eggs, beaten
- Salt and black pepper, to taste

Preparation:
1. Heat the olive oil in a large pan placed over medium heat and sauté the tomatoes and spinach for about 4 minutes.
2. Add the eggs and cook for about 1 minute, stirring continuously.
3. Stir in the feta cheese and cook for another 2 minutes until set.
4. Stir in the salt and black pepper and remove from the heat.
5. Serve immediately.
Serving Suggestion: Serve with toasted whole-wheat bread.
Variation Tip: You can also add some fresh cilantro.
Nutritional Information per Serving:
Calories: 188 | Fat: 15.7g | Sat Fat: 4.5g | Carbohydrates: 2.6g | Fiber: 0.7g | Sugar: 1.7g | Protein: 10.3g

Tuna Lemon Avocado Salad

Prep Time: 10 minutes
Cook Time: 5 minutes
Serves: 2
Ingredients:
- 5 ounces can tuna, drained
- ½ onion, chopped
- 3 cups cherry tomatoes, halved
- 2 avocados, chopped
- 1 tablespoon fresh lemon juice
- ¼ cup fresh cilantro, chopped
- Pepper
- Salt

Directions:
1. Add tuna and remaining ingredients into the mixing bowl and mix until well combined.
Serving Suggestion: Serve with toast.
Variation Tip: You can also use grape tomatoes.
Nutritional Information per Serving:
Calories 554 | Fat 40.4g | Sodium 142mg | Carbs 30.6g | Fiber 17.4g | Sugar 9.5g | Protein 24.7g

Cucumber Avocado Salad

Prep Time: 10 minutes
Cook Time: 5 minutes
Serves: 4
Ingredients:
- 1 avocado, diced
- 2 tablespoons olive oil
- 1 cup cucumber, diced
- 1 cup cherry tomatoes, halved
- 1 tablespoon fresh parsley, chopped
- 1 teaspoon garlic, minced
- ½ cup onion, chopped
- Pepper
- Salt

Directions:
1. Add onion, cucumber, avocado, cherry tomatoes and garlic into the bowl and mix well.
2. Drizzle with olive oil and season with pepper and salt.
Serving Suggestion: Garnish with parsley and serve.
Variation Tip: Add your choice of seasonings.
Nutritional Information per Serving:
Calories 182 | Fat 16.9g | Sodium 46mg | Carbs 8.7g | Fiber 4.4g | Sugar 2.5g | Protein 1.8g

Oatmeal Pancakes

Prep Time: 10 minutes
Cook Time: 20 minutes
Serves: 4
Ingredients:
- 4 large egg whites
- 1 large egg
- 1 cup low-fat cottage cheese
- 2 tablespoons honey
- 1 teaspoon vanilla extract
- ½ teaspoon ground cinnamon
- 1 cup gluten-free rolled oats
- Coconut oil, for cooking

Preparation:
1. In a large bowl, whisk together the egg whites, egg, cottage cheese, honey, vanilla, and cinnamon until well blended and most of the lumps are gone.
2. Whisk in the rolled oats until blended.
3. Place a large skillet over medium heat and lightly coat it with coconut oil.
4. Pour about ¼ cup of batter onto the skillet for each pancake, being sure not to overfill the skillet.
5. Cook for about 3 minutes, then flip the pancake over.
6. Cook until the other side is golden brown, about two more minutes.
7. Repeat with the rest of the batter.
8. Serve warm or cold.
Serving Suggestion: Top the pancakes with bananas, nuts, and a drizzle of dry berries.
Variation Tip: Cold pancakes are a perfect snack wrapped around fresh fruit.
Nutritional Information per Serving:
Calories 164 | Fat 3g | Sodium 281mg | Carbs 19g | Fiber 1g | Sugar 9g | Protein 15g

Italian Feta Cheese Tomato Salad

Prep Time: 10 minutes
Cook Time: 5 minutes
Serves: 4
Ingredients:
- 4 large tomatoes, chopped
- ¼ cup fresh basil, chopped
- ¼ cup fresh chives, chopped
- 1 cup Feta cheese, crumbled
- 2 tablespoons fresh lime juice
- ¼ cup olive oil
- ¼ cup fresh dill, chopped
- Pepper
- Salt

Directions:
1. Add tomatoes into the mixing bowl.
2. In a small bowl, whisk together lime juice, chives, dill, oil, basil, pepper and salt and pour over tomatoes.
3. Sprinkle crumbled cheese on top of tomatoes.
Serving Suggestion: Mix well and serve.
Variation Tip: You can also use crumbled Goat cheese instead of Feta cheese.
Nutritional Information per Serving:
Calories 254 | Fat 21.1g | Sodium 473mg | Carbs 12.3g | Fiber 2.8g | Sugar 6.8g | Protein 7.8g

Yogurt with Berries

Prep Time: 10 minutes
Cook Time: 5 minutes
Serves: 1
Ingredients:
- 1 cup yogurt
- 1 teaspoon honey
- ¼ cup fresh blackberries
- ¼ cup fresh strawberries, sliced
- 2 tablespoons walnuts, chopped

Directions:
1. In a bowl, mix together yogurt and honey.
Serving Suggestion: Top with chopped walnuts and fresh berries.
Variation Tip: Add your choice of nuts.
Nutritional Information per Serving:
Calories 319 | Fat 12.5g | Sodium 173mg | Carbs 30.8g | Fiber 3.7g | Sugar 26.7g | Protein 18.5g

Fruity Quinoa Bowl

Prep Time: 15 minutes
Cook Time: 15 minutes
Serves: 2
Ingredients:
- ½ cup skim milk
- ½ teaspoon vanilla extract
- ½ cup uncooked quinoa, rinsed and drained
- ½ cup water
- ½ teaspoon ground cinnamon
- ½ cup cashews, chopped
- ½ cup fresh blackberries
- ½ cup dried cherries
- 1 tablespoon honey

Preparation:
1. In a preheated saucepan over medium heat, add the milk, quinoa, water, cinnamon, and bring to a boil.
2. Lower the heat to medium-low and simmer, covered, for about 15 minutes or until all the liquid is absorbed, stirring occasionally.
3. Remove from the heat and stir in the cashews, cherries, and honey.
4. Divide the quinoa mixture into serving bowls evenly.
5. Serve with a topping of blackberries.
Serving Suggestion: Top with additional honey before serving.
Variation Tip: You can substitute the blackberries with blueberries and strawberries.
Nutritional Information per Serving:
Calories: 477 | Fat: 18.6g | Sat Fat: 3.5g | Carbohydrates: 66.2g | Fiber: 6.8g | Sugar: 24.7g | Protein: 13.8g

Buckwheat Pancakes

Prep Time: 10 Minutes
Cook Time: 10 Minutes
Serves: 4
Ingredients:
- ¼ teaspoon vanilla extract
- 1 cup buckwheat flour
- 1¼ teaspoons baking powder
- ½ teaspoon sugar
- ¼ teaspoon salt
- 1¼ cups buttermilk
- 1 egg
- 1 tablespoon olive oil

Preparation:
1. Whisk the wet ingredients in one bowl and the dry ingredients in another.
2. Mix the content of both bowls together.
3. Heat the olive oil in a skillet over medium heat.
4. Pour in the batter in batches and cook on both sides, about five minutes.
Serving Suggestion: Top with some honey and fresh berries.
Variation Tip: You can use almond or peanut butter for more protein.
Nutritional Information per Serving:
Calories 196.4 | Fat 5.8g | Sodium 269mg | Carbs 25.7g | Fiber 6g | Sugar 5.2g | Protein 9.1g

Quinoa Muffins

Prep Time: 10 Minutes
Cook Time: 30 Minutes
Serves: 12
Ingredients:
- 1 cup quinoa, cooked
- 6 eggs, whisked
- Salt and black pepper, to taste
- 1 cup Swiss cheese, grated
- 1 small yellow onion, chopped
- 1 cup white mushrooms, sliced
- ½ cup sun-dried tomatoes, chopped

Preparation:
1. Combine the eggs with salt, pepper, and the rest of the ingredients in a bowl and whisk well.
2. Divide this mixture into a silicone muffin pan, bake at 350°F for 30 minutes and serve for breakfast.
Serving Suggestion: Serve with yogurt.
Variation Tip: You can add other spices or seasonings or play with different veggie variations.
Nutritional Information per Serving:
Calories 123 | Fat 5.6g | Sodium 50mg | Carbs 10.8g | Fiber 1.3g | Sugar 0.8g | Protein 7.5g

Broccoli Tart

Prep Time: 10 minutes
Cook Time: 7 minutes
Serves: 6
Ingredients:
- 12 eggs
- 1½ cups mozzarella, shredded
- 1½ cups almond milk
- ½ teaspoon dried thyme
- Salt, to taste
- 1 red bell pepper, sliced
- ½ cup broccoli, chopped
- 1 clove garlic, minced
For the tart:
- ¾ cup almond flour
- 2 ounces cold almond butter
- 1 tablespoon cold water
- 2 eggs

Preparation:
1. Preheat the oven to 400°F.
2. Make breadcrumbs by rubbing the butter into the almond flour with a pinch of salt in a bowl.
3. Add the cold water and two eggs and mix everything until a dough forms.
4. Press the dough into a greased baking dish and refrigerate it for 25 minutes.
5. Beat the 12 eggs with the almond milk, thyme, and salt.
6. Stir in the bell pepper, broccoli, and garlic; set aside.
7. Remove the dough from the fridge and prick it with a fork. Bake it for 20 minutes.
8. Spread the mozzarella cheese over the cooked pie crust and top with the egg mixture.
9. Bake for 30 minutes until the tart sets.
10. Slice into pieces to serve.
Serving Suggestion: Serve with a garden salad.
Variation Tip: Substitute almond milk with dairy milk.
Nutritional Information per Serving:
Calories 367 | Fat 30.6g | Sodium 227mg | Carbs 8.3g | Fiber 2.7g | Sugar 4.3g | Protein 18.6g

Breakfast Berry Oats

Prep Time: 10 minutes
Cook Time: 5 minutes
Serves: 2

Ingredients:
- ½ cup rolled oats
- 1 cup almond milk
- ¼ cup chia seeds
- A pinch of cinnamon powder
- 2 teaspoons honey
- 1 cup pureed berries
- 1 tablespoon yogurt

Preparation:
1. Mix all the ingredients in a bowl until the honey is thoroughly incorporated.
2. Divide between two serving bowls or glasses, serve and enjoy.

Serving Suggestion: Top with fresh berries of your choice.
Variation Tip: Substitute honey with dry berries.
Nutritional Information per Serving:
Calories 420 | Fat 30.3g | Sodium 346mg | Carbs 35.3g | Fiber 7.2g | Sugar 16.1g | Protein 6.4g

Olive Scrambled Eggs

Prep Time: 10 minutes
Cook Time: 10 minutes
Serves: 2

Ingredients:
- 1 yellow bell pepper, chopped
- 2 spring onions, chopped
- 1 tablespoon olive oil
- 1 tablespoon capers, drained
- 8 cherry tomatoes, cubed
- 2 tablespoons pitted black olives, sliced
- 4 eggs, beaten
- Salt and black pepper, to taste
- ¼ teaspoon dried oregano
- 1 tablespoon fresh parsley, chopped

Preparation:
1. Heat the oil in a pan over medium heat.
2. When the oil warms up, add the spring onions and bell pepper and sauté for about 2 minutes.
3. Stir in the capers, tomatoes, and black olives; sauté for three more minutes.
4. Add in the salt, pepper, oregano, and eggs. Scramble for five more minutes.
5. Place the cooked egg mixture on two plates, serve and enjoy.

Serving Suggestion: Top with the fresh parsley.
Variation Tip: Switch up yellow bell pepper with red bell pepper.
Nutritional Information per Serving:
Calories 249 | Fat 17g | Sodium 633mg | Carbs 13.3g | Fiber 3.2g | Sugar 0.9g | Protein 13.5g

Tahini and Feta Toast

Prep Time: 5 minutes
Cook Time: 20 minutes
Serves: 2

Ingredients:
- 1½ tablespoons tahini
- 2 whole-wheat bread slices, toasted
- 1 tablespoon fresh lemon juice
- 2 teaspoons feta cheese, crumbled
- Ground black pepper, to taste
- 1 teaspoon water
- 2 teaspoons pine nuts

Preparation:
1. Add the tahini, water, and lemon juice to a small bowl and combine until a thick mixture forms.
2. Place the toasted bread slices onto serving plates.
3. Spread the tahini mixture in an even layer over each bread slice.
4. Top each slice with the pine nuts and feta cheese.
5. Sprinkle with the black pepper and serve immediately.

Serving Suggestion: Serve with hot tea.
Variation Tip: You can add any nuts of your choice.
Nutritional Information per Serving:
Calories: 166 | Fat: 9.7g | Sat Fat: 1.7g | Carbohydrates: 14.6g | Fiber: 3.1g | Sugar: 2g | Protein: 6.4g

Breakfast Chives Frittata

Prep Time: 10 minutes
Cook Time: 35 minutes
Serves: 6

Ingredients:
- 8 whisked eggs
- 1 teaspoon red pepper flakes
- 2 garlic cloves, minced
- ½ cups goat's cheese, crumbled
- 2 tablespoons chives, chopped
- 2 tablespoons dill, chopped
- 4 tomatoes, diced
- 1 tablespoon olive oil
- Salt and pepper, to taste

Preparation:
1. Grease a baking pan and preheat the oven to 325 °F.
2. Mix all the ingredients thoroughly in a large bowl and pour into the prepared pan.
3. Place in the oven and bake until the middle is cooked through, around 30–35 minutes.
4. Remove from the oven and serve.

Serving Suggestion: Garnish with fresh chopped cilantro.

Variation Tip: For a milder taste, omit the red pepper flakes

Nutritional Information per Serving:
Calories 149 | Fat 10.28g | Sodium 210mg | Carbs 9.93g | Fiber 2.3g | Sugar 2g | Protein 13.26g

Spinach and Egg Scramble

Prep Time: 10 minutes
Cook Time: 15 minutes
Serves: 1

Ingredients:
- 1 tablespoon olive oil
- 1½ cups baby spinach
- 2 eggs, beaten

- Kosher salt and black pepper, to taste
- 1 slice whole-grain bread, toasted
- ½ cup raspberries, chopped

Preparation:
1. Heat the oil in a non-stick skillet on medium-high heat.
2. Add the spinach and cook for 5–7 minutes.
3. Add the eggs to the same skillet and cook for 5 minutes, stirring every 2 minutes.
4. Add salt and pepper to your taste.
5. Serve and enjoy!

Serving Suggestion: Serve with the toast and raspberries as a garnish.

Variation Tip: Replace raspberries with your favorite berries or with avocado.

Nutritional Information per Serving:
Calories 296 | Fat 16g | Sodium 394mg | Carbs 21g | Fiber 7g | Sugar 5g | Protein 18g

Quinoa Porridge

Prep Time: 10 minutes
Cook Time: 15 minutes
Serves: 4

Ingredients:
- ½ cup quinoa, rinsed
- 1 cup water
- 1 cup gluten-free rolled oats
- ½ cup unsweetened vanilla almond milk, plus more if needed
- ¼ cup pumpkin seeds
- ¼ cup pecans, chopped
- 1 tablespoon honey

Preparation:
1. In a small saucepan, combine the quinoa and water. Bring to a boil over medium heat.
2. Reduce the heat to low and simmer, uncovered until the liquid is absorbed, 10–15 minutes. Set aside to cool.
3. In a medium bowl, stir the cooled quinoa, oats, almond milk, pumpkin seeds, pecans, and honey until well mixed.
4. Transfer to a storage container and store in the refrigerator, sealed, overnight.
5. If needed, stir in more almond milk in the morning to adjust the texture. Serve.

Serving Suggestion: Top with blueberries and chopped nuts.

Variation Tip: Make sure you use cooked quinoa because raw quinoa has a bitter taste.

Nutritional Information per Serving:
Calories 282 | Fat 9g | Sodium 27mg | Carbs 42g | Fiber 5g | Sugar 5g | Protein 10g

Cheesy Potato Frittata

Prep Time: 10 minutes
Cook Time: 10 minutes
Serves: 4
Ingredients:
- 8 large eggs
- ⅓ cup milk
- ⅔ cup baby spinach
- 2 cups russet potatoes, diced
- ¾ cup white onion, chopped
- ½ cup parmesan cheese, grated
- ½ cup fresh basil, chopped
- 2 tablespoons olive oil
- Salt and pepper, to taste

Preparation:
1. Whisk the eggs, milk, salt, and pepper in a large bowl.
2. Add the olive oil, potatoes, and chopped onion to a skillet over medium heat.
3. Allow the onions to become translucent, then add the spinach, which should begin to wilt after about a minute.
4. Add the egg and milk mixture to the skillet and top with parmesan cheese.
5. Let the frittata cook for about 5 minutes until the edges are brown.
Serving Suggestion: Garnish with rosemary sprigs.
Variation Tip: Substitute spinach with kale.
Nutritional Information per Serving:
Calories 281 | Fat 17.9g | Sodium 329mg | Carbs 15.9g | Fiber 2.4g | Sugar 3.5g| Protein 15.5g

Breakfast Hummus Toast

Prep Time: 10 minutes
Cook Time: 5 minutes
Serves: 2
Ingredients:
- 4 slices of rye bread, toasted

- ⅓ cup hummus
- 1 tomato, sliced
- ¼ cup mixed greens
- ½ cup red onion, sliced
- 1 teaspoon each of salt and pepper

Preparation:
1. Prepare the sliced vegetables while the bread is toasting.
2. Once the bread is toasted, layer with the hummus, tomatoes, onions, and mixed greens to create open-faced sandwiches.
3. Season with salt and pepper to taste.
Serving Suggestion: Top with chopped cilantro.
Variation Tip: Substitute rye bread with whole-wheat pita bread.
Nutritional Information per Serving:
Calories 148 | Fat 4.6g | Sodium 261mg | Carbs 30.2g | Fiber 5.6g | Sugar 3.3g | Protein 6.1g

Creamy Millet

Prep Time: 10 minutes
Cook Time: 15 minutes
Serves: 8
Ingredients:
- 2 cups millet
- 1 cup almond milk, unsweetened
- 1 cup water
- 1 cup coconut milk, unsweetened
- 1 teaspoon ground cinnamon
- ½ teaspoon ground ginger
- ¼ teaspoon salt
- 1 tablespoon chia seeds
- 1 tablespoon cashew butter
- 4 ounces shredded coconut

Preparation:
1. Combine the coconut milk, almond milk, and water in a saucepan over medium heat; stir gently.
2. Add the millet, mix well and close the lid.
3. Cook the millet for 5 minutes.
4. Add in the cinnamon, ground ginger, salt, and chia seeds. Stir well and continue to cook on medium heat for 5 minutes more.
5. Add the cashew butter and cook for 5 more minutes.
6. Remove the mixture from the heat and transfer it to serving bowls.
7. Serve and enjoy.
Serving Suggestion: Sprinkle the coconut.
Variation Tip: Substitute cashew butter with any nut butter.
Nutritional Information per Serving:
Calories 384 | Fat 19.8g | Sodium 215mg | Carbs 42.9g | Fiber 6.6g | Sugar 3.6g | Protein 11.7g

Pumpkin Pancakes

Prep Time: 10 minutes
Cook Time: 15 minutes
Serves: 6
Ingredients:
- 3 large eggs
- ⅔ cup organic oats
- 6 ounces pumpkin puree
- 1 teaspoon stevia powder
- ½ teaspoon ground cinnamon
- Cooking spray

Preparation:
1. Blend all the ingredients into a smooth batter.
2. Thoroughly coat a skillet with cooking spray.
3. Pour 2–3 tablespoons of the batter into the skillet and swirl it around.
4. Wait till the edges of the pancake brown up a little bit.
5. Flip it over and cook the other side.
6. Repeat the process with the remaining batter.

Serving Suggestion: Serve with blueberries and honey.
Variation Tip: Substitute stevia with a sweetener of your choice.

Nutritional Information per Serving:
Calories 70 | Fat 3g | Sodium 37mg | Carbs 16g | Fiber 1.8g | Sugar 1.2g | Protein 3g

Cherry Oats Bowl

Prep Time: 10 minutes
Cook Time: 0 minutes
Serves: 1
Ingredients:
- ½ cup organic rolled oats
- ½ cup unsweetened almond milk
- 1 tablespoon chia seeds
- 1 teaspoon hemp seeds
- 2 teaspoons almonds, sliced

- 1 tablespoon almond butter
- 1 teaspoon vanilla extract
- ½ cup fresh berries
- 1 cup frozen cherries
- 1 cup plain Greek yogurt

Preparation:
1. Soak the oats in the unsweetened almond milk.
2. Prepare a smooth blend of the soaked oats, frozen cherries, yogurt, chia seeds, almond butter, and vanilla extract.
3. Pour the mixture into two bowls.
4. Add equal amounts of hemp seeds, sliced almonds, and fresh cherries to each bowl.

Serving Suggestion: Top with a drizzle of honey.
Variation Tip: Substitute almond milk with a milk of your choice.

Nutritional Information per Serving:
Calories 889 | Fat 35.3g | Sodium 126mg | Carbs 112g | Fiber 21.7g | Sugar 85.4g | Protein 33.6g

Blue Cheese Egg Scramble

Prep Time: 10 minutes
Cook Time: 6 minutes
Serves: 4
Ingredients:
- 2 tablespoons olive oil
- 1 cup white mushrooms, sliced
- 2 cloves garlic, minced
- 16 ounces blue cheese
- ½ cup spinach, sliced
- 6 fresh eggs

Preparation:
1. Heat the oil in a skillet over medium heat and sauté the mushrooms and garlic for 5 minutes.
2. Crumble the blue cheese into the skillet and cook for 6 minutes.
3. Add the spinach and sauté for five more minutes.
4. Crack the eggs into a bowl, whisk until well combined and creamy in color, and pour all over the spinach.
5. Use a spatula to immediately stir the eggs while cooking until they're scrambled and no longer runny (about 5 minutes).
6. Serve and enjoy.

Serving Suggestion: Serve with arugula salad.
Variation Tip: Add a tablespoon of paprika for a vibrant flavor.

Nutritional Information per Serving:
Calories 562 | Fat 46.2g | Sodium 1679mg | Carbs 4.4g | Fiber 0.3g | Sugar 1.4g | Protein 33.3g

Oat and Berry Parfait

Prep Time: 10 minutes
Cook Time: 12 minutes
Serves: 2
Ingredients:
- ½ cup whole-grain rolled oats
- ¾ cup walnut pieces
- 1 teaspoon honey
- 1 cup fresh blueberries
- 1½ cups vanilla low-fat Greek yogurt
- Fresh mint leaves, for garnish

Preparation:
1. Preheat the oven to 300°F.
2. Spread the oats and walnuts in a single layer on a baking sheet.
3. Toast the oats and nuts just until you begin to smell them cooking, 10 to 12 minutes. Take the sheet out from the oven.
4. In a microwave-safe bowl, heat the honey until it's just warm, about 30 seconds. Add the blueberries and stir to coat.
5. Place one tablespoon of the berries in the bottom of two dessert dishes or 8-ounce glasses.
6. Add a portion of yogurt and then a portion of oats and repeat the layers until the containers are full, ending with the berries.
7. Serve.
Serving Suggestion: Garnish with the mint leaves.
Variation Tip: Substitute honey with maple syrup.
Nutritional Information per Serving:
Calories 916 | Fat 35.8g | Sodium 360mg | Carbs 115.7g | Fiber 7.6g | Sugar 90.9g | Protein 39.9g

Yogurt with Berries and Nuts

Prep Time: 5 minutes
Cook Time: 0 minutes
Serves: 1
Ingredients:

- 6 ounces non-fat plain Greek yogurt
- ½ cup fresh berries of your choice
- ¼ ounce crushed walnuts
- 1 tablespoon honey

Preparation:
1. In a jar with a lid, add the yogurt.
2. Add the berries, nuts, and honey.
3. Seal with the lid and store in the fridge for 2–3 days.
Serving Suggestion: Garnish with mint.
Variation Tip: Substitute honey with maple syrup.
Nutritional Information per Serving:
Calories 243 | Fat 4.6g | Sodium 136mg | Carbs 42.5g | Fiber 5.3g | Sugar 36g | Protein 10.6g

Polenta Frittata

Prep Time: 2 hours 10 minutes
Cook Time: 35 minutes
Serves: 6
Ingredients:
- 6 cloves garlic, minced
- 1 bunch kale
- 1 teaspoon oregano
- 1 teaspoon Italian seasoning blend (no salt added)
- 1 teaspoon dry mustard
- ¼ teaspoon black pepper
- 3 tablespoons nutritional yeast
- 1 cup coarsely ground whole-grain cornmeal (not instant)

Preparation:
1. Sauté the garlic in a skillet for 2–3 minutes over moderate heat.
2. Add the kale, oregano, and Italian seasoning and simmer for 10 minutes until the kale is just starting to wilt.
3. Bring 4 cups of water to a boil in a different pot.
4. Add the dry mustard, pepper, and yeast, then whisk in the cornmeal, and cook for 5 minutes.
5. Reduce the heat to medium and mix in the greens.
6. Cook, stirring for the next 10 minutes (until a wooden spoon will almost be able to stand up in the pot).
7. Stretch the mixture to fit a pie pan greased with a bit of olive oil, and cool for 2 hours to allow it to the firm.
8. Serve.
Serving Suggestion: Serve with a dab of almond butter.
Variation Tip: Substitute kale with collards.
Nutritional Information per Serving:
Calories 114 | Fat 0.6g | Sodium 17mg | Carbs 23g | Fiber 3.2g | Sugar 0.2g | Protein 4g

Eggs Florentine

Prep Time: 10 minutes
Cook Time: 10 minutes
Serves: 3
Ingredients:
- 2 tablespoons olive oil
- 2 cloves garlic
- 3 tablespoons cream cheese
- ½ cup mushroom
- ½ cup fresh spinach
- Salt and black pepper, to taste
- 6 eggs

Preparation:
1. Put the oil in a non-stick skillet and heat. Mix in the mushrooms and garlic until the garlic is fragrant for about 1 minute.
2. Add the spinach to the mushroom paste and cook until the spinach softens for 2–3 minutes.
3. Combine the mushroom-spinach mixture, then add salt and pepper.
4. Add the eggs and cook, mixing, until the eggs are stiff; turn.
5. Pour the cream cheese over the egg mixture and cook until the cheese starts melting, about 5 minutes.
Serving Suggestion: Serve over toasted bread slices.
Variation Tip: Feel free to add in more seasoning.
Nutritional Information per Serving:
Calories 278.9 | Fat 22.9g | Sodium 191mg | Carbs 4.1g | Fiber 22.9g | Sugar 1.1g | Protein 15.7g

Breakfast Burrito

Prep Time: 10 minutes
Cook Time: 18 minutes
Serves: 2
Ingredients:
- 2 whole-wheat tortillas
- 3 eggs
- 2 tablespoons sun-dried tomatoes, chopped
- ¼ cup canned beans
- ¼ cup feta cheese, crumbled
- 1 tablespoon pitted black olives, sliced
- ½ cup fresh baby spinach, roughly diced
- 2 tablespoons olive oil
- Salt and black pepper, to taste

Preparation:
1. In a small saucepan on medium heat, add the olive oil and cook the eggs on both sides.
2. Add the tomatoes, spinach, olives, and tomatoes and continue to stir.
3. Season with salt and pepper, then stir in the feta cheese.
4. Heat each tortilla in the microwave and divide the beans onto each one.
5. Divide the egg mixture onto each tortilla.
6. Grill on a panini press or lightly fry in a pan until golden brown.
Serving Suggestion: Serve with salsa and guacamole.
Variation Tip: Add chili for a spicier result.
Nutritional Information per Serving:
Calories 248 | Fat 11g | Sodium 356mg | Carbs 20g | Fiber 2.4g | Sugar 2g | Protein 14g

Chickpea Pancakes

Prep Time: 10 minutes
Cook Time: 5 minutes
Serves: 4
Ingredients:
- 1 cup water
- 1 cup chickpea flour
- ½ teaspoon salt
- ½ teaspoon pepper
- 1 teaspoon turmeric
- 1 tablespoon of olive oil
- 3 spring onions, diced
- 1 red bell pepper, diced, optional
- ½ teaspoon chili flakes, optional

Preparation:
1. Add the water, flour, salt, pepper, chili flakes (optional), and turmeric to a blender. Blend and then set aside.
2. Heat the oil in a non-stick pan.
3. Add the spring onions to the flour mixture.
4. Add a tablespoon of the mixture to the hot pan and cook for 3 minutes.
5. Flip the pancake with a spatula and cook for another 2 minutes.
6. Serve warm.
Serving Suggestion: Garnish with green onions.
Variation Tip: For a milder taste, omit the chili flakes.
Nutritional Information per Serving:
Calories 253| Fat 11g | Sodium 107mg | Carbs 34g | Fiber 9g | Sugar 6g | Protein 10g

Shakshuka

Prep Time: 10 Minutes
Cook Time: 20 Minutes
Serves: 6

Ingredients:
- 1 teaspoon ground cumin
- 2 tablespoons olive oil
- 1 red bell pepper, chopped
- 6 eggs
- ¼ teaspoon salt
- 3 cloves garlic, minced
- Ground black pepper, to taste
- 2 tablespoons tomato paste
- ½ teaspoons moked paprika
- 1 yellow onion, chopped
- ¼ teaspoon red pepper flakes, plus more for garnish
- 2 tablespoons cilantro, chopped, for garnish
- ½ cup feta cheese, crumbled, for garnish
- 28 ounces fire-roasted tomatoes, crushed
- Crusty bread, for serving

Preparation:
1. Preheat the oven to 375°F.
2. Heat the oil in a skillet over medium heat. Add and cook the bell pepper, onions, and salt for six minutes, constantly stirring the mixture.
3. Stir in the tomato paste, red pepper flakes, cumin, garlic, and paprika. Cook for another two minutes.
4. Add the crushed tomatoes and cilantro to the onion mixture. Let it simmer.
5. Reduce the heat and simmer for five minutes.
6. Use salt and pepper to adjust the flavor.
7. Crack the eggs in small wells made in different areas of the pan using a spoon.
8. Pour the tomato mixture over the eggs to help them cook while staying intact.
9. Bake the skillet in the preheated oven for 12 minutes.
10. Garnish with the cilantro, red pepper flakes, and feta cheese, and serve.

Serving Suggestion: Serve with crusty bread.
Variation Tip: Adjust the timing to cook your eggs how you like them.
Nutritional Information per Serving:
Calories 216 | Fat 12.8g | Sodium 381mg | Carbs 16.6g | Fiber 4.4g | Sugar 6.5g | Protein 11.2g

Artichoke Casserole

Prep Time: 10 minutes
Cook Time: 35 minutes
Serves: 8

Ingredients:
- 16 eggs
- ¼ cup milk
- 10 ounces frozen chopped spinach, thawed and drained well
- 14 ounces artichoke hearts, drained
- 1 cup white cheddar, shredded
- 1 garlic clove, minced
- 1 teaspoon salt
- ½ cup parmesan cheese
- ½ cup ricotta cheese
- ½ teaspoon dried thyme
- ½ teaspoon crushed red pepper
- ¼ cup onion, chopped
- Cooking spray

Preparation:
1. Grease a baking dish with the cooking spray and preheat the oven to 350°F.
2. In a mixing bowl, mix the milk and eggs thoroughly.
3. Squeeze out the excess moisture from the spinach leaves with a paper towel and add to the egg mixture.
4. Break the artichoke hearts into small pieces and separate the leaves. Add to the egg mixture.
5. Add the remaining ingredients except for the ricotta cheese to the eggs and mix thoroughly.
6. Pour the egg mixture into the baking dish.
7. Evenly add dollops of ricotta cheese on top of the eggs and then pop in the oven; bake for about 35 minutes.
8. Remove from the oven and evenly divide into suggested servings.
9. Enjoy.

Serving Suggestion: Top with chopped fresh cilantro.
Variation Tip: Feel free to use half the spinach and twice the artichokes.
Nutritional Information per Serving:
Calories 302 | Fat 18.7g | Sodium 546mg | Carbs 10.8g | Fiber 1g | Sugar 1g | Protein 22.6g

Minestrone Soup

Prep Time: 10 Minutes
Cook Time: 30 Minutes
Serves: 6

Ingredients:
- 2 tablespoons olive oil
- ⅓ cup parmesan cheese, shredded
- 4 shredded garlic cloves, shredded
- 1 onion, chopped
- 2 celery stalks, chopped
- ⅓ pound green beans, chopped
- 1 carrot, diced
- 1 teaspoon dried oregano
- Salt and black pepper, to taste
- 1 teaspoon dried basil
- 14 ounces crushed tomatoes
- 28 ounces diced tomatoes
- 6 cups chicken stock
- 1 cup elbow pasta
- 15 ounces kidney beans
- 2 tablespoons fresh basil, chopped

Preparation:
1. Sauté the onions in heated olive oil over medium heat for five minutes.
2. Stir in the garlic and cook for half a minute.
3. Mix in the carrot and celery and cook for five more minutes, stirring occasionally.
4. Add the oregano, green beans, salt, basil, and black pepper and cook for another three minutes, stirring constantly.
5. Pour in the broth followed by the tomatoes and let it boil.
6. Lower the heat to low and let it simmer for ten minutes.
7. Add the pasta and kidney beans and cook for another ten minutes.
8. Add some salt and serve.

Serving Suggestion: Garnish with cheese and basil.
Variation Tip: Feel free to add whatever vegetables that are in season.

Nutritional Information per Serving:
Calories 260 | Fat 8g | Sodium 961mg | Carbs 37g | Fiber 10g | Sugar 10.2g | Protein 15g

Veggie Soup

Prep Time: 20 minutes
Cook Time: 25 minutes
Serves: 8

Ingredients:
- 4 small zucchinis, chopped
- 2 (14-ounce) cans diced tomatoes with juice (low-sodium)
- 8 carrots, peeled and chopped
- 4 small onions, chopped
- 1 leek, chopped
- 1 teaspoon ground cumin
- ¼ teaspoon paprika
- 1 whole-meal bread slice, toasted and chopped into small croutons
- 2 garlic cloves, minced
- ¼ teaspoon ground cayenne pepper
- Salt and black pepper, to taste
- 4¼ cups vegetable broth

Preparation:
1. In a big soup pan placed over high heat, add all the ingredients except the croutons. Allow the mixture to boil.
2. Reduce the heat to low, cover partially, and simmer for about 20 minutes.
3. Remove from the heat and set aside to cool slightly.
4. In batches, pour the soup into a blender and pulse until smooth.
5. Transfer the pureed mixture back into the same pan over medium heat and let it simmer for about 4 minutes.
6. Remove from the heat and serve topped with the croutons.

Serving Suggestion: Serve with a garnish of fresh parsley.
Variation Tip: You can use any veggies of your choice.

Nutritional Information per Serving:
Calories: 105 | Fat: 1.3g | Sat Fat: 0.3g | Carbohydrates: 19.2g | Fiber: 4.6g | Sugar: 9.2g | Protein: 5.7g

White Bean Soup

Prep Time: 10 Minutes
Cook Time: 8 hours
Serves: 6
Ingredients:
- 1 cup celery, chopped
- 1 cup carrot, chopped
- 1 yellow onion, chopped
- 6 cups veggie stock
- 4 garlic cloves, minced
- 2 cups navy beans, dried
- ½ teaspoon basil, dried
- ½ teaspoon sage, dried
- 1 teaspoon thyme, dried
- A pinch of salt and black pepper

Preparation:
1. In your slow cooker, combine the beans with the stock and the rest of the ingredients.
2. Put the lid on and cook on Low for 8 hours.
3. Divide the soup into bowls and serve right away.
Serving Suggestion: Serve with roasted vegetables and crusty bread.
Variation Tip: Add other vegetables of your choice for a healthier result!
Nutritional Information per Serving:
Calories 264 | Fat 17.5g | Sodium 751mg | Carbs 23.7g | Fiber 4.5g | Sugar 6.6g | Protein 11.5g

Cucumber and Tomato Salad

Prep Time: 10 Minutes
Cook Time: 0 Minutes
Serves: 4
Ingredients:
- Salt and black pepper, to taste
- 1 tablespoon fresh lemon juice
- 1 onion, chopped
- 1 cucumber, peeled and diced
- 2 tomatoes, chopped
- 4 cups spinach

Preparation:
1. In a salad bowl, mix the onions, cucumbers, and tomatoes.
2. Season with pepper and salt to taste.
3. Add the lemon juice and mix well.
4. Add the spinach, toss to coat, serve and enjoy.
Serving Suggestion: Top with feta cheese and chickpeas.
Variation Tip: Remove the seeds from the cucumber if you don't want any bitterness.
Nutritional Information per Serving:
Calories 70.3 | Fat 0.3g | Sodium 50mg | Carbs 8.9g | Fiber 2.4g | Sugar 4.3g | Protein 2.2g

Roasted Pepper Soup

Prep Time: 10 Minutes
Cook Time: 55 Minutes
Serves: 4
Ingredients:
- 2 tomatoes, halved
- 3 red bell peppers, halved and seeded
- 1 yellow onion, quartered
- 2 garlic cloves, peeled and halved
- 2 tablespoons olive oil
- 2 cups veggie stock
- A pinch of salt and black pepper
- 2 tablespoons tomato paste
- ¼ cup fresh parsley, chopped
- ¼ teaspoon Italian seasoning
- ¼ teaspoon sweet paprika

Preparation:
1. Spread the bell peppers, tomatoes, onion, and garlic on a baking sheet lined with parchment paper.
2. Add the oil, salt, and pepper and bake at 375°F for 45 minutes.
3. Heat a pot with the stock over medium heat, add the roasted vegetables and the rest of the ingredients, stir, bring to a simmer and cook for 10 minutes.
4. Blend the mix using an immersion blender. Divide the soup into bowls and serve.
Serving Suggestion: Serve with ciabatta bread.
Variation Tip: You can also use sun-dried tomatoes.
Nutritional Information per Serving:
Calories 273 | Fat 11.2g | Sodium 21mg | Carbs 15.7g | Fiber 3.4g | Sugar 9.7g | Protein 5.6g

Cauliflower and Farro Salad

Prep Time: 20 minutes
Serves: 4
Ingredients:
For the salad
- ¾ cup pearled farro
- Kosher salt, to taste
- 2 tablespoons olive oil
- ½ medium red onion, thinly sliced
- ¼ cup fresh parsley, chopped
- 1 medium cauliflower head, cut into bite-sized florets
- 1-ounce parmesan cheese, shaved

For the dressing
- 2 tablespoons fresh lemon juice
- 3 tablespoons extra-virgin olive oil
- 1 tablespoon tahini paste
- ½ teaspoon kosher salt
- 1 small garlic clove, minced

Preparation:
1. Heat a pan over medium heat. Toast the farro for about 5 minutes or until nutty and browned, occasionally shaking the pan.
2. Stir in the water to cover the farro by about 1-inch, sprinkle with the salt, and bring to a boil.
3. Cook for about 25 minutes until the farro is tender but still chewy.
4. Strain the farro using a fine mesh strainer.
5. Transfer the farro to a large bowl and set it aside to cool slightly.
6. Heat the olive oil in a skillet over medium-high heat and cook the cauliflower for about 6 minutes, frequently stirring.
7. Stir in the onion and sauté for about 3 minutes.
8. Remove from the heat and set aside.
9. For the dressing: In a bowl, beat all the dressing ingredients until well combined.
10. Add the farro, dressing, and cauliflower mixture to a large serving bowl and toss to coat well.
11. Serve with a garnish of the parsley and parmesan cheese.

Serving Suggestion: Serve with your favorite main dish.
Variation Tip: You can also add some rosemary to this salad.
Nutritional Information per Serving:
Calories: 286 | Fat: 14.3g | Sat Fat: 2.9g | Carbohydrates: 33.1g | Fiber: 6.7g | Sugar: 4.3g | Protein: 10.6g

Greek Chicken Gyro Salad

Prep Time: 10 Minutes
Cook Time: 7 Minutes
Serves: 4
Ingredients:
Chicken
- 3 teaspoons dried oregano
- 2 tablespoons olive oil
- 1 tablespoon red wine vinegar
- 1¼ pound boneless chicken breasts
- 1 teaspoon ground black pepper
- 1 tablespoon lemon juice
- 1 teaspoon kosher salt

Salad
- 1 cup English cucumber, diced
- 6 cups lettuce
- 1 cup feta cheese, diced
- 1 cup tomatoes, diced
- ½ cup red onion, diced
- 1 cup pita chips, crushed

Tzatziki sauce
- 1 tablespoon white wine vinegar
- ¾ teaspoon kosher salt
- 8 ounces Greek yogurt
- 1 clove garlic, minced
- ⅔ cup English cucumber, grated
- 1 tablespoon lemon juice
- ¾ teaspoon ground black pepper
- 2 teaspoons dried dill weed
- A pinch of sugar

Preparation:
1. Heat the oil in a skillet over medium heat and add the chicken, salt, oregano, and black pepper.
2. Cook for five minutes.
3. Reduce the heat to low and add the lemon juice and vinegar and simmer for five minutes.
4. Continue cooking until the chicken is done. When the chicken is ready, remove the pan from the heat and set it aside.
5. Combine the tomatoes, pita chips, chicken, lettuce, cucumber, and onions in a large serving bowl. Mix and set aside. The salad is ready.
6. Whisk the yogurt, cucumber, garlic, lemon juice, vinegar, dill, salt, pepper, and sugar in another bowl. Mix well. The sauce is ready.

Serving Suggestion: Pour the sauce over the salad and serve with the cooked chicken.
Variation Tip: Marinate your chicken beforehand for a tastier result.
Nutritional Information per Serving:
Calories 737 | Fat 29g | Sodium 1253mg | Carbs 54g | Fiber 6g | Sugar 5.7g | Protein 64g

Tuscan Veggie Soup

Prep Time: 10 Minutes
Cook Time: 20 Minutes
Serves: 6

Ingredients:
- 1 (15 ounces) can low-sodium cannellini beans (drained and rinsed)
- 1 tablespoon olive oil
- ½ large-sized onion, diced
- 2 carrots, diced
- 2 stalks celery, diced
- 1 small-sized zucchini, diced
- 1 garlic clove, minced
- 1 tablespoon fresh thyme leaves, chopped
- 2 teaspoons fresh sage, chopped
- ½ teaspoon salt
- ¼ teaspoon freshly ground black pepper
- 32 ounces low-sodium chicken broth
- 14 ounces no-salt diced tomatoes
- 2 cups baby spinach leaves, chopped
- ⅓ cup parmesan, freshly grated, for serving

Preparation:
1. Take a small-sized bowl and add half of the beans. Mash them using the back of a spoon. Set them aside.
2. Place a large-sized soup pot over medium-high heat.
3. Add the oil and allow it to heat up. Add the carrots, onion, garlic, celery, zucchini, thyme, ½ a teaspoon of salt, sage, ¼ teaspoon of pepper, and cook for 15 minutes until the veggies are tender.
4. Add the broth and tomatoes (with their juice) and bring the whole mixture to a boil.
5. Add the beans (both mashed and whole) alongside the spinach.
6. Cook for 3 minutes until the spinach has wilted. Serve with a topping of parmesan.
7. Enjoy!

Serving Suggestion: Serve with grilled baguette slices.

Variation Tip: Add chili for a spicier result.

Nutritional Information per Serving:
Calories 145 | Fat 4g | Sodium 261mg | Carbs 21g | Fiber 4.7g | Sugar 3.5g | Protein 8g

Greek Avocado Salad

Prep Time: 10 Minutes
Cook Time: 0 Minutes
Serves: 8

Ingredients:
- 2 English cucumbers, sliced
- 1½ pound tomatoes, chopped
- ¼ red onion, sliced
- ½ cup Kalamata olives, sliced
- ¼ cup fresh parsley, chopped
- 3 avocados, peeled, cored, and sliced
- 1 cup feta cheese, crumbled
- ½ cup extra-virgin olive oil
- ½ cup red wine vinegar
- 2 garlic cloves, minced
- 1 tablespoon dried oregano
- 2 teaspoons sugar
- 1 teaspoon kosher salt
- 1 teaspoon ground black pepper

Preparation:
1. Mix the tomatoes, parsley, onions, cucumbers, avocado, and olives in a large serving bowl. Set aside.
2. Whisk the vinegar, sugar, olive oil, salt, oregano, garlic, and pepper in a jar.
3. Close the lid and shake to get an emulsified mixture.
4. You can add salt, black pepper, and sugar to adjust the taste according to your preference. The dressing is now ready!
5. Transfer the dressing to the salad bowl and toss well.
6. Serve.

Serving Suggestion: Garnish with the crumbled feta cheese.

Variation Tip: Avoid using mushy avocados.

Nutritional Information per Serving:
Calories 360 | Fat 32.5g | Sodium 586mg | Carbs 16.2g | Fiber 7.2g | Sugar 5.9g | Protein 5.6g

Pecan Salmon Salad

Prep Time: 10 minutes
Cook Time: 0 minutes
Serves: 4
Ingredients:
• 6 cups mixed baby greens (spinach, kale, and Swiss chard)
• 2 large oranges, peeled, and cut into chunks
• 2 red grapefruits, peeled and cut into chunks
• 1 avocado, peeled, pitted, and chopped
• 2 (5-ounce) cans boneless, skinless salmon, drained
• ½ cup pecan halves
• ½ cup pesto vinaigrette
Preparation:
1. Arrange the greens on a large platter and top with the oranges, grapefruits, avocado, salmon, and pecans.
2. Drizzle the salad with the vinaigrette and serve.
Serving Suggestion: Top with chopped cilantro.
Variation Tip: Swap the pecans for sunflower or pumpkin seeds.
Nutritional Information per Serving:
Calories 459 | Fat 34g | Sodium 191mg | Carbs 28g | Fiber 8g | Sugar 13g | Protein 19g

Lebanese Bean Salad

Prep Time: 2 hours 10 minutes
Cook Time: 0 minutes
Serves: 5
Ingredients:
• 1 (15-ounce) can of fava beans, drained and rinsed
• 1 (15-ounce) can of chickpeas, drained and rinsed
• 1 can (15½-ounce) can of white beans, drained and rinsed
• ¼ cup flat-leaf parsley, chopped
• 3 tablespoons olive oil

• 2 cloves garlic, minced
• 1 lemon, juiced
• Kosher salt and black pepper, to taste
Preparation:
1. Thoroughly combine all the ingredients in a bowl.
2. Refrigerate for two hours to marinate.
3. Serve and enjoy!
Serving Suggestion: Top with fresh cilantro.
Variation Tip: Add chili flakes for a hint of heat.
Nutritional Information per Serving:
Calories 312 | Fat 9.3g | Sodium 418mg | Carbs 44.7g | Fiber 10g | Sugar 1.5g | Protein 13.2 g

Asparagus, Arugula, and Pasta Salad

Prep Time: 20 minutes
Cook Time: 10 minutes
Serves: 8
Ingredients:
• 1-pound fresh asparagus, trimmed into bite-sized pieces
• 1-pound whole-wheat pasta
• 1 tablespoon red wine vinegar
• 2 tablespoons lemon zest, grated
• 2 large handfuls fresh baby arugula
• ⅔ cup feta cheese, crumbled
• Black pepper, to taste
• 3 tablespoons fresh lemon juice
• 1 tablespoon olive oil
• ¼ cup fresh basil, julienned
• ¼ cup pine nuts, toasted
Preparation:
1. In a large saucepan of salted water, cook the whole-wheat pasta for about 10minutes or until al dente.
2. Stir in the asparagus and mix well.
3. Remove the pan from the heat and transfer the pasta and asparagus to a strainer.
4. Run cold water over the pasta and asparagus and drain well.
5. Mix the pasta, vinegar, asparagus, olive oil, lemon zest, and lemon juice and toss to coat well.
6. Shift the pasta mixture into a large serving bowl.
7. Stir in the arugula, feta cheese, basil, pine nuts, and black pepper.
8. Gently toss to coat well and serve immediately.
Serving Suggestion: Top with some walnuts before serving if you like.
Variation Tip: You can use fresh parsley instead of basil.
Nutritional Information per Serving:
Calories: 299 | Fat: 10.3g | Sat Fat: 4g | Carbohydrates: 42.1g | Fiber: 5.5g | Sugar: 6.7g | Protein: 11.7g

Spicy Tomato Soup

Prep Time: 15 minutes
Cook Time: 28 minutes
Serves: 8

Ingredients:
- 2 medium yellow onions, sliced thinly
- 3 tablespoons olive oil
- Salt, to taste
- 1 teaspoon ground cumin
- ½ teaspoon red pepper flakes, crushed
- 1 (28-ounce) can low-sodium plum tomatoes with juices
- ½ cup ricotta cheese, crumbled
- 3 teaspoons curry powder
- 1 teaspoon ground cilantro
- 1 (15-ounce) can low-sodium diced tomatoes with juice
- 5½ cups low-sodium vegetable broth

Preparation:
1. Place a large wok over medium-low heat and add the olive oil, onions, and 1 teaspoon of salt.
2. Cook for about 12 minutes, occasionally stirring.
3. Add the curry powder, cilantro, cumin, and red pepper flakes and sauté for about 1 minute.
4. Stir in the broth and all the tomatoes with their juices and simmer for about 15 minutes.
5. Remove from the heat and blend the soup with a hand blender until smooth.
6. Serve immediately topped with ricotta cheese.

Serving Suggestion: Serve alongside mozzarella sticks.

Variation Tip: Ricotta cheese can be replaced with feta cheese.

Nutritional Information per Serving:
Calories: 120 | Fat: 6.7g | Sat Fat: 1.5g | Carbohydrates: 9.8g | Fiber: 1.3g | Sugar: 2.6g | Protein: 5g

Cheesy Beet Soup

Prep Time: 10 minutes
Cook Time: 30 minutes
Serves: 4

Ingredients:
- 1 tablespoon olive oil
- 6 large beets, peeled and chopped
- 1 fennel bulb, coarsely chopped
- 1 sweet onion, chopped
- 1 teaspoon garlic, minced
- 6 cups low-sodium chicken stock
- Sea salt and black pepper, to taste
- ½ cup goat's cheese, crumbled
- 1 tablespoon fresh parsley, chopped

Preparation:
1. In a pot, heat the olive oil over medium-high heat.
2. Sauté the beets, fennel, onion, and garlic until they soften, occasionally stirring, about 10 minutes.
3. Add the chicken stock and bring the soup to a boil.
4. Reduce the heat to low and simmer until the vegetables are very tender, about 20 minutes.
5. Transfer the soup to a food processor or, using an immersion blender, purée until smooth.
6. Return the soup to the saucepan and season with salt and pepper.
7. Serve.

Serving Suggestion: Top with the goat's cheese and parsley.

Variation Tip: Substitute chicken stock with vegetable stock.

Nutritional Information per Serving:
Calories 309 | Fat 13g | Sodium 1984mg | Carbs 32g | Fiber 5g | Sugar 17g | Protein 17g

Mediterranean Watermelon Salad

Prep Time: 10 Minutes
Cook Time: 0 Minutes
Serves: 6

Ingredients:
- 6 cups mixed salad greens, torn
- 3 cups watermelon, seeded and cubed
- ½ cup onion, sliced
- 1 tablespoon extra-virgin olive oil
- ⅓ cup feta cheese, crumbled
- Cracked black pepper, to taste

Preparation:
1. In a large bowl, mix all the ingredients.
2. Toss to combine everything well.
3. Allow chilling before serving.

Serving Suggestion: Serve with your favorite barbequed meat.

Variation Tip: For a creamier result, add avocado slices.

Nutritional Information per Serving:
Calories 91| Fat 4.3g | Sodium 130mg | Carbs 11.4g | Fiber 0.5g | Sugar 5.4g | Protein 3.5g

Quinoa and Veggie Salad

Prep Time: 20 minutes
Cook Time: 20 minutes
Serves: 8

Ingredients:
- 1½ cups dry quinoa, rinsed and drained
- Salt and black pepper, to taste
- 1 tablespoon balsamic vinegar
- ½ teaspoon dried thyme, crushed
- 1 (15-ounce) can low-sodium garbanzo beans, rinsed and drained
- ⅓ cup roasted red bell pepper, drained and sliced
- ¼ cup fresh basil, slivered thinly
- 3 cups water
- ½ cup extra-virgin olive oil
- 2 small garlic cloves, pressed
- ½ teaspoon dried basil, crushed
- 3 cups fresh arugula
- ⅓ cup fresh Kalamata olives, pitted and sliced
- ⅓ cup feta cheese, crumbled

Preparation:
1. Fill a saucepan with water and add ½ teaspoon of salt and the quinoa. Bring to a boil over high heat.
2. Reduce the heat, cover, and cook for about 20 minutes or until all the liquid is absorbed.
3. Remove from the heat, and with a fork, fluff the quinoa.
4. Set aside to completely cool.
5. For the dressing: In a bowl, mix the olive oil with the garlic, vinegar, dried herbs, salt, and black pepper until well combined.
6. Mix the garbanzo beans, quinoa, arugula, bell pepper, olives, and feta cheese in a large serving bowl.
7. Sprinkle the dressing over the salad and toss to coat well.
8. Serve garnished with the dried basil.

Serving Suggestion: Serve alongside your favorite meal.
Variation Tip: You can use any beans of your choice.
Nutritional Information per Serving:
Calories: 304 | Fat: 16.9g | Sat Fat: 3g | Carbohydrates: 31.3g | Fiber: 2.7g | Sugar: 3.2g | Protein: 8.3g

Spicy Lentil Soup

Prep Time: 20 minutes
Cook Time: 1 hour 15 minutes
Serves: 6

Ingredients:
- 2 carrots, peeled and chopped
- 2 tablespoons olive oil
- 2 celery stalks, chopped
- 3 garlic cloves, minced
- 1 (14½-ounce) can low-sodium diced tomatoes
- ¼ teaspoon dried oregano, crushed
- 1 teaspoon ground cumin
- ½ teaspoon paprika
- 3 cups fresh spinach, chopped
- 2 tablespoons fresh lemon juice
- Salt and black pepper, to taste
- 2 sweet onions, chopped
- 1½ cups brown lentils, picked over and rinsed
- ¼ teaspoon dried basil, crushed
- ¼ teaspoon dried thyme, crushed
- ½ teaspoon ground cilantro
- 6 cups low-sodium vegetable broth

Preparation:
1. In a big soup pan placed over medium heat, add the carrots, celery, and onion.
2. Cook for about 5 minutes and then stir in the garlic.
3. Sauté for about 1 minute and add the brown lentils, stir-frying for about 3 minutes.
4. Add the tomatoes, herbs, spices, and broth and allow the mixture to boil.
5. Reduce the heat to low, partially cover, and simmer for about 1 hour.
6. Stir in the spinach, salt, and black pepper, and cook for about 4 minutes.
7. Squeeze in the lemon juice and serve hot.

Serving Suggestion: You can serve the soup alongside your favorite rice.
Variation Tip: You can also use yellow lentils.
Nutritional Information per Serving:
Calories: 128 | Fat: 5.1g | Sat Fat: 0.7g | Carbohydrates: 14.9g | Fiber: 3g | Sugar: 4.5g | Protein: 5.7g

Chickpea, Bean, and Veggie Salad

Prep Time: 20 minutes
Serves: 6
Ingredients:
- 1 (15-ounce) can low-sodium black beans, rinsed and drained
- 2 cups fresh cherry tomatoes, halved
- ¼ cup fresh cilantro, chopped
- 2 tablespoons fresh lime juice
- 1 (15-ounce) can low-sodium chickpeas, rinsed and drained
- ¼ teaspoon red chili powder
- ¼ cup feta cheese, crumbled
- 2 medium avocados, peeled, pitted, and chopped
- 1 (15-ounce) can low-sodium corn, rinsed and drained
- 1 (2¼-ounce) can diced olives, drained
- 2 tablespoons extra-virgin olive oil
- 1 teaspoon ground cumin
- ¼ teaspoon salt

Preparation:
1. Add the chickpeas, corn, beans, olives, avocados, and tomatoes to a large bowl and combine well.
2. Mix the remaining ingredients, except the feta cheese, in another bowl until well combined.
3. Sprinkle the dressing over the salad and toss to coat well.
4. Serve garnished with feta cheese.
Serving Suggestion: You can also add some chopped onion.
Variation Tip: Cilantro can be replaced by parsley.
Nutritional Information per Serving:
Calories: 573 | Fat: 23.3g | Sat Fat: 4.5g | Carbohydrates: 75.4g | Fiber: 23.3g | Sugar: 13g | Protein: 22.9g

Chicken and Mushroom Soup

Prep Time: 10 minutes
Cook Time: 7 hours on low
Serves: 8
Ingredients:
- 3 cups chicken breasts, diced
- 1 cup chicken broth
- 2 cups hot water
- 1 can of diced Italian tomatoes
- 2 red bell peppers, sliced
- 1 red onion, diced
- ¾ cup mushrooms, washed, dried, and sliced
- 4 cloves garlic, minced
- 1 teaspoon dried oregano
- 1 teaspoon ground cumin
- Salt and pepper to taste
- 2 tablespoons fresh parsley, chopped

Preparation:
1. Preheat the slow cooker on low.
2. Add all the ingredients, then cover and cook on low for 6 hours.
3. Break up the chicken with a fork, cover the slow cooker again, and cook for an additional hour until ready.
4. Serve warm with a garnish of fresh parsley.
Serving Suggestion: Serve with sour cream.
Variation Tip: Switch up red bell peppers with yellow bell peppers.
Nutritional Information per Serving:
Calories 129 | Fat 4.3g | Sodium 146mg | Carbs 5.5g | Fiber 1.2g | Sugar 2.9g | Protein 16.8g

Zucchini and Basil Soup

Prep Time: 15 minutes
Cook Time: 25 minutes
Serves: 6
Ingredients:
- 2½ pounds zucchini, chopped
- 2 tablespoons olive oil
- 1 medium onion, chopped
- 4 garlic cloves, chopped
- ⅓ cup fresh basil leaves, chopped
- ⅓ cup heavy cream
- 4 cups chicken broth
- Salt and black pepper, to taste
- 2 tablespoons extra-virgin olive oil

Preparation:
1. In a large pan placed over medium-low heat, add the olive oil, zucchini, and onion.
2. Cook for about 6 minutes, frequently stirring.
3. Stir in the garlic and sauté for about 1 minute.
4. Add the chicken broth and allow to boil over medium-high heat.
5. Reduce the heat to medium-low and simmer for about 15 minutes.
6. Sprinkle in the basil, salt, and black pepper, and remove from the heat.
7. Blend the soup using an immersion blender until a smooth puree is formed.
8. Ladle out the soup into serving bowls and drizzle with the extra-virgin olive oil.
9. Top with the heavy cream and serve immediately.
Serving Suggestion: Serve with toasted whole-wheat bread slices.
Variation Tip: You can use vegetable broth instead of chicken broth.
Nutritional Information per Serving:
Calories: 170 | Fat: 13.1g | Sat Fat: 3.2g | Carbohydrates: 9.6g | Fiber: 2.5g | Sugar: 4.5g | Protein: 6g

Zucchini Avocado Carpaccio

Prep Time: 10 minutes
Cook Time: 0 minutes
Serves: 2
Ingredients:
- 3 cups zucchini, thinly sliced
- 1 ripe avocado, thinly sliced
- 1 tablespoon freshly squeezed lemon juice
- 1 tablespoon extra-virgin olive oil
- ¼ tablespoon lemon zest, finely grated
- ½ teaspoon freshly ground black pepper
- 1-ounce almonds, sliced and chopped
- Sea salt, to taste

Preparation:
1. Place the avocado and zucchini on a plate in an overlapping manner.
2. Mix the lemon juice with the lemon zest in a bowl.
3. Add in the olive oil along with black pepper and sea salt.
4. Now drizzle the lemon juice mixture over the salad.
Serving Suggestion: Top the salad with the finely chopped almonds.
Variation Tip: Substitute almonds with walnuts.
Nutritional Information per Serving:
Calories 378 | Fat 34.1g | Sodium 142mg | Carbs 18g | Fiber 10.6g | Sugar 4.2g | Protein 7.1g

Portuguese Salad

Prep Time: 10 minutes
Cook Time: 0 minutes
Serves: 4
Ingredients:
- 1 medium head iceberg lettuce, washed, dried, and torn into pieces
- 4 medium tomatoes, sliced
- 1 medium carrot, shredded
- 1 small cucumber, sliced
- 1 small green bell pepper, seeded and sliced thinly
- 1 small onion, cut into rings
- ½ cup pitted olives (black or green)
- Lemon wedges, to serve
- Fresh parsley, chopped, for garnish
For the dressing:
- 2 tablespoons olive oil
- 2 tablespoons balsamic or red wine vinegar
- Salt and pepper, to taste

Preparation:
1. Whisk the dressing ingredients together in a small bowl and set aside.
2. Arrange the lettuce on a serving dish and top with the tomatoes, carrot, cucumber, green bell pepper, onion, and olives.
3. Drizzle with the dressing.
Serving Suggestion: Serve with lemon wedges and garnish with chopped parsley.
Variation Tip: Substitute the iceberg lettuce with crisphead lettuce.
Nutritional Information per Serving:
Calories 141 | Fat 8.6 g | Sodium 260 mg | Carbs 16.1g | Fiber 4.4g | Sugar 8.9g | Protein 3g

Chicken and Carrot Salad

Prep Time: 10 minutes
Cook Time: 45 minutes
Serves: 3
Ingredients:
- 1 celery root
- 1 chicken breast
- 1 apple
- 3 carrots
- ½ lemon, juice only
- 8½ ounces mayonnaise
- Kosher salt, to taste
- Black pepper, to taste

Preparation:
1. Fill a pot with water. Boil the chicken breast until cooked through, about 45 minutes.
2. Grate the apple, carrots, and celery root. Transfer to a medium bowl.
3. Drizzle the grated veggies and apple with the lemon juice and mix well.
4. Cut the chicken breast into strips. Add to the bowl.
5. Add the salt, pepper, and mayo. Mix until all the ingredients are combined.
6. Allow the salad to chill in your refrigerator until you serve.
Serving Suggestion: Serve over whole-wheat bread.
Variation Tip: Substitute kosher salt with sea salt.
Nutritional Information per Serving:
Calories 490 | Fat 28.9g | Sodium 738mg | Carbs 39.9g | Fiber 4g | Sugar 18.4g | Protein 20.5g

Quinoa Mango Salad

Prep Time: 10 minutes
Cook Time: 20 minutes
Serves: 4

Ingredients:
- 1 cup dry quinoa
- 1 cucumber, chopped
- 1 ripe mango, peeled and diced
- 2 pints cherry or grape tomatoes, halved
- ¼ cup fresh basil leaves, finely chopped
- 2 tablespoons balsamic vinegar
- 1½ cups cooked garbanzo beans
- 5 ounces mixed baby greens

Preparation:
1. Put the quinoa in a fine-mesh sieve and rinse under cool water for a few seconds.
2. Boil 2 cups of water in a saucepan.
3. Add the quinoa and reduce the heat to medium.
4. Cover and boil gently for about 15 minutes until all the moisture is absorbed.
5. Combine the cooked quinoa, cucumber, mango, onion, basil, vinegar, and beans in a large dish.
6. Serve on a mixed-greens bed.

Serving Suggestion: Garnish with fresh parsley.
Variation Tip: Substitute mango with two fresh peaches, pitted and chopped.
Nutritional Information per Serving:
Calories 335 | Fat 3.3g | Sodium 39mg | Carbs 65g | Fiber 10.6g | Sugar 12.1g | Protein 15g

Carrot Soup

Prep Time: 10 minutes
Cook Time: 25 minutes
Serves: 2

Ingredients:
- ½ onion, chopped
- 2 teaspoons fresh ginger, minced
- 1 teaspoon fresh garlic, minced
- 4 cups water
- 3 carrots, chopped
- 1 teaspoon turmeric powder
- ½ cup coconut milk
- 1 tablespoon fresh cilantro, chopped
- 1 tablespoon olive oil

Preparation:
1. Heat the olive oil in a saucepan on medium heat.
2. Sauté the onion, garlic, and ginger until softened (3 minutes). Stir in the water, carrots, and turmeric.
3. Bring the mixture to a boil, reduce the heat, and simmer until the carrots are tender (20 minutes).
4. Transfer the soup to a blender, add the coconut milk, and pulse until the soup becomes smooth.

Serving Suggestion: Serve the soup topped with the cilantro.
Variation Tip: Substitute water with vegetable broth.
Nutritional Information per Serving:
Calories 259 | Fat 21.6g | Sodium 89mg | Carbs 17.4g | Fiber 4.7g | Sugar 7.8g | Protein 2.8g

Lentil Soup

Prep Time: 10 minutes
Cook Time: 35 minutes
Serves: 4

Ingredients:
- 1 tablespoon olive oil
- 1 onion, chopped
- 2 celery stalks, chopped
- 1 tablespoon garlic, minced
- 6 cups low-sodium vegetable stock
- 2 (28-ounce) cans low-sodium diced tomatoes
- 1 (15-ounce) can low-sodium red lentils, rinsed and drained
- 1 tablespoon fresh basil, chopped
- A pinch of red pepper flakes
- Sea salt and black pepper, to taste

Preparation:
1. In a pot, heat the olive oil over medium-high heat.
2. Sauté the onion, celery, and garlic until softened, about 3 minutes.
3. Stir in the stock, salt, pepper, and tomatoes with their juices, and bring to a boil.
4. Reduce the heat to low and simmer for 20 minutes.
5. Transfer the mixture to a food processor and purée until smooth.
6. Return the soup to the pot, stir in the lentils, basil, and red pepper flakes, and simmer for about 10 minutes.
7. Serve.

Serving Suggestion: Serve with toasted whole-wheat bread.
Variation Tip: Substitute vegetable stock with chicken stock.
Nutritional Information per Serving:
Calories 211 | Fat 4g | Sodium 336mg | Carbs 36g | Fiber 13g | Sugar 11g | Protein 12g

Squash Pasta Salad

Prep Time: 10 minutes
Cook Time: 40 minutes
Serves: 6
Ingredients:
- 1 red bell pepper, cut into ½-inch pieces
- 1 yellow bell pepper, chopped
- 1 medium eggplant, cubed
- 3 small yellow squash, cut in ¼-inch slices
- 6 tablespoons extra-virgin olive oil
- Salt and black pepper, to taste
- 1½ ounces sun-dried tomatoes, soaked in ½ cup boiling water
- ½ cup arugula leaves, torn
- ½ cup fresh basil, chopped
- 2 tablespoons balsamic vinegar
- 2 tablespoons garlic, minced
- 4 ounces feta cheese, crumbled
- 12 ounces farfalle pasta

Preparation:
1. Preheat the oven to 450℉.
2. Cover a casserole dish with foil and grease the foil with non-stick spray.
3. Combine the bell peppers, salt, pepper, eggplant, 2 tablespoons of olive oil, and squash in a bowl.
4. Place the mixture in the prepared casserole dish. Cook in the oven for thirty minutes, stirring the contents halfway through.
5. Boil the pasta in water and salt for 11 minutes, then drain.
6. Place the pasta in a bowl with the basil, liquid from the tomatoes, pepper, veggies, salt, arugula, feta, pasta, garlic, sun-dried tomatoes, balsamic, and olive oil.
7. Place the mix in the fridge for 60 minutes, then serve.
8. Enjoy!
Serving Suggestion: Top with chopped cilantro.
Variation Tip: Switch up balsamic vinegar with apple cider vinegar.
Nutritional Information per Serving:
Calories 446 | Fat 19.5g | Sodium 324mg | Carbs 56.9g | Fiber 6.7g | Sugar 7.4g | Protein 13.8g

Lentil Salad

Prep Time: 10 minutes
Cook Time: 20 minutes
Serves: 4
Ingredients:
For the salad
- 1 cup lentils
- 2½ cups water
- 1 bay leaf
- 2 tablespoons extra-virgin olive oil
- 1 cup onion, chopped
- 1 cup carrot, chopped
- 1 garlic clove, minced
For the dressing
- ¼ cup extra-virgin olive oil
- 2 tablespoons white wine vinegar
- 1 teaspoon Dijon mustard
- Salt and black pepper, to taste
Preparation:
1. In a large saucepan, combine the lentils, water, and bay leaf and bring to a boil over medium-high heat.
2. Reduce the heat to low and simmer for 30 minutes until the lentils are tender.
3. Drain the lentils and discard the bay leaf.
4. Heat the olive oil over medium heat in a skillet and add the onion and carrot.
5. Sauté for about 5 minutes, until softened. Add the garlic and cook for one more minute.
6. Whisk together the dressing ingredients in a small bowl to make the dressing.
7. In another bowl, combine the warm lentils with the onion-carrot-garlic mixture.
8. Add the dressing and toss to combine.
Serving Suggestion: Serve with hot brown rice.
Variation Tip: Add a tablespoon of paprika for more vibrancy.
Nutritional Information per Serving:
Calories 380 | Fat 21g | Sodium 56mg | Carbs 37g | Fiber 7g | Sugar 4g | Protein 13g

Beets and Walnut Salad

Prep Time: 10 minutes
Cook Time: 10 minutes
Serves: 3
Ingredients:
- 2 ounces beets
- 3 ounces arugula
- 2 ounces bibb lettuce
- 9 ounces romaine lettuce
- ¼ cup dry breadcrumbs
- ¼ tablespoon dried thyme
- ¼ tablespoon dried basil
- $1/3$ teaspoon black pepper
- 6 ounces goat's cheese (preferably in log shape)
- $1/8$ cup walnut pieces
- ¼ cup red wine vinaigrette

Preparation:
1. Preheat the oven to 425℉.
2. Trim, wash, and dry all the salad greens. Tear the greens into small pieces and toss well.
3. Combine the herbs, pepper, and crumbs.
4. Slice the cheese into 1-ounce pieces. Roll the pieces of cheese in the seasoned crumbs mixture to coat them.
5. Place the cheese on a sheet pan.
6. Bake for 10 minutes.
7. Meanwhile, toast the walnuts in a dry sauté pan or in the oven with the cheese.
8. Toss the greens with the vinaigrette and arrange them on plates.

Serving Suggestion: Top each plate of greens with two pieces of cheese and sprinkle with walnuts.
Variation Tip: Substitute dried thyme and basil with fresh thyme and basil.
Nutritional Information per Serving:
Calories 460 | Fat 40g | Sodium 787mg | Carbs 21.4g | Fiber 2g | Sugar 9.1g | Protein 17g

Mushroom Leek Salad

Prep Time: 2 days 10 minutes
Cook Time: 10 minutes
Serves: 6
Ingredients:
- 24 fresh medium mushrooms
- 6 medium leeks, roots trimmed
- Sea salt and black pepper, to taste
- 12 green or black olives, pitted
- 1 lemon, sliced
- $1/3$ cup extra-virgin olive oil
- 1 teaspoon fennel seeds
- ¼ teaspoon dried thyme
- 1 bay leaf
- 3 tablespoons fresh parsley, chopped

Preparation:
1. Cut the green leaves from the leeks and wash the white parts, removing any grit. Cut them into pieces of 1½ inches each.
2. Cook, covered in boiling, salted water until the leeks are tender. Drain them and allow them to cool.
3. Clean the mushrooms by wiping them off or rinsing them quickly. Make sure all dirt is removed. Snip the tough ends of the stems off.
4. Cook, covered in boiling, salted water for 5 minutes. Drain them and allow them to cool.
5. In a bowl, combine the olives, leeks, and mushrooms with the rest of the ingredients, excluding the parsley.
6. Cover and refrigerate for two days. Stir the mixture occasionally.
7. Remove the bay leaf and lemon slices and discard.
8. Sprinkle the parsley over the top and serve.

Serving Suggestion: Garnish with chopped parsley.
Variation Tip: Feel free to use fresh thyme.
Nutritional Information per Serving:
Calories 179 | Fat 12.5g | Sodium 79mg | Carbs 16.8g | Fiber 3.1g | Sugar 5g | Protein 3.9g

Moroccan Chickpea Soup

Prep Time: 10 minutes
Cook Time: 40 minutes
Serves: 6

Ingredients:
- ¼ cup fresh parsley or mint, minced
- ¼ teaspoon ground cumin
- ¼ teaspoon ground ginger
- ¼ teaspoon saffron threads, crumbled
- ½ teaspoon hot paprika
- 1 (14½-ounce) can diced tomatoes
- 1 onion, chopped fine
- 1-pound red potatoes, unpeeled, cut into ½-inch pieces
- 1 teaspoon sugar
- 1 zucchini, cut into ½-inch pieces
- 2 (15-ounce) cans garbanzo beans, rinsed
- 3 tablespoons extra-virgin olive oil
- 3½ cups chicken or vegetable broth
- 4 garlic cloves, minced
- Lemon wedges, for serving
- Salt and pepper, to taste

Preparation:
1. Heat the oil in a Dutch oven on moderate to high heat until it starts to shimmer.
2. Put in the onion, sugar, and ½ teaspoon salt and cook until the onion softens, approximately 5 minutes.
3. Mix in the garlic, paprika, saffron, ginger, and cumin and cook until aromatic, approximately half a minute.
4. Mix in the beans, potatoes, tomatoes and their juice, zucchini, and broth.
5. Bring to simmer and cook, stirring intermittently until the potatoes are tender for 20 to 30 minutes.
6. Using a wooden spoon, mash some potatoes against the side of the pot to thicken the soup.
7. Remove from the heat, mix in the parsley or mint and sprinkle with salt and pepper to taste.

Serving Suggestion: Serve with lemon wedges.
Variation Tip: Substitute chicken with vegetable stock.

Nutritional Information per Serving:
Calories 120 | Fat 26.9g | Sodium 276mg | Carbs 105.5g | Fiber 28g | Sugar 19.8g | Protein 135.1g

Roasted Tomato Basil Soup

Prep Time: 10 minutes
Cook Time: 50 minutes
Serves: 6

Ingredients:
- 3 pounds halved Roma tomatoes
- Olive oil
- 2 carrots, chopped
- Salt and black pepper, to taste
- 2 yellow onions, chopped
- 5 garlic cloves, minced
- 2 ounces basil leaves
- 1 cup crushed tomatoes
- 3 thyme sprigs
- 1 teaspoon dry oregano
- 2 teaspoon thyme leaves
- ½ teaspoon paprika
- 2½ cups water
- ½ teaspoon cumin
- 1 tablespoon lemon juice

Preparation:
1. Mix the salt, olive oil, carrot, black pepper, and to-matoes in a bowl.
2. Transfer the carrot mixture to a baking tray and bake in a preheated oven at 450℉ for 30 minutes.
3. Blend the baked mixture in a blender. You can use a little water if needed during blending.
4. Sauté the onions heated in olive oil over medium flame in a pot for three minutes.
5. Mix in the garlic and cook for one more minute.
6. Transfer the blended tomato mixture to the pot, followed by the crushed tomatoes, water, spices, thyme, salt, basil, and pepper.
7. Let the mixture boil. Reduce the heat and simmer for 20 minutes.
8. Drizzle with lemon juice and serve.

Serving Suggestion: Serve with bread slices.
Variation Tip: Add chili for a spicier taste.

Nutritional Information per Serving:
Calories 104 | Fat 0.8g | Sodium 117mg | Carbs 23.4g | Fiber 5.4g | Sugar 8.5g | Protein 4.3g

Grilled Veggie Sandwich

Prep Time: 25 minutes
Cook Time: 5 minutes
Serves: 4
Ingredients:
- ¼ cup mayonnaise
- Olive oil cooking spray
- ½ teaspoon fresh lemon juice
- 2 small zucchinis, thinly sliced lengthwise
- 2 portobello mushrooms, cut into ¼-inch thick slices
- Salt, to taste
- ½ cup feta cheese, crumbled
- 2 cups fresh baby arugula
- 2 garlic cloves, minced
- 1 eggplant, cut into ¼-inch thick slices
- 2 tablespoons olive oil
- ¾ of a ciabatta loaf, split horizontally
- 2 medium tomatoes, cut into slices

Preparation:
1. Set the broiler on high and grease a baking pan with the cooking spray.
2. In a bowl, add the mayonnaise, garlic, and lemon juice and toss well. Set aside.
3. Evenly coat the zucchini, eggplant, and mushrooms with oil and sprinkle with salt.
4. Place the vegetable slices onto the baking pan and broil for about 1½ minutes per side.
5. Shift the vegetable slices onto a plate.
6. Arrange the loaves onto the broiler rack, cut side down, and cook for about 2 minutes.
7. Remove from the broiler and cut each half-loaf into four equal-sized pieces.
8. Layer the mayonnaise mixture evenly onto each bread piece and top with the vegetable slices, followed by the tomatoes, arugula, and feta cheese.
9. Cover with the top pieces and serve.
Serving Suggestion: Serve these sandwiches with your favorite dip.
Variation Tip: You can use any type of mushrooms.
Nutritional Information per Serving:
Calories: 268 | Fat: 16.9g | Sat Fat: 8.3g | Carbohydrates: 25g | Fiber: 6.2g | Sugar: 8.7g | Protein: 7.4g

Chicken and Veggie Flatbread Pizza

Prep Time: 15 minutes
Cook Time: 10 minutes
Serves: 4
Ingredients:
- 1 tablespoon Greek vinaigrette
- 2 flatbreads
- ½ cup feta cheese, crumbled
- ½ cup water-packed artichoke hearts, rinsed, drained, and chopped
- ½ cup cooked chicken breast strips, chopped
- ⅛ teaspoon dried oregano, crushed
- 1 cup part-skim mozzarella cheese, shredded
- ¼ cup parmesan cheese, grated
- ½ cup black olives, pitted and sliced
- ⅛ teaspoon dried basil, crushed
- Pinch of black pepper

Preparation:
1. Preheat the oven to 390°F.
2. Organize the flatbreads onto a large baking sheet and glaze each with the vinaigrette.
3. Place the feta cheese on each bread, followed by the veggies, parmesan cheese, and chicken.
4. Sprinkle with the black pepper and dried herbs.
5. Top each bread evenly with the mozzarella cheese.
6. Bake for 10 minutes until the cheese is melted.
7. Remove from the oven and set aside for about 2 minutes.
8. Slice each flatbread into two pieces and serve.
Serving Suggestion: Serve with your favorite sauce.
Variation Tip: Black olives can be replaced with green olives.
Nutritional Information per Serving:
Calories: 200 | Fat: 11.4g | Sat Fat: 5.3g | Carbohydrates: 12.3g | Fiber: 2.4g | Sugar: 1.9g | Protein: 14.1g

Avocado Caprese Wrap

Prep Time: 10 Minutes
Cook Time: 0 Minutes
Serves: 2

Ingredients:
- 2 tortillas
- Balsamic vinegar, as needed
- 1 ball mozzarella cheese, grated
- ½ cup arugula
- 1 tomato, sliced
- 2 tablespoons fresh basil leaves, chopped
- Kosher salt, to taste
- 1 avocado, sliced
- Olive oil, as required
- Black pepper, to taste

Preparation:
1. Divide the tomato slices and cheese evenly among the tortilla wraps. Then add the avocado and basil.
2. Drizzle olive oil and vinegar over the top.
3. Season with salt and pepper.
4. Wrap the tortilla and serve.

Serving Suggestion: Garnish with parsley.

Variation Tip: Add chicken or fish for an even tastier snack!

Nutritional Information per Serving:
Calories 791 | Fat 47g | Sodium 280mg | Carbs 71g | Fiber 16g | Sugar 5.5g | Protein 23g

Sautéed Apricots

Prep Time: 10 Minutes
Cook Time: 15 Minutes
Serves: 4

Ingredients:
- 2 tablespoons olive oil
- 1 cup almonds, blanched, skinless, and unsalted
- ½ teaspoon fine sea salt
- ⅛ teaspoon red pepper flakes
- ⅛ teaspoon ground cinnamon
- ½ cup dried apricots, chopped

Preparation:
1. Place a frying pan over high heat, adding in your almonds, salt, and olive oil.
2. Sauté until the almonds turn light gold, which will take five to ten minutes. Make sure to stir often because they can burn easily.
3. Spoon your almonds into a serving dish, adding the cinnamon, red pepper flakes, and chopped apricot.
4. Allow the mixture to cool before serving.

Serving Suggestion: Serve with a dash of cinnamon.

Variation Tip: Omit the red pepper flakes for a milder taste.

Nutritional Information per Serving:
Calories 207 | Fat 19g | Sodium 235mg | Carbs 7g | Fiber 3.4g | Sugar 2.8g | Protein 5g

Spicy Berry Dip

Prep Time: 10 Minutes
Cook Time: 15 Minutes
Serves: 4

Ingredients:
- 10 ounces cranberries
- ¼ cup fresh orange juice
- ¾ teaspoon paprika
- ½ teaspoon chili powder
- 1 teaspoon lemon zest
- 1 tablespoon lemon juice

Preparation:
1. Add all the ingredients into the inner pot of an Instant Pot and stir well.
2. Seal the pot with the lid and cook on High for 15 minutes.
3. Once done, allow for natural pressure release for 5 minutes, and then use the quick release. Remove the lid.
4. Blend the cranberry mixture using a blender until it reaches the desired consistency.
5. Serve and enjoy.

Serving Suggestion: Serve with a variety of meats like chicken, pork, turkey, etc.

Variation Tip: You may omit the chili for a milder taste.

Nutritional Information per Serving:
Calories 49 | Fat 0.2 g | Sodium 1mg | Carbs 8.6g | Sugar 4.1g | Protein 0.3g

Baked Cheese Crisp

Prep Time: 10 Minutes
Cook Time: 8 Minutes
Serves: 4
Ingredients:
- ¾ cup cheddar cheese, shredded
- ¾ cup parmesan cheese, shredded
- 1 teaspoon Italian seasoning

Preparation:
1. Mix the cheese and spread it on a baking tray.
2. Bake for eight minutes in the oven at 400°F.

Serving Suggestion: Serve with marinara sauce.
Variation Tip: Add in some dried herbs and ground spices of your liking.
Nutritional Information per Serving:
Calories 152 | Fat 11g | Sodium 520mg | Carbs 1g | Fiber 0g | Sugar 0.2g | Protein 12g

Zucchini Fritters

Prep Time: 10 Minutes
Cook Time: 30 Minutes
Serves: 6
Ingredients:
- 2 zucchinis, peeled and grated
- 1 sweet onion, finely diced
- 2 cloves garlic, minced
- 1 cup fresh parsley, chopped
- ½ teaspoon fine sea salt
- ½ teaspoon black pepper
- ½ teaspoon ground allspice
- 2 tablespoons olive oil
- 4 large eggs

Preparation:
1. Line a plate with paper towels and set it aside.

2. Mix the onion, parsley, garlic, zucchini, pepper, all-spice, and sea salt in a large bowl.
3. In a different bowl, beat the eggs before adding them to the zucchini mixture. Make sure it's mixed well.
4. Place a large skillet over medium heat.
5. Heat the olive oil, and then scoop ¼ cup of the mixture at a time into the skillet to create your fritters.
6. Cook for three minutes or until the bottom sets.
7. Flip and cook for an additional three minutes.
8. Transfer the fritters to the lined plate so they can drain.
9. Serve.
Serving Suggestion: Serve with pita bread.
Variation Tip: You can substitute the eggs for a dairy-free option.
Nutritional Information per Serving:
Calories 103 | Fat 8g | Sodium 216mg | Carbs 5g | Fiber 1.5g | Sugar 2.3g | Protein 5g

Chicken Caprese Sandwich

Prep Time: 10 Minutes
Cook Time: 6 Minutes
Serves: 4
Ingredients:
- 4 tablespoons olive oil
- 1 tablespoon lemonjuice
- ¼ cup basil leaves
- 1 teaspoon fresh parsley, minced
- Kosher, salt to taste
- 2 boneless chicken breasts, cut into bite-size pieces
- Black pepper, to taste
- 8 slices sourdough bread
- 11 Campari tomatoes
- 8 ounces mozzarella cheese, sliced
- Balsamic vinegar, as required

Preparation:
1. Add the chicken pieces, olive oil, lemon juice, salt, parsley, and pepper to a bowl.
2. Toss well to evenly coat the chicken in the mixture. Set aside.
3. Heat a skillet with some oil on medium heat. Add the chicken and cook for six minutes on both sides.
4. Drizzle the bread slices with olive oil and toast them in the oven.
5. Place the chicken pieces, cheese, and tomato slices over each slice of bread.
6. Sprinkle vinegar, oil, salt, basil, and pepper over the bread slices and serve.
Serving Suggestion: Top with basil leaves.
Variation Tip: You can use crusty ciabatta instead of sourdough bread.
Nutritional Information per Serving:
Calories 612.73 | Fat 32.06g | Sodium 891mg | Carbs 46.5g | Fiber 2.2g | Sugar 2.4g | Protein 34.4 g

Peanut Butter Balls

Prep Time: 10 minutes
Cook Time: 10 minutes
Serves: 16
Ingredients:
- 2 cups rolled oats
- ¼ cup unsweetened shredded coconut
- ¼ cup chocolate chips
- ½ cup honey
- 1 cup peanut butter

Directions:
1. Add oats and remaining ingredients into the mixing bowl and mix until well combined.
2. Make small balls from oats mixture and place onto the dish then place in refrigerator for 15 minutes.
Serving Suggestion: Serve chilled and enjoy.
Variation Tip: You can also use other nut butter.
Nutritional Information per Serving:
Calories 191 | Fat 10.6g | Sodium 78mg | Carbs 20.8g | Fiber 2.4g | Sugar 11.8g | Protein 5.7g

Veggie Tortilla Wraps

Prep Time: 20 minutes
Cook Time: 5 minutes
Serves: 2
Ingredients:
- ½ small zucchini, thinly sliced
- ½ teaspoon olive oil
- ½ medium red bell pepper, seeded and thinly sliced
- 2 whole-grain tortillas
- ½ cup fresh baby spinach
- 1 teaspoon dried oregano
- 1 red onion, thinly sliced
- ¼ cup hummus
- 2 tablespoons feta cheese, crumbled
- 1 tablespoon black olives, pitted and sliced

Preparation:

1. Heat the olive oil in a small skillet placed over medium-low heat. Add the bell pepper, zucchini, and onion.
2. Sauté for about 5 minutes.
3. Meanwhile, in another skillet, heat the tortillas one by one until they are warm.
4. Place the hummus evenly onto the middle of each wrap.
5. Place the spinach onto each tortilla, then add the sautéed vegetables, feta cheese, oregano, and olives.
6. Carefully fold the edges of each tortilla over the filling and roll them up.
7. Slice each roll in half crosswise and serve.
Serving Suggestion: Serve with a healthy dip of your choice.
Variation Tip: You can also use corn tortillas.
Nutritional Information per Serving:
Calories: 282 | Fat: 10.4g | Sat Fat: 3.6g | Carbohydrates: 39.2g | Fiber: 8.4g | Sugar: 6.8g | Protein: 10.4g

Chickpea Spinach Patties

Prep Time: 10 minutes
Cook Time: 10 minutes
Serves: 12
Ingredients:
- 1 egg
- 2 cups can chickpeas, rinsed & drained
- 1 teaspoon ground cumin
- 1 tablespoon paprika
- 1 teaspoon garlic, minced
- ½ onion, chopped
- 1 carrot, grated
- 1 cup baby spinach, cooked & drained
- Pepper
- Salt

Directions:
1. Add chickpeas into the mixing bowl and mash using the fork.
2. Add remaining ingredients into the bowl and mix until well combined.
3. Spray pan with cooking spray and heat over medium-high heat.
4. Make patties from chickpea mixture and place onto the hot pan and cook for 4-5 minutes on each side or until golden brown.
Serving Suggestion: Serve with your choice of dip.
Variation Tip: Add ¼ cup of chopped scallions.
Nutritional Information per Serving:
Calories 60 | Fat 1g | Sodium 143mg | Carbs 10.6g | Fiber 2.3g | Sugar 0.5g | Protein 2.7g

Crispy Chickpeas

Prep Time: 10 minutes
Cook Time: 4 minutes
Serves: 6
Ingredients:
- 30 ounces can chickpeas, rinsed
- 2 tablespoons everything bagel seasoning
- 3 tablespoons olive oil

Directions:
1. Preheat the oven to 400° F.
2. In a bowl, toss chickpeas with oil and spread onto the baking sheet and roast in preheated oven for 30 minutes. Stir halfway through.
3. Transfer chickpeas into the bowl and toss with bagel seasoning.

Serving Suggestion: Allow to cool completely then serve.
Variation Tip: Add your choice of seasonings.
Nutritional Information per Serving:
Calories 238 | Fat 1.2g | Sodium 439mg | Carbs 33.9g | Fiber 6.4g | Sugar 0.2g | Protein 7.3g

Cauliflower Fritters

Prep Time: 10 Minutes
Cook Time: 50 Minutes
Serves: 4
Ingredients:
- 30 ounces canned chickpeas, drained and rinsed
- 2½ tablespoons olive oil
- 1 small yellow onion, chopped
- 2 cups cauliflower florets, chopped
- 2 tablespoons garlic, minced
- A pinch of salt and black pepper

Preparation:
1. Spread half of the chickpeas on a baking sheet lined with parchment pepper, add 1 tablespoon of oil, season with salt and pepper, toss, and bake at 400°F for 30 minutes.
2. Transfer the baked chickpeas to a food processor, pulse well, and put the mixture into a bowl.
3. Heat a pan with ½ tablespoon of oil over medium-high heat; add the garlic and the onion and sauté for 3 minutes.
4. Add the cauliflower and cook for 6 minutes more. Transfer the mixture to a blender, add the rest of the uncooked chickpeas, and pulse.
5. Pour the blended mixture over the crispy chickpea mixture. Stir the mixture and then shape it into medium fritters.
6. Heat a pan with the rest of the oil over medium-high heat. Add the fritters, cook them for 3 minutes on each side, and serve.

Serving Suggestion: Garnish with parsley.
Variation Tip: Use fresh cauliflower as the frozen ones tend to have more liquid, making the fritters mushy.
Nutritional Information per Serving:
Calories 333 | Fat 12.6g | Sodium 65mg | Carbs 44.7g | Fiber 12.8g | Sugar 21.5g | Protein 13.6g

Carrot Cake Balls

Prep Time: 10 minutes
Cook Time: 10 minutes
Serves: 22
Ingredients:
- ½ cup old-fashioned rolled oats
- 1 cup dates, pitted
- ¼ teaspoon turmeric
- ½ teaspoon ground cinnamon
- 1 teaspoon vanilla
- 2 medium carrots, grated
- ¼ cup chia seeds
- ¼ cup pecans, chopped
- ¼ teaspoon salt

Directions:
1. Add dates, chia seeds, pecans, and oats into the food processor and process until well combined.
2. Add remaining ingredients and process until just combined.
3. Make small balls from oat mixture and place onto the dish then place dish in the refrigerator for 20 minutes.

Serving Suggestion: Serve chilled and enjoy.
Variation Tip: Add ½ teaspoon of ground ginger.
Nutritional Information per Serving:
Calories 54 | Fat 2g | Sodium 32mg | Carbs 9g | Fiber 1.9g | Sugar 5.5g | Protein 1g

Salsa Dip

Prep Time: 10 minutes
Cook Time: 5 minutes
Serves: 16
Ingredients:
- 2 cups cucumber, peeled & chopped
- 2 teaspoons Greek seasoning
- 2 tablespoons olive oil
- 1 cup Feta cheese, crumbled
- 1 teaspoon garlic, minced
- 4 ounces can black olives, sliced
- 1 cup onion, chopped
- 2 cups tomatoes, chopped

Directions:
1. Add all ingredients into the large bowl and stir until well combined.
2. Cover and place in refrigerator for 8 hours.
Serving Suggestion: Serve with pita chips.
Variation Tip: Add ¼ cup of chopped basil.
Nutritional Information per Serving:
Calories 59 | Fat 4.3g | Sodium 185mg | Carbs 3.6g | Fiber 0.5g | Sugar 1.5g | Protein 1.8g

Lamb-Filled Pita with Yogurt Sauce

Prep Time: 15 minutes
Cook Time: 6 minutes
Serves: 4
Ingredients:
- 1 tablespoon fresh rosemary, minced
- 2 garlic cloves, minced
- Salt and black pepper, to taste
- 2 teaspoons olive oil
- 1½ cups cucumber, finely chopped
- 4 (6-ounce) whole-wheat pitas, warmed
- ¾ pound boneless leg of lamb, cut into bite-sized pieces
- 1 (6-ounce) container Greek yogurt, fat-free and plain
- 1 tablespoon fresh lemon juice
Preparation:

1. Add the rosemary, garlic, salt, and black pepper to a bowl and mix well.
2. Add the lamb pieces and toss to coat well.
3. Add the olive oil to a non-stick skillet placed over medium-high heat.
4. Transfer the lamb mixture to the skillet and stir fry for about 6 minutes.
5. Meanwhile, mix the cucumber, yogurt, lemon juice, salt, and black pepper in a bowl for the yogurt sauce.
6. Arrange the lamb mixture evenly between all the pitas.
7. Drizzle the yogurt sauce over the top of the lamb and serve immediately.
Serving Suggestion: Top with mint leaves before serving.
Variation Tip: You can also use plain yogurt instead of Greek yogurt.
Nutritional Information per Serving:
Calories: 675 | Fat: 14.1g | Sat Fat: 4g | Carbohydrates: 97.8g | Fiber: 13.2g | Sugar: 3.9g | Protein: 45.3g

Chicken Skewers

Prep Time: 10 minutes
Cook Time: 10 minutes
Serves: 4
Ingredients:
- 1 pound chicken breast, boneless and cut into ¾-inch pieces
- 1 tablespoon fresh lemon juice
- 1 ¾ cups green grapes, seedless, rinsed
- 1 teaspoon lemon zest
- 1 tablespoon fresh rosemary, minced
- 1 tablespoon fresh oregano, minced
- ½ teaspoon chili flakes, crushed
- 1 teaspoon garlic, minced
- ¼ cup olive oil
- ½ teaspoon salt

Directions:
1. Add chicken and remaining ingredients into the zip-lock bag. Seal bag and place in refrigerator for overnight.
2. Thread marinated chicken pieces onto the soaked wooden skewers.
3. Preheat the grill.
4. Arrange chicken skewers onto the hot grill and cook for 3-5 minutes on each side.
Serving Suggestion: Drizzle with lemon juice and serve.
Variation Tip: Add your choice of seasonings.
Nutritional Information per Serving:
Calories 273 | Fat 15.9g | Sodium 351mg | Carbs 8.6g | Fiber 1.3g | Sugar 6.7g | Protein 24.5g

Tempeh Snack

Prep Time: 10 minutes
Cook Time: 25 minutes
Serves: 6
Ingredients:
- 11 ounces soy tempeh, cut into sticks
- 1 teaspoon olive oil
- ½ teaspoon ground black pepper
- ¼ teaspoon garlic powder

Preparation:
1. Preheat the oven to 400℉. Line a baking sheet with parchment paper.
2. Toss the tempeh sticks in the salt, black pepper, garlic powder, and olive oil.
3. Spread the sticks out evenly onto the prepared baking sheet and bake in the oven for 25 minutes.
4. When ready, the cooked tempeh sticks will be golden and crispy.
Serving Suggestion: Serve with ginger soy dressing.
Variation Tip: For a more varied flavor, add ¼ teaspoon of onion powder or other seasonings of your choice.
Nutritional Information per Serving:
Calories 88 | Fat 2.5g | Sodium 18mg | Carbs 10.2g | Fiber 22g | Sugar 0g | Protein 6.5g

Parsley Nachos

Prep Time: 10 minutes
Cook Time: 0 minutes
Serves: 3
Ingredients:
- 3 ounces tortilla chips
- ¼ cup Greek yogurt
- 1 tablespoon fresh parsley, chopped
- ¼ teaspoon garlic, minced
- 2 kalamata olives, chopped
- 1 teaspoon paprika
- ¼ teaspoon ground thyme

Preparation:
1. Combine all the ingredients except for the tortilla chips in a bowl.
2. Add the tortilla chips and mix up gently.
3. Serve immediately.
Serving Suggestion: Garnish with fresh chopped parsley.
Variation Tip: Add more paprika if needed.
Nutritional Information per Serving:
Calories 81 | Fat 1.6g | Sodium 39mg | Carbs 14.1g | Fiber 2.2g | Sugar 0.3g | Protein 3.5g

Chickpeas and Veggie Gazpacho

Prep Time: 15 minutes (plus 2 hours for chilling)
Serves: 10
Ingredients:
- 1 large fresh plum tomato, chopped
- 1 (15½-ounce) can low-sodium chickpeas, rinsed and drained
- 1 large cucumber, peeled, seeded, and chopped finely
- ½ yellow bell pepper, seeded and chopped
- 2 tablespoons sweet onion, finely chopped
- 1 large garlic clove, minced
- 1 (46 fluid ounces) can low-sodium tomato juice
- Dash of hot pepper sauce
- ½ cup fresh parsley, chopped
- 1 celery stalk, chopped finely
- ½ red bell pepper, seeded and chopped
- 2 scallions, chopped
- ¼ cup fresh parsley, chopped
- 1 tablespoon fresh lemon juice
- 1 teaspoon curry powder
- Black pepper, to taste

Preparation:
1. Place all the ingredients except the parsley in a large bowl and toss thoroughly to combine.
2. Cover the bowl tightly with plastic wrap and place it in the refrigerator.
3. Chill for about 2 hours and serve garnished with parsley.
Serving Suggestion: Serve with a sprinkling of oregano on top.
Variation Tip: More vegetables can also be added.
Nutritional Information per Serving:
Calories 200 | Fat 2.9g | Sodium 0.3g | Carbs 36.2g | Fiber 9g | Sugar 11.3g | Protein 10.2g

Butternut Squash Fries

Prep Time: 10 minutes
Cook Time: 20 minutes
Serves: 2
Ingredients:
- 1 butternut squash, seeded
- 1 tablespoon extra-virgin olive oil
- ½ tablespoon grapeseed oil
- Sea salt, to taste

Preparation:
1. Preheat the oven to 425°F.
2. Cut the squash into thin slices and place the slices into a bowl.
3. Coat the slices with the extra-virgin olive oil and grapeseed oil.
4. Add a sprinkle of salt and toss to coat well.
5. Arrange the squash slices onto three baking sheets and bake for 20 minutes, tossing halfway through.

Serving Suggestion: Serve with your preferred sauce.
Variation Tip: Add ½ teaspoon paprika and ½ teaspoon dried thyme for a varied flavor.
Nutritional Information per Serving:
Calories 153 | Fat 10g | Sodium 123mg | Carbs 10g | Fiber 16.4g | Sugar 2.8g | Protein 1.5g

Sweet Potato Chips

Prep Time: 10 minutes
Cook Time: 35 minutes
Serves: 4
Ingredients:
- 1 large sweet potato, thinly sliced
- 1 tablespoon extra-virgin olive oil
- Salt, to taste

Preparation:
1. Preheat your oven to 400°F.
2. Toss the potato slices in the salt and extra-virgin olive oil in a bowl.

3. Bake for about 35 minutes, flipping every 15 minutes until crispy and browned.
Serving Suggestion: Serve with yogurt-mint sauce.
Variation Tip: Sprinkle with pepper for more heat.
Nutritional Information per Serving:
Calories 71 | Fat 3.6g | Sodium 55mg | Carbs 9.4g | Fiber 1.5g | Sugar 2.9g | Protein 1g

Pita Pizza with Shrimp

Prep Time: 15 minutes
Cook Time: 10 minutes
Serves: 1
Ingredients:
- 2 tablespoons spaghetti sauce
- Olive oil cooking spray
- 1 tablespoon pesto sauce
- 2 tablespoons mozzarella cheese, shredded
- ⅛ cup bay shrimp
- Pinch of dried basil
- 1 (6-inch) pita bread
- 5 cherry tomatoes, halved
- Pinch of garlic powder

Preparation:
1. Preheat the oven to 330°F.
2. Grease a baking sheet lightly with the cooking spray.
3. Combine the spaghetti sauce and pesto in a bowl.
4. Layer the pesto mixture thinly over the pita bread.
5. Arrange the cheese, tomatoes, and shrimp over the pita bread.
6. Dust with the garlic powder and basil.
7. Place the pita bread onto the baking sheet and bake for about 10 minutes.
8. Take out from the oven and set aside for about 5 minutes.
9. Cut into the desired size of slices and serve.

Serving Suggestion: Serve with barbecue sauce.
Variation Tip: You can use dried oregano instead of basil.
Nutritional Information per Serving:
Calories: 571 | Fat: 18.8g | Sat Fat: 7.7g | Carbohydrates: 73.4g | Fiber: 9.6g | Sugar: 18g | Protein: 31.9g

Easy Avocado Hummus

Prep Time: 10 minutes
Cook Time: 10 minutes
Serves: 10
Ingredients:
- 15 ounces can chickpeas
- 1 teaspoon ground cumin
- 1 garlic clove
- ¼ cup fresh lemon juice
- ¼ cup olive oil
- ¼ cup tahini
- 1 avocado, halved & pitted
- ½ teaspoon salt

Directions:
1. Add chickpeas and remaining ingredients into the food processor and process until smooth.
Serving Suggestion: Serve with veggie or pita chips.
Variation Tip: Add 2 tablespoons of chopped cilantro.
Nutritional Information per Serving:
Calories 173 | Fat 12.8g | Sodium 253mg | Carbs12.9g | Fiber 3.8g | Sugar 0.3g | Protein 3.6g

Baked Italian Fries

Prep Time: 10 minutes
Cook Time: 40 minutes
Serves: 4
Ingredients:
- 12 baby red potatoes, cut into wedges
- 1 tablespoon Italian seasoning
- 3 tablespoons olive oil
- 1 teaspoon turmeric
- ½ teaspoon of sea salt
- ½ teaspoon dried rosemary
- 1 tablespoon dried dill

Preparation:
1. Preheat the oven to 375℉.
2. Put the potato wedges in a large bowl.

3. Add the Italian seasoning, olive oil, turmeric, sea salt, dried rosemary, and dried dill. Toss well to coat the wedges.
4. Line a baking tray with parchment paper.
5. Place the potatoes wedges in the tray in a single layer.
6. Bake in the oven for 40 minutes, occasionally gently stirring the wedges using a spatula.
Serving Suggestion: Garnish with rosemary sprigs.
Variation Tip: You can add some paprika.
Nutritional Information per Serving:
Calories 122 | Fat 11.6g | Sodium 252mg | Carbs 4.5g | Fiber 3.3g | Sugar 3.3g | Protein 0.6g

Parmesan Zucchini Tots

Prep Time: 10 minutes
Cook Time: 20 minutes
Serves: 10
Ingredients:
- 1 teaspoon paprika
- 1 teaspoon basil
- 1 teaspoon cilantro
- 2 eggs
- 1-pound green zucchini, peeled and grated
- 1 teaspoon salt
- 1 cup breadcrumbs
- 9 ounces parmesan, grated
- 1 teaspoon chili flakes
- 3 tablespoons fresh dill

Preparation:
1. Preheat the oven to 365℉
2. Combine the grated zucchini with the eggs and mix well.
3. Sprinkle the zucchini mixture with salt, paprika, basil, cilantro, chili flakes, breadcrumbs, and fresh dill.
4. Add the parmesan cheese to the zucchini mixture and knead the dough smooth.
5. Cover a baking sheet with parchment paper.
6. Make zucchini tots from the zucchini dough and place them on the prepared sheet.
7. Bake the tots in the oven for 20 minutes.
8. Chill the tots before serving.
Serving Suggestion: Serve with tomato sauce.
Variation Tip: For a milder taste, omit the chili flakes.
Nutritional Information per Serving:
Calories 145 | Fat 3.8g | Sodium 563mg | Carbs 14.94g | Fiber 1.6g | Sugar 1.7g | Protein 13g

Salmon and Celery Salad Wraps

Prep Time: 10 minutes
Cook Time: 0 minutes
Serves: 4
Ingredients:
- 1-pound salmon fillet, cooked and flaked
- 1 carrot, diced
- 1 celery stalk, diced
- 3 tablespoons fresh dill, chopped
- 1 small red onion, diced
- 2 tablespoons capers
- 1½ tablespoons extra-virgin olive oil
- 1 tablespoon aged balsamic vinegar
- Sea salt and black pepper, to taste
- 4 whole-wheat tortillas

Preparation:
1. Mix the salmon, carrots, celery, dill, red onion, ca-pers, oil, vinegar, pepper, and salt in a large bowl.
2. Divide the salmon salad among the flatbreads.
3. Fold up the bottoms of the tortillas, then roll them up and serve.
Serving Suggestion: Garnish with chopped cilantro.
Variation Tip: Substitute tortillas with whole-wheat flatbread.
Nutritional Information per Serving:
Calories 336 | Fat 16g | Sodium 628mg | Carbs 23g | Fiber 2.8g | Sugar 2.5g | Protein 20.3g

Easy Toasted Almonds

Prep Time: 10 minutes
Cook Time: 10 minutes
Serves: 2 cups
Ingredients:
- 1 tablespoon extra-virgin olive oil
- 1 teaspoon salt
- 2 cups skin-on raw whole almonds
Preparation:

1. Heat the oil in a 12-inch non-stick frying pan on moderate to high heat until it barely starts to shim-mer.
2. Put in the almonds, salt, and pepper and reduce the heat to moderate to low.
3. Cook, frequently stirring, until the almonds be-come aromatic and their color becomes somewhat deep, approximately 8 minutes.
4. Move the almonds to a plate lined with paper tow-els and allow them to cool before serving.
Serving Suggestion: Serve over ice cream.
Variation Tip: Add chili for a spicier result.
Nutritional Information per Serving:
Calories 230 | Fat 22g | Sodium 1163mg | Carbs 6g | Fiber 4g | Sugar 1g | Protein 6g

Spicy Deviled Eggs

Prep Time: 10 minutes
Cook Time: 0 minutes
Serves: 8
Ingredients:
- 8 eggs, boiled
- 3 tablespoons Romano cheese, grated
- 1 teaspoon paprika
- 2 tablespoons pesto
- 1 tablespoon mayonnaise
- 1 teaspoon mustard
- ½ teaspoon ground black pepper
- 1 tablespoon dill
- 1 teaspoon lime juice
Preparation:
1. Peel the eggs and cut them into halves.
2. Remove the egg yolks from the eggs and mash them carefully in a separate bowl with a fork.
3. Add the mustard, mayo, pesto, and lime juice. Blend the mixture with a hand blender.
4. Season the smooth mixture with ground black pepper and paprika.
5. Add the dill and Romano cheese to the egg yolk mixture and stir it carefully with the fork again.
6. Fill a pastry bag with the egg yolk mixture and fill the egg whites with it.
7. Put the cooked eggs in the fridge and chill until serving.
Serving Suggestion: Garnish with chopped green onions.
Variation Tip: Substitute lime juice with lemon juice.
Nutritional Information per Serving:
Calories 157 | Fat 12g | Sodium 119mg | Carbs 2.3g | Fiber 0.3g | Sugar 0.7g | Protein 10g

Baked Eggplant Fries

Prep Time: 10 minutes
Cook Time: 15 minutes
Serves: 8

Ingredients:
- 2 eggs
- 2 cups almond flour
- 2 tablespoons coconut oil spray
- 2 eggplants, peeled and cut thinly
- Salt and pepper, to taste

Preparation:
1. Preheat the oven to 400°F.
2. Put the almond flour with a little salt and pepper in a shallow bowl.
3. Beat the eggs until frothy in a bowl.
4. Dip the eggplant pieces into the egg, then coat them in the flour mixture.
5. Add another layer of flour and egg.
6. Take a baking sheet and grease it with the coconut oil spray. Arrange the coated eggplant on the sheet. Bake for about 15 minutes.
7. Serve and enjoy.

Serving Suggestion: Serve with a ranch dip.
Variation Tip: Substitute almond flour with coconut flour.

Nutritional Information per Serving:
Calories 119 | Fat 8.2g | Sodium 21mg | Carbs 9.7g | Fiber 5.6g | Sugar 4.4g | Protein 4.2g

Zucchini Chips

Prep Time: 10 minutes
Cook Time: 12 minutes
Serves: 4

Ingredients:
- 1 zucchini, thinly sliced
- A pinch of sea salt
- Black pepper, to taste

- 1 teaspoon dried thyme
- 1 egg
- 1 teaspoon garlic powder
- 1 cup almond flour

Preparation:
1. Preheat the oven to 450°F.
2. In a bowl, whisk the egg with a pinch of salt.
3. Put the flour in another bowl and mix it with the thyme, black pepper, and garlic powder.
4. Dredge the zucchini slices in the egg mix and then in the flour.
5. Arrange the chips on a lined baking sheet, place the sheet in the oven, and bake for 6 minutes on each side.
6. Serve and enjoy.

Serving Suggestion: Serve with your favorite dip.
Variation Tip: Feel free to add in more seasoning.

Nutritional Information per Serving:
Calories 67 | Fat 8.2g | Sodium 82mg | Carbs 3.9g | Fiber 1.5g | Sugar 1.4g | Protein 3.6g

Beet Fries

Prep Time: 10 minutes
Cook Time: 30 minutes
Serves: 4

Ingredients:
- 3 beets, cut in strips similar to French fries
- 3 tablespoons olive oil
- 1 cup spring onions, finely cut
- 2 garlic cloves, crushed
- 1 teaspoon salt

Preparation:
1. Preheat the oven to 425 ℉. Line a baking dish with baking paper.
2. Toss the beets with the olive oil, spring onions, garlic, and salt.
3. Arrange them on the prepared baking sheet and place them in the oven for 30 minutes, flipping halfway through.

Serving Suggestion: Serve with your favorite dip.
Variation Tip: Add black pepper for a varied flavor.

Nutritional Information per Serving:
Calories 133 | Fat 10.7g | Sodium 643mg | Carbs 9.8g | Fiber 2.2g | Sugar 6.6g | Protein 1.8g

Bruschetta

Prep Time: 10 minutes
Cook Time: 15 minutes
Serves: 24

Ingredients:
- 6 kalamata olives, pitted and chopped
- 2 tablespoons green onion, minced
- ¼ cup parmesan cheese, grated, divided
- ¼ cup extra-virgin olive oil for brushing, or as needed
- ¼ cup cherry tomatoes, thinly sliced
- 1 teaspoon lemon juice
- 1 tablespoon extra-virgin olive oil
- 1 tablespoon basil pesto
- 1 red bell pepper, halved and seeded
- 1 piece (12 inches) whole-wheat baguette, cut into ½-inch-thick slices
- 1 package (4 ounces) feta cheese with basil and sun-dried tomatoes, crumbled
- 1 clove garlic, minced

Preparation:
1. Set the broiler on medium and place the oven rack 6 inches below the heat source.
2. Brush both sides of the baguette slices with ¼ cup of olive oil.
3. Arrange the bread slices on a baking sheet; toast in the oven for about 1 minute on each side, carefully watching to avoid burning.
4. Remove the toasted slices, transferring them to another baking sheet.
5. With the cut sides down, place the red peppers on a baking sheet; broil for about 8 to 10 minutes or until the skin is charred and blistered.
6. Transfer the roasted peppers to a bowl; cover with plastic wrap.
7. Let the peppers cool, then remove the charred skin. Discard the skin and chop the roasted peppers.
8. Mix the roasted red peppers, cherry tomatoes, feta cheese, green onion, olives, pesto, one tablespoon olive oil, garlic, and lemon juice in a bowl.
9. Top each bread with one tablespoon of the roasted pepper mixture and sprinkle lightly with the parmesan cheese.
10. Broil for 2 minutes or until the topping is lightly browned.

Serving Suggestion: Top with chopped green onions and fresh basil.
Variation Tip: Switch up whole-wheat baguette with whole-wheat sourdough.
Nutritional Information per Serving:
Calories 73 | Fat 4.8g | Sodium 188mg | Carbs 5.3g | Fiber 0.2g | Sugar 0.4g | Protein 2.1g

Eggplant Pie

Prep Time: 10 minutes
Cook Time: 35 minutes
Serves: 6

Ingredients:
- 2 eggplants
- 1 tablespoon olive oil
- 3½ ounces feta cheese
- 3½ ounces provolone cheese, grated
- 1 potato, cooked and mashed
- 2 eggs

Preparation:
1. Preheat the oven to 350°F.
2. Place the eggplants on a baking sheet and roast them until evenly charred.
3. Cut a slit at the bottom of each eggplant and place them in a sieve. Leave them to drain.
4. Once cool enough to handle, peel the burnt skin off the eggplants, remove the dark seeds, and roughly chop.
5. Mix the chopped eggplants with the olive oil, cheeses, mashed potato, and eggs until thoroughly combined.
6. Put in a baking pan and bake for 35 minutes, until lightly browned on the top.
7. Remove from the oven and cool for a few minutes before serving.

Serving Suggestion: Serve with tomato sauce.
Variation Tip: Use boiled, chopped leeks instead of eggplant.
Nutritional Information per Serving:
Calories 210 | Fat 12.1g | Sodium 355mg | Carbs 16.8g | Fiber 7.1g | Sugar 6.6g | Protein 10.8g

Greek-Style Potatoes

Prep Time: 10 Minutes
Cook Time: 1 hour 30 Minutes
Serves: 4
Ingredients:
- ⅓ cup olive oil
- 2 garlic cloves, chopped
- 1½ cups water
- Salt and black pepper, to taste
- ¼ cup lemon juice
- 1 teaspoon rosemary
- 1 teaspoon thyme
- 2 chicken bouillon cubes
- 6 potatoes, chopped

Preparation:
1. Place the potatoes in a baking tray.
2. Mix all the ingredients in a large bowl and pour over the potatoes.
3. Bake in a preheated oven at 350°F for 90 minutes.
4. Serve and enjoy.
Serving Suggestion: Serve with tomato sauce.
Variation Tip: Use 1 teaspoon of smoked and hot paprika for more flavor.
Nutritional Information per Serving:
Calories 418 | Fat 18.5g | Sodium 331mg | Carbs 58.6g | Fiber 9g | Sugar 4.3g | Protein 7g

Cauliflower Curry

Prep Time: 10 Minutes
Cook Time: 25 Minutes
Serves: 4
Ingredients:
- 2 tablespoons olive oil
- ½ cauliflower, chopped into florets
- ¼ teaspoon salt
- 1 teaspoon curry paste
- 1 cup unsweetened coconut milk
- ¼ cup fresh cilantro, chopped
- 1 tablespoon lime juice

Preparation:
1. Sauté the cauliflower in heated olive oil over medium heat for 10 minutes.
2. Mix the coconut milk and curry powder, add to the cauliflower, and simmer for ten minutes.
3. Add the lime juice and cilantro and toss well.
4. Serve and enjoy!
Serving Suggestion: Garnish with chives and serve over hot rice.
Variation Tip: Use black pepper for a more vibrant taste.
Nutritional Information per Serving:
Calories 243 | Fat 24g | Sodium 179mg | Carbs 9g | Fiber 2g | Sugar 3.9g | Protein 3g

Spicy Zucchini

Prep Time: 10 Minutes
Cook Time: 5 Minutes
Serves: 4
Ingredients:
- 4 zucchinis, cut into ½-inch pieces
- 1 cup water
- ½ teaspoon Italian seasoning
- ½ teaspoon red pepper flakes
- 1 teaspoon garlic, minced
- 1 tablespoon olive oil
- ½ can crushed tomatoes
- Salt, to taste

Preparation:
1. Add the water and zucchini to an Instant Pot.
2. Seal the pot with the lid and cook on High for 2 minutes.
3. Once done, release the pressure using quick release. Remove the lid.
4. Drain the zucchini well and clean the Instant Pot.
5. Add the oil to the Instant pot and set it to Sauté mode.
6. Add the garlic and sauté for 30 seconds.
7. Add the remaining ingredients and stir well. Cook for 2–3 minutes.
8. Serve and enjoy.
Serving Suggestion: Serve over rice.
Variation Tip: Add in chili for a hotter dish.
Nutritional Information per Serving:
Calories 69 | Fat 4.1g | Sodium 95mg | Carbs 7.9g | Fiber 2.7g | Sugar 3.5g | Protein 2.7g

Balsamic Roasted Green Beans

Prep Time: 10 Minutes
Cook Time: 17 Minutes
Serves: 1 cup
Ingredients:
- 1-pound green beans
- 2 garlic cloves, chopped
- 1 tablespoon balsamic vinegar
- 1 tablespoon olive oil
- ⅛ teaspoon salt
- ⅛ teaspoon pepper

Preparation:
1. Preheat the oven to 425°F.
2. Mix the green beans along with the olive oil, pepper, and salt in a large bowl.
3. Evenly spread the green beans on a baking sheet lined with foil or parchment paper.
4. Place in the oven and bake for 10–12 minutes until the beans turn light brown.
5. Sprinkle the garlic over the green beans and mix well to combine.
6. Bake the beans for another 5 minutes.
7. Remove from the oven and toss with balsamic vinegar.
Serving Suggestion: Garnish with pine nuts.
Variation Tip: Use lemon-flavored balsamic vinegar for a twist.
Nutritional Information per Serving:
Calories 93 | Fat 5g | Sodium 1227mg | Carbs 12g | Fiber 4g | Sugar 3.2g | Protein 4g

Simple Sautéed Cauliflower

Prep Time: 10 Minutes
Cook Time: 15 Minutes
Serves: 4
Ingredients:
- 1 onion, chopped
- 1 head cauliflower
- ¼ cup olive oil
- 1 cup cherry tomatoes
- 2 tablespoons raisins
- 1 teaspoon white sugar
- 1 garlic clove, minced
- 1 teaspoon dried parsley

- ¼ teaspoon red pepper flakes
- 1 tablespoon lemon juice

Preparation:
1. Heat someolive oil in a wide skillet onmedium heat. Mix in the onion and cook until soft (about 5–10 minutes are enough).
2. Add the cauliflower, cherry tomatoes, raisins, and white sugar to the onion. Cover the skillet and cook, stirring regularly, until the cauliflower is soft, for about 4–5 minutes.
3. Mix thegarlic, parsley, and somered pepper flakes inthe cauliflower mixture. Turn the heat up to maximum. Sautéfor 1–3 minutes until the cauliflower getsbrowned.
4. Drizzle the juice of the lemon over the cauliflower.
Serving Suggestion: Serve over hot rice.
Variation Tip: You can also use fresh parsley.
Nutritional Information per Serving:
Calories 196.5 | Fat 13.9g | Sodium 25mg | Carbs 17.8g | Fiber 4.8g | Sugar 7.7g | Protein 3.7g

Brussels Sprouts and Pistachios

Prep Time: 10 Minutes
Cook Time: 30 Minutes
Serves: 4
Ingredients:
- 1 pound Brussels sprouts, trimmed and halved lengthwise
- 4 shallots, peeled and quartered
- ½ cup roasted pistachios, chopped
- ½ lemon, zested and juiced
- ¼ teaspoon fine sea salt
- ¼ teaspoon black pepper
- 1 tablespoon olive oil

Preparation:
1. Preheat the oven to 400°F. Line a baking sheet with foil.
2. In a bowl, toss the shallots and Brussels sprouts in olive oil. Make sure the sprouts are well coated.
3. Season with the salt and pepper before spreading them onto the baking sheet.
4. Bake for 15 minutes. Your vegetables should be lightly caramelized as well as tender.
5. Take the sheet out of the oven and toss the sprouts with the lemon zest, lemon juice, and pistachios.
6. Serve and enjoy!
Serving Suggestion: Serve with lime wedges on the side.
Variation Tip: When the sprouts are cooked, add in pomegranate seeds, if desired.
Nutritional Information per Serving:
Calories 126 | Fat 7g | Sodium 188mg | Carbs 14g | Fiber 5.2g | Sugar 3.1g | Protein 6g

Mediterranean Sautéed Kale

Prep Time: 10 Minutes
Cook Time: 10 Minutes
Serves: 6
Ingredients:
- 12 cups kale, chopped
- 2 tablespoons lemon juice
- 1 tablespoon olive oil
- 1 tablespoon garlic, minced
- 1 teaspoon soy sauce
- Salt and black pepper, to taste

Preparation:
1. Add a steamer insert into a saucepan.
2. Fill up the saucepan with water up until the bottom of the steamer insert.
3. Cover and bring the water to a boil over medium-high heat.
4. Add the kale to the steamer insert and steam for 7–8 minutes.
5. Add the lemon juice, olive oil, garlic, salt, soy sauce, and black pepper to a large bowl. Mix well.
6. Add the steamed kale, toss well, and serve.
Serving Suggestion: Serve the kale on its own or add to a grain bowl.
Variation Tip: Add chili for spice.
Nutritional Information per Serving:
Calories 91 | Fat 4g | Sodium 109mg | Carbs 14g | Fiber 2.1g | Sugar 0.1g | Protein 5g

Green Bean Stew

Prep Time: 10 Minutes
Cook Time: 40 Minutes
Serves: 4
Ingredients:
- ¼ cup extra-virgin olive oil
- 3 garlic cloves, chopped
- 1 sweet onion, chopped
- Sea salt and ground black pepper, to taste

- 1-pound fresh green beans, ends snipped and cut into 2-inch pieces
- 1 (8-ounce) can tomato sauce
- ½ cup water
Preparation:
1. In a small skillet over medium heat, add the olive oil and allow it to heat up.
2. Add the garlic and onion and sauté for 3 minutes until the garlic is fragrant.
3. Season with salt and pepper.
4. Add the beans to the skillet and stir gently with a spoon; cover and cook for 10 minutes.
5. Stir in the tomato sauce and water.
6. Cover and cook for 25 minutes more.
7. Serve and enjoy!
Serving Suggestion: Garnish with freshly chopped parsley and serve over rice.
Variation Tip: Use three large peeled tomatoes instead of the canned tomatoes.
Nutritional Information per Serving:
Calories 159 | Fat 13g | Sodium 306mg | Carbs 12g | Fiber 5.4g | Sugar 5.2g | Protein 3g

Cauliflower and Carrot Stir Fry

Prep Time: 10 Minutes
Cook Time: 10 Minutes
Serves: 4
Ingredients:
- 1 large onion, chopped
- 1 tablespoon garlic, minced
- 2 cups carrots, diced
- 4 cups cauliflower florets, washed
- ½ teaspoon ground cumin
- 3 tablespoons olive oil
Preparation:
1. In a large frying pan on medium heat, heat the olive oil.
2. Add the onion, garlic, and carrots and cook for 3 minutes.
3. Cut the cauliflower into 1-inch or bite-size pieces.
4. Add the cauliflower, salt, and cumin to the pan and toss to combine with the carrots and onions. Cover and cook for 3 minutes.
5. Continue to cook uncovered for an additional 3–4 minutes.
6. Serve warm.
Serving Suggestion: Serve with flatbread or rice.
Variation Tip: Make sure to chop the cauliflower into small florets.
Nutritional Information per Serving:
Calories 159 | Fat 0.2g | Sodium 70mg | Carbs 15g | Fiber 4.7g | Sugar 6.7g | Protein 3g

Mushroom and Tomato Bake

Prep Time: 10 Minutes
Cook Time: 20 Minutes
Serves: 6

Ingredients:
- 2 pounds mushrooms, washed and dried with a paper towel
- 1 cup red wine
- ½ cup extra-virgin olive oil
- 3 tomatoes, sliced
- ¼ teaspoon salt
- 1 teaspoon dried oregano

Preparation:
1. Preheat the oven to 400°F.
2. Put the mushrooms in a baking tray.
3. Top with the olive oil, oregano, wine, and salt. Mix well, and then bake for around 20 minutes.
4. Add the seasoning.
5. Serve.

Serving Suggestion: Serve with steak, chicken, or pork.
Variation Tip: Add other dried herbs of your liking.
Nutritional Information per Serving:
Calories 156 | Fat 18g | Sodium 220mg | Carbs 14g | Fiber 2.4g | Sugar 4.5g | Protein 6g

Parmesan Potatoes

Prep Time: 10 Minutes
Cook Time: 6 Minutes
Serves: 4

Ingredients:
- 2 pounds potatoes, rinsed and cut into chunks
- 2 tablespoons parmesan cheese, grated
- 2 tablespoons olive oil
- ½ teaspoon parsley
- ½ teaspoon Italian seasoning
- 1 teaspoon garlic, minced
- 1 cup vegetable broth
- ½ teaspoon salt

Preparation:
1. Add all ingredients except the cheese to an Instant Pot and stir well.

2. Seal the pot with the lid and cook on High for 6 minutes.
3. Once done, release the pressure using quick release.
4. Remove the lid.
5. Add the parmesan cheese and stir until it has melted.
6. Serve and enjoy.

Serving Suggestion: Garnish with freshly chopped parsley.
Variation Tip: Feel free to add in other seasonings of your choice.
Nutritional Information per Serving:
Calories 237 | Fat 8.3g | Sodium 521mg | Carbs 36.3g | Fiber 5.5g | Sugar 2.8g | Protein 5.9g

Mediterranean Gnocchi

Prep Time: 5 minutes
Cook Time: 2 minutes
Serves: 2

Ingredients:
- 1 cup chargrilled vegetables, chopped
- 2 cups gnocchi
- 2 tablespoons red pesto
- ¼ cup Pecorino cheese
- ½ cup basil leaves

Preparation:
1. Boil water in a large pot, add some salt and add the gnocchi.
2. Cook the gnocchi for 2 minutes and then carefully drain.
3. Return the gnocchi to the pot and add a splash of water.
4. Stir in the chargrilled vegetables, basil leaves, and red pesto.
5. Top with the Pecorino and serve immediately.

Serving Suggestion: Serve with a side salad.
Variation Tip: Pecorino can be replaced with parmesan cheese.
Nutritional Information per Serving:
Calories: 398 | Fat: 12.2g | Sat Fat: 2g | Carbohydrates: 56.4g | Fiber: 1.1g | Sugar: 0g | Protein: 12.7g

Mediterranean Slices

Prep Time: 10 minutes
Cook Time: 20 minutes
Serves: 4
Ingredients:
- 13-ounce pack ready-rolled puff pastry
- 4 tablespoons green pesto
- ¾ cup frozen roasted peppers, sliced
- ¾ cup frozen artichokes
- ½ cup mozzarella cheese, grated

Preparation:
1. Preheat the oven to 400°F and lightly grease a baking sheet.
2. Unfold the puff pastry and cut it into four rectangles.
3. Cut an edge of 0.4 inches inside each rectangle with a sharp knife and transfer the rectangles to the baking sheet.
4. Layer all the rectangles with the pesto, followed by the peppers and artichokes.
5. Put the baking sheet in the oven and bake for 15 minutes.
6. Top with mozzarella cheese and bake for another 7 minutes.
Serving Suggestion: Serve alongside a green salad.
Variation Tip: You can use cheddar cheese instead of mozzarella.
Nutritional Information per Serving:
Calories: 606 | Fat: 42.6g | Sat Fat: 9.8g | Carbohydrates: 46.2g | Fiber: 2.9g | Sugar: 1.7g | Protein: 9.5g

Goat's Cheese and Lentil Filo Pie

Prep Time: 5 minutes
Cook Time: 30 minutes
Serves: 2
Ingredients:
- 1 pouch pre-cooked puy lentils
- 1 tray Mediterranean roasting vegetables
- ¾ cup goat's cheese
- 3 sheets filo pastry
- 1 tablespoon olive oil
- Salt and black pepper, to taste

Preparation:
1. Preheat the oven to 390°F and lightly grease a pie dish.
2. Put the olive oil in a pan and add the Mediterranean roasting vegetables.
3. Stir-fry for about 10 minutes, and then add the lentils.
4. Cook for 2 more minutes and season with salt and black pepper.
5. Transfer the mixture to the pie dish and top with the goat's cheese.
6. Top with scrunched-up ruffles of the pastry. Brush with the olive oil and bake for about 20 minutes.
7. Serve warm.
Serving Suggestion: Serve with a side salad.
Variation Tip: Goat's cheese can be replaced with feta cheese.
Nutritional Information per Serving:
Calories: 428 | Fat: 30.9g | Sat Fat: 12.5g | Carbohydrates: 20.2g | Fiber: 1.2g | Sugar: 5.5g | Protein: 17.5g

Greek Green Beans

Prep Time: 10 minutes
Cook Time: 50 minutes
Serves: 8
Ingredients:
- ¾ cup olive oil
- 2 cups onions, chopped
- 1 clove garlic, minced
- 2 pounds fresh green beans, rinsed and trimmed
- 3 large tomatoes, diced
- 2 teaspoons sugar
- Salt, to taste

Preparation:
1. Stir fry the garlic and onions in the olive oil until soft.
2. Add in the salt, beans, sugar, and tomatoes.
3. Lower the heat and cook everything for 50 more minutes until tender.
4. Enjoy.
Serving Suggestion: Top with red pepper flakes.
Variation Tip: Feel free to omit the sugar.
Nutritional Information per Serving:
Calories 243 | Fat 20.6g | Sodium 12mg | Carbs 14.6g | Fiber 5.3g | Sugar 5.6g | Protein 3g

Falafels with Tahini Sauce

Prep Time: 25 minutes
Cook Time: 6 minutes
Serves: 8
Ingredients:
For the falafel
- 1 garlic clove, minced
- 1 (15½-ounce) can low-sodium chickpeas, rinsed and drained
- ½ cup fresh parsley leaves, chopped roughly
- Salt and black pepper, to taste
- 1 egg, beaten
- 8 cups lettuce leaves, torn
- ¼ teaspoon ground cumin
- ¼ cup all-purpose flour, divided
- 2 tablespoons olive oil
For the tahini sauce
- ¼ cup fresh lemon juice
- 4 large garlic cloves, minced
- ½ cup tahini
- Pinch of ground cumin
- ½ teaspoon fine sea salt
- 6 tablespoons ice water
Preparation:
1. For the falafel: Put the chickpeas, garlic, cumin, parsley, salt, and black pepper in a food processor and pulse until mixed.
2. Shift the mixture into a bowl and set it aside.
3. Mix 2 tablespoons of the all-purpose flour and egg until well combined.
4. Form eight equal-sized patties from the mixture.
5. Put the rest of the all-purpose flour in a shallow dish.
6. Dredge the patties evenly in the flour.
7. Heat the olive oil in a non-stick skillet placed over medium-high heat.
8. Cook the patties for about 3 minutes per side until golden brown.
9. For the tahini sauce: Mix the garlic and lemon juice in a bowl.
10. Strain the garlic mixture through a fine-mesh sieve into another bowl, thoroughly pressing the garlic solids.
11. Discard the drained garlic solids.
12. In the bowl containing the strained lemon juice, beat the tahini, cumin, and salt until well combined.

13. Add the water in batches, 2 tablespoons at a time, and beat well after each addition.
14. Divide the lettuce evenly between serving plates.
15. Place two patties onto each serving plate over the lettuce.
16. Serve drizzled with the tahini sauce.
Serving Suggestion: Serve along with rice of your choice.
Variation Tip: You can replace the tahini sauce with any other sauce of your choice.
Nutritional Information per Serving:
Calories: 355 | Fat: 15.7g | Sat Fat: 2.2g | Carbohydrates: 42.2g | Fiber: 11.6g | Sugar: 6.8g | Protein: 14.8g

Vegetable Stew

Prep Time: 10 minutes
Cook Time: 15 minutes
Serves: 1
Ingredients:
- 1 teaspoon olive oil
- 1 sweet onion, chopped
- 1 teaspoon garlic, minced
- 2 zucchinis, chopped
- 1 red bell pepper, diced
- 2 carrots, chopped
- Salt and black pepper, to taste
- 2 cups broccoli florets
- 2 cups low-sodium vegetable stock
- 2 large tomatoes, chopped
- 1 teaspoon ground coriander
- ½ teaspoon ground cumin
- 2 tablespoons fresh cilantro, chopped
- 1 teaspoon cayenne pepper
Preparation:
1. Heat the olive oil on moderate heat in a saucepan.
2. Add the garlic and onion and cook until softened for about 3 minutes.
3. Add the carrots, bell pepper, and zucchini. Sauté until softened for almost 5 minutes.
4. Stir in the vegetable stock, coriander, tomatoes, broccoli, and cayenne pepper.
5. Cook until boiled and then reduce the heat.
6. Simmer until the vegetables are tender and stir for 5 minutes.
7. Season with salt and pepper and serve hot.
Serving Suggestion: Garnish with cilantro.
Variation Tip: For a milder taste, omit the cayenne pepper.
Nutritional Information per Serving:
Calories 416 | Fat 7.7g | Sodium 491mg | Carbs 81.1g | Fiber 23.1g | Sugar 42.3g | Protein 19.1g

Stewed Okra

Prep Time: 10 Minutes
Cook Time: 25 Minutes
Serves: 4
Ingredients:
* 4 cloves garlic, finely chopped
* 1 pound fresh or frozen okra, cleaned
* 1 (15 ounces) can plain tomato sauce
* 2 cups water
* ¼ cup olive oil
* 1 onion, sliced
* ½ cup fresh cilantro, finely chopped

Preparation:
1. In a big pot on medium heat, add the olive oil, onion, garlic, and salt. Cook until the onion is softened and the garlic is fragrant.
2. Stir in the okra and cook for 3 minutes.
3. Add the tomato sauce, water, cilantro, and black pepper; stir, cover, and let cook for 15 minutes, stirring occasionally.
4. Serve warm.
Serving Suggestion: Serve over rice.
Variation Tip: Replace the canned tomatoes with two fresh and peeled ones.
Nutritional Information per Serving:
Calories 201| Fat 12.9g | Sodium 43mg | Carbs 18g | Fiber 5.8g | Sugar 7.3g | Protein 4g

Tortellini with Pesto and Broccoli

Prep Time: 5 minutes
Cook Time: 5 minutes
Serves: 2
Ingredients:
* 9 ounces fresh tortellini

* 1 medium broccoli, cut into florets
* 3 tablespoons pesto
* 1 tablespoon balsamic vinegar
* 2 tablespoons toasted pine nuts
* 8 cherry tomatoes, halved

Preparation:
1. Boil water in a heavy pot and add the broccoli.
2. Cook for about 2 minutes and add the tortellini.
3. Cook for 2 more minutes and drain.
4. Put the broccoli and tortellini in a bowl and add the pine nuts, pesto, tomatoes, and balsamic vinegar.
5. Serve and enjoy!
Serving Suggestion: Top with walnuts before serving.
Variation Tip: Pine nuts can be replaced with your favorite nuts.
Nutritional Information per Serving:
Calories: 654 | Fat: 27.4g | Sat Fat: 6g | Carbohydrates: 79.1g | Fiber: 12.5g | Sugar: 19.1g | Protein: 27.9g

Vegetarian Chili

Prep Time: 2 minutes
Cook Time: 30 minutes
Serves: 2
Ingredients:
* 14 ounces oven-roasted vegetables
* 1 can chopped tomatoes
* 1 can kidney beans in chili sauce
* Salt and black pepper, to taste

Preparation:
1. Preheat the oven to 390°F and lightly grease a casserole dish.
2. Arrange the vegetables in the casserole dish and place them in the oven.
3. Bake for about 15 minutes and then stir in the kidney beans, tomatoes, salt, and black pepper.
4. Bake for 15 more minutes.
5. Remove from the oven and serve.
Serving Suggestion: Serve with ready-made mixed grains.
Variation Tip: You can replace the kidney beans with navy beans.
Nutritional Information per Serving:
Calories: 366 | Fat: 15g | Sat Fat: 2.5g | Carbohydrates: 43.8g | Fiber: 15.4g | Sugar: 8.5g | Protein: 14.4g

Veggie Pasta

Prep Time: 20 minutes
Cook Time: 45 minutes
Serves: 6
Ingredients:
- 1 large sweet onion, chopped finely
- ½ pound fresh baby portobello mushrooms, chopped finely
- 1 tablespoon olive oil
- 2 medium carrots, peeled and chopped finely
- 1 large zucchini, chopped finely
- ½ cup dry red wine
- 1 (14½-ounce) can low-sodium diced tomatoes with juices
- ½ teaspoon dried oregano, crushed
- ⅛ teaspoon red pepper flakes, crushed
- 4½ cups uncooked whole-wheat Rigatoni
- 3 garlic cloves, minced
- 1 (28-ounce) can low-sodium crushed tomatoes with juices
- ½ cup parmesan cheese, grated
- ½ teaspoon black pepper
- Pinch of ground nutmeg

Preparation:
1. In a large pan placed over medium-high heat, heat the olive oil and sauté the onion and carrots for about 5 minutes.
2. Add the mushrooms, garlic, and zucchini and cook and for about 6 minutes.
3. Stir in the dry red wine and allow the mixture to come to a boil.
4. Cook for about 3 minutes until all the liquid is absorbed.
5. Stir in the tomatoes, oregano, cheese, and spices and let it come to a boil.
6. Reduce the heat to low, cover, and simmer for about 30 minutes until the desired thickness is reached.
7. Meanwhile, cook the rigatoni pasta in salted boiling water until al dente according to the package's instructions.
8. Drain the rigatoni well and transfer to a serving dish.
9. Top with the veggie sauce and serve.

Serving Suggestion: Serve with stuffed tomatoes.
Variation Tip: You can omit the nutmeg.
Nutritional Information per Serving:
Calories: 286 | Fat: 5.7g | Sat Fat: 1.7g | Carbohydrates: 43.3g | Fiber: 8.5g | Sugar: 9g | Protein: 12.6g

Ratatouille

Prep Time: 10 Minutes
Cook Time: 40 Minutes
Serves: 8
Ingredients:
Veggies
- 2 zucchinis, sliced
- 2 eggplants, sliced
- 2 yellow squashes, sliced
- 6 Roma tomatoes, sliced

Sauce
- 1 onion, diced
- 4 cloves garlic, minced
- 2 tablespoon olive oil
- 1 red bell pepper, diced
- 1 yellow bell pepper, diced
- Salt and pepper, to taste
- 28 ounces tomatoes, crushed
- 2 tablespoons fresh basil, chopped

Herb seasoning
- 2 tablespoons fresh basil, chopped
- 1 teaspoon garlic, minced
- 2 tablespoons fresh parsley, chopped
- 2 teaspoons thyme
- Salt and pepper, to taste
- 4 tablespoons olive oil

Preparation:
1. Preheat the oven to 375°F.
2. Heat the olive oil in an oven-safe pan. Sauté the onion, garlic, and bell peppers for about 10 minutes.
3. Season with the salt and pepper, then add the crushed tomatoes. Mix well.
4. Remove the pan from the heat, and then add 2 tablespoons of freshly chopped basil. Stir until smooth.
5. Arrange the sliced veggies on top of the sauce and then season with salt and pepper.
6. Mix the basil, parsley, thyme, garlic, salt, pepper, and olive oil. Spoon this herb seasoning onto the vegetables.
7. Cover the pan with foil, place it in the oven, and bake for 40 minutes.
8. Uncover, and bake for another 20 minutes until the vegetables are softened.
9. Serve!

Serving Suggestion: Serve with seared flank steak.
Variation Tip: You can either cut the veggies into chunks or slices.
Nutritional Information per Serving:
Calories 230 | Fat 11g | Sodium 1112mg | Carbs 32g | Fiber 8g | Sugar 6g | Protein 5g

Couscous with Cauliflower and Dates

Prep Time: 20 minutes
Cook Time: 40 minutes
Serves: 4
Ingredients:
* 4 tablespoons olive oil, divided
* 2 cups cauliflower florets
* Salt and black pepper, to taste
* 1¼ cups vegetable broth
* 1 tablespoon fresh lemon juice
* 3 tablespoons dates, pitted and chopped
* 1 teaspoon red wine vinegar
* 2 garlic cloves, minced
* 1 cup pearl couscous
* 1 shallot, chopped
* 2 tablespoons fresh parsley, chopped
Preparation:
1. Preheat the oven to 390°F and line a baking sheet with parchment paper.
2. In a bowl, thoroughly toss the cauliflower florets, salt, and black pepper with 2 tablespoons of the olive oil.
3. Place the cauliflower florets on the prepared baking sheet and layer evenly.
4. Bake for 40 minutes until the cauliflower is golden brown.
5. Take out the cauliflower from the oven and set it aside to cool slightly.
6. In the meantime, for the couscous: In a large pan placed on medium-high heat, heat 1 tablespoon of the olive oil and sauté the garlic for about 1 minute.
7. Stir in the vegetable broth and let it come to a boil.
8. Stir in the couscous and reduce the heat to medium.
9. Cover the pan and simmer for about 10 minutes, stirring occasionally.
10. Squeeze in the lemon juice and remove the pan from the heat.
11. Meanwhile, in a skillet placed over medium heat, heat the rest of the olive oil and sauté the shallots for about 6 minutes.
12. Add the dates and cook for about 2 minutes.
13. Whisk in the vinegar, salt, and black pepper and remove from the heat.
14. Shift the date mixture into the pan with the couscous and stir well to combine.
15. Remove from the heat and set aside to cool slightly.
16. Put the couscous and cauliflower in a serving bowl and stir lightly to combine.
17. Serve warm garnished with parsley.
Serving Suggestion: Serve with vegetable curry.

Variation Tip: Red wine can be replaced with balsamic vinegar.
Nutritional Information per Serving:
Calories: 342 | Fat: 15g | Sat Fat: 2.2g | Carbohydrates: 45g| Fiber: 2g | Sugar: 6.8g | Protein: 8.6g

Spelt-Stuffed Peppers

Prep Time: 20 minutes
Cook Time: 25 minutes
Serves: 4
Ingredients:
* 4 large red peppers, halved and deseeded
* ½ cup sundried tomatoes
* 2 tablespoons olive oil
* 1 red onion, spiralized on the flat blade of the spiralizer
* 1 large zucchini, spiralized into thin noodles
* 9-ounce pouch pre-cooked spelt
* ½ cup mixed olives
* ½ cup basil, chopped
* Salt and black pepper, to taste
Preparation:
1. Preheat the oven to 390°F and lightly grease a roasting tray.
2. Arrange the red peppers on the roasting tray, cut-side up, and sprinkle with 1 tablespoon of olive oil.
3. Season with salt and black pepper, and bake for 25 minutes.
4. In the meantime, in a pan placed over medium heat, heat the rest of the olive oil and add the spiralized onion.
5. Cook for 3 minutes until softened and transfer to a bowl.
6. Stir in the zucchini, spelt, olives, sundried tomatoes, and basil.
7. Generously fill the red peppers with the mixture.
8. Roast for approximately 5 minutes and serve.
Serving Suggestion: Serve with a green salad.
Variation Tip: You can use any other variety of tomatoes too.
Nutritional Information per Serving:
Calories: 412 | Fat: 12.5g | Sat Fat: 1.5g | Carbohydrates: 64.3g | Fiber: 12.4g | Sugar: 7.6g | Protein: 12.2g

Couscous Salad

Prep Time: 10 minutes
Cook Time: 15 minutes
Serves: 6
Ingredients:
- 1 cup couscous
- 1 lemon juice
- ½ cucumber, sliced
- ¼ cup fresh parsley, chopped
- ½ cup onion, diced
- 1 cup cherry tomatoes, cut in half
- 15 ounces can chickpeas, drained & rinsed
- 12 ounces chicken broth
- Pepper
- Salt

Directions:
1. Add couscous and broth into the pot and cook over medium-high heat. Bring to boil.
2. Turn heat to medium and simmer for 15 minutes. Remove pot from heat.
3. In a large mixing bowl, mix together cooked couscous and the remaining ingredients.
Serving Suggestion: Mix well and serve.
Variation Tip: Add ¼ cup of crumbled Feta cheese.
Nutritional Information per Serving:
Calories 218 | Fat 1.5g | Sodium 428mg | Carbs 41.9g | Fiber 5.4g | Sugar 2g | Protein 9g

Roasted Vegetables

Prep Time: 10 minutes
Cook Time: 15 minutes
Serves: 4
Ingredients:
- 1 zucchini, chopped

- ½ teaspoon dried oregano
- ½ teaspoon garlic powder
- 1 teaspoon basil
- ½ teaspoon parsley
- 2 tablespoons olive oil
- 2 small onions, sliced
- 10 grape tomatoes
- 3 bell peppers, sliced
- ½ teaspoon salt

Directions:
1. Preheat the oven to 425° F.
2. In a bowl, add all ingredients and toss until well coated.
3. Transfer vegetables onto the baking sheet and roast in preheated oven for 15 minutes. Stir halfway through.
Serving Suggestion: Allow to cool completely and serve.
Variation Tip: Add your choice of seasonings.
Nutritional Information per Serving:
Calories 168 | Fat 8g | Sodium 314mg | Carbs 24g | Fiber 6.3g | Sugar 15g | Protein 4.7g

Lentil Curry

Prep Time: 10 minutes
Cook Time: 8 hours
Serves: 6
Ingredients:
- 2 cups dry brown lentils
- 14 ounces can unsweetened coconut milk
- 2 teaspoon turmeric
- 1 tablespoon garam masala
- 1 tablespoon garlic, minced
- 1 medium onion, chopped
- 3 cups vegetable broth
- 28 ounces can crushed tomatoes
- Pepper
- Salt

Directions:
1. Add lentils and remaining ingredients except coconut milk into the slow cooker and stir well.
2. Cover and cook on low for 8 hours.
3. Stir in coconut milk.
Serving Suggestion: Garnish with cilantro and serve.
Variation Tip: Add ½ teaspoon of chili powder.
Nutritional Information per Serving:
Calories 416 | Fat 16.6g | Sodium 1037mg | Carbs 56.1g | Fiber 12.6g | Sugar 1.2g | Protein 19.5g

Roasted Potatoes

Prep Time: 10 minutes
Cook Time: 25 minutes
Serves: 4
Ingredients:
- 1 pound baby potatoes, cut into half
- 1 tablespoon parsley, chopped
- 2 tablespoons Feta cheese, crumbled
- ¼ cup caramelized onions
- 1 teaspoon thyme, chopped
- 1 tablespoon olive oil
- 1 tablespoon rosemary, chopped
- 2 garlic cloves, minced
- Pepper
- Salt

Directions:
1. Preheat the oven to 400° F.
2. In a bowl, toss potatoes with thyme, rosemary, garlic, and oil until well coated.
3. Spread potatoes onto the baking sheet and top with caramelized onions. Season with pepper and salt.
4. Bake in preheated oven for 20-25 minutes.
Serving Suggestion: Toss with Feta cheese and parsley and serve.
Variation Tip: You can also use crumbled Goat cheese instead of Feta cheese.
Nutritional Information per Serving:
Calories 123 | Fat 5g | Sodium 17.1mg | Carbs 17.1g | Fiber 3.6g | Sugar 1.1g | Protein 4g

Chickpeas with Veggies

Prep Time: 10 minutes
Cook Time: 7 minutes
Serves: 2
Ingredients:
- 2 cups can chickpeas, drained & rinsed

- ¼ cup basil, chopped
- 1 teaspoon Nigella seeds
- 1 tablespoon sesame seeds
- 1 tablespoon olive oil
- 1 teaspoon garlic, minced
- 1 teaspoon chili powder
- 1 bell pepper, sliced
- 1 small onion, chopped
- 1 small zucchini, chopped
- 4 medium tomatoes, chopped

Directions:
1. Add onion and tomatoes in a large pan and simmer over medium-high heat for 3-4 minutes.
2. Add chickpeas and stir well, cover and simmer for 5 minutes.
3. Add bell peppers, zucchini and garlic and stir for 2 minutes.
4. Turn off the heat. Add oil and basil.
5. Sprinkle Nigella seeds, chili powder and sesame seeds.
Serving Suggestion: Stir well and serve hot.
Variation Tip: Add ¼ teaspoon of paprika.
Nutritional Information per Serving:
Calories 487 | Fat 15.5g | Sodium 752mg | Carbs 75.9g | Fiber 16.8g | Sugar 12.1g | Protein 16.9g

Garlic Cauliflower and Zucchini

Prep Time: 10 minutes
Cook Time: 8 minutes
Serves: 2
Ingredients:
- 1 cup cauliflower florets
- ½ teaspoon cumin
- 1 teaspoon mint
- 2 garlic cloves
- 1 tablespoon olive oil
- 1 bell pepper, sliced
- 1 cup zucchini, chopped
- Pepper
- Salt

Directions:
1. Heat oil in a pan over medium heat.
2. Add vegetables, garlic, cumin, pepper and salt to the pan and stir well.
3. Cover and cook for 3-4 minutes.
4. Remove cover and stir well and cook for 2 minutes more. Remove pan from heat.
Serving Suggestion: Allow to cool completely then serve.
Variation Tip: Drizzle with tablespoon of fresh lemon juice.
Nutritional Information per Serving:
Calories 108 | Fat 7.5g | Sodium 101mg | Carbs 10.4g | Fiber 2.9g | Sugar 5.2g | Protein 2.6g

Pesto Brussels Sprouts

Prep Time: 10 minutes
Cook Time: 30 minutes
Serves: 4
Ingredients:
- 1 pound brussels sprouts, halved
- 1 tablespoon olive oil
- Pepper
- Salt

For Pesto:
- 1 tablespoon olive oil
- 1 tablespoon nutritional yeast
- 1 tablespoon Pine nuts
- 1 cup basil leaves
- ½ cup sun-dried tomatoes
- 2 garlic cloves
- Pepper
- Salt

Directions:
1. Preheat the oven to 400° F.
2. In a bowl, toss Brussels sprouts with oil, pepper and salt.
3. Spread Brussels sprouts onto the baking sheet and roast in preheated oven for 15-20 minutes.
4. Add all pesto ingredients into the blender and blend until smooth.
5. Toss roasted Brussels sprouts with pesto.
Serving Suggestion: Stir well and serve.
Variation Tip: Add your choice of seasonings.
Nutritional Information per Serving:
Calories 140 | Fat 9.1g | Sodium 109mg | Carbs 13.3g | Fiber 5.4g | Sugar 3.2g | Protein 5.8g

Tabbouleh

Prep Time: 20 minutes
Serves: 3
Ingredients:
- 3 tablespoons olive oil, divided

- ½ cup bulgur, uncooked
- 2 cups boiling vegetable broth
- 3 cups fresh Italian flat-leaf parsley, chopped
- ¼ cup scallions, chopped
- ½ teaspoon salt
- 3 fresh Roma tomatoes, cored and chopped
- ½ cup fresh mint, chopped
- 2 tablespoons fresh lemon juice

Preparation:
1. In a large bowl, mix the bulgur thoroughly with 1 tablespoon of the olive oil.
2. Pour in the hot vegetable broth and cover the bowl tightly with plastic wrap.
3. Set aside for about 1 hour until the bulgur has softened.
4. Strain the bulgur through a fine-mesh strainer.
5. In a large serving bowl, mix the bulgur and 2 tablespoons of olive oil and the rest of the ingredients until well combined.
6. Serve immediately.
Serving Suggestion: Serve with grilled vegetables.
Variation Tip: Scallions can be replaced with red onions.
Nutritional Information per Serving:
Calories: 244 | Fat: 14.8g | Sat Fat: 2.2g | Carbohydrates: 26.6g | Fiber: 7.7g | Sugar: 5.1g | Protein: 4.7g

Asparagus Stir-Fry

Prep Time: 10 minutes
Cook Time: 15 minutes
Serves: 4
Ingredients:
- 1-pound fresh asparagus spears, trimmed
- 3 tablespoons olive oil
- Coarse salt, to taste
- 3 cloves garlic, minced

Preparation:
1. Stir fry the garlic in the olive oil, then add some salt.
2. Let the garlic fry for another minute, then add the asparagus and fry them for 12 minutes.
3. Enjoy.
Serving Suggestion: Sprinkle ground black pepper on top before serving.
Variation Tip: Add a tablespoon of paprika for more vibrancy.
Nutritional Information per Serving:
Calories 188 | Fat 18.4g | Sodium 525mg | Carbs 5.2g | Fiber 3.4g | Sugar 3.2g | Protein 2.8g

Creamy Farro

Prep Time: 10 minutes
Cook Time: 15 minutes
Serves: 4
Ingredients:
- 1 cup Farro, rinsed
- 1 tablespoon olive oil
- ¼ cup Asiago cheese, shredded
- 2 tablespoons garlic, minced
- 10 ounces fresh spinach
- 2 ½ cups water
- Pepper
- Salt

Directions:
1. Add Farro and water into the saucepan and bring to boil.
2. Cover and reduce heat and simmer until the water is absorbed, about 15 minutes.
3. Turn off the heat. Add spinach and remaining ingredients and stir until spinach is wilted.
Serving Suggestion: Stir well and serve warm.
Variation Tip: Add 2 tablespoons of crumbled feta cheese.
Nutritional Information per Serving:
Calories 166 | Fat 9.4g | Sodium 332mg | Carbs 16g | Fiber 4g | Sugar 1.7g | Protein 7.7g

Marinated Tomatoes

Prep Time: 10 minutes
Cook Time: 10 minutes
Serves: 4
Ingredients:
- 1 pound tomatoes, cut into ⅓-inch slices
- 1 teaspoon parsley, chopped
- 1 teaspoon basil, chopped
- ½ lemon juice
- 2 tablespoons red wine vinegar
- ¼ cup olive oil

- 1 garlic clove, minced
- ½ onion, chopped
- Pepper
- Salt

Directions:
1. Arrange tomato slices onto the plate.
2. Mix together remaining ingredients and pour over tomato slices.
3. Cover and place in refrigerator for 2 hours.
Serving Suggestion: Serve with your meal.
Variation Tip: Add ¼ teaspoon of paprika.
Nutritional Information per Serving:
Calories 138 | Fat 12.9g | Sodium 47mg | Carbs 6.2g | Fiber 1.7g | Sugar 3.7g | Protein 1.3g

Couscous with Olives and Tomato

Prep Time: 10 minutes
Cook Time: 25 minutes
Serves: 4
Ingredients:
- 1 cup Couscous
- 1 tablespoon basil, sliced
- ¼ cup olive oil
- 2 tablespoons red wine vinegar
- 2 teaspoons garlic, minced
- ½ cup shallots, minced
- ½ cup olives, pitted & sliced
- 4 cups baby tomatoes, cut in half
- 1 ½ cups water
- 1 teaspoon Kosher salt

Directions:
1. Add water and ½ teaspoon salt into the saucepan and bring to boil.
2. Add couscous and reduce heat to simmer. Cover and cook until the water is absorbed, about 10 minutes.
3. Remove saucepan from heat and let it cool couscous for 5 minutes. Fluff with fork.
4. In a medium bowl, mix together tomatoes, vinegar, garlic, shallots, olives, and ½ teaspoon salt.
5. Heat oil in a pan over medium heat.
6. Add tomato mixture to the pan and cook for 8-10 minutes.
7. Add couscous and basil to the tomatoes and stir to combine.
Serving Suggestion: Allow to cool completely then serve.
Variation Tip: Add 2 tablespoons of freshly chopped parsley.
Nutritional Information per Serving:
Calories 339 | Fat 14.7g | Sodium 753mg | Carbs 44.5g | Fiber 4.3g | Sugar 3.1g | Protein 7.8g

Roasted Cauliflower

Prep Time: 10 minutes
Cook Time: 20 minutes
Serves: 4

Ingredients:
- 2 pounds cauliflower florets
- 2 tablespoons Parmesan cheese, shredded
- ½ teaspoon dried thyme
- ½ teaspoon dried oregano
- ½ teaspoon onion powder
- ½ teaspoon garlic powder
- 1 tablespoon olive oil
- ½ teaspoon dried basil
- 2 tablespoons Balsamic vinegar
- 2 tablespoons fresh lemon juice
- Pepper
- Salt

Directions:
1. Add cauliflower florets and remaining ingredients except cheese into the mixing bowl and mix well.
2. Cover and place in refrigerator for 30 minutes.
3. Preheat the oven to 425° F.
4. Spread cauliflower florets onto the baking sheet and bake in preheated oven for 15-20 minutes.
5. Toss roasted cauliflower florets with cheese.

Serving Suggestion: Garnish with parsley and serve.
Variation tip: You can also use Romano and Asiago cheese instead of Parmesan cheese.
Nutritional Information per Serving:
Calories 113 | Fat 5.1g | Sodium 165mg | Carbs 13.2g | Fiber 5.9g | Sugar 5.8g | Protein 6.6g

White Beans with Tomato and Arugula

Prep Time: 10 minutes
Cook Time: 5 minutes
Serves: 6

Ingredients:
- 30 ounces can, Cannellini beans, drained & rinsed
- 1 teaspoon dried thyme
- 5 ounces baby arugula
- 1 tablespoon olive oil
- ½ cup sun-dried tomatoes, drained
- Pepper
- Salt

Directions:
1. Heat oil in a pot over medium-high heat.
2. Add arugula and stir until wilted, about 3 minutes.
3. Add thyme, beans, tomatoes, pepper, and salt and cook for 2-3 minutes.

Serving Suggestion: Stir well and serve warm.
Variation Tip: You can also use cooked spinach instead of arugula.
Nutritional Information per Serving:
Calories 133 | Fat 3.5g | Sodium 76mg | Carbs 19.1g | Fiber 5.7g | Sugar 0.9g | Protein 7g

Vegetarian Falafel

Prep Time: 10 minutes
Cook Time: 15 minutes
Serves: 4

Ingredients:
- 1 can chickpeas
- 3 tablespoons flour
- 4 cloves garlic, minced
- 2 shallots, minced
- 2 tablespoons sesame seeds
- 4 tablespoons olive oil
- ⅓ cup fresh parsley
- Salt and pepper, to taste
- 1 teaspoon cumin
- 1 teaspoon cardamom
- 1 teaspoon coriander

Preparation:
1. In a food processor or blender, combine the chickpeas, garlic, shallots, sesame seeds, parsley, salt, pepper, cumin, cardamom, and coriander.
2. Pulse until a crumbly dough forms.
3. Add the flour and pulse until the dough becomes smooth. Refrigerate the mixture for up to 2 hours.
4. Form the falafel into 2-inch balls.
5. In a medium-heat skillet, add the olive oil and fry the falafel on all sides for about 5 minutes.

Serving Suggestion: Garnish with fresh cilantro.
Variation Tip: Add chili flakes for heat.
Nutritional Information per Serving:
Calories 545 | Fat 22.4g | Sodium 20mg | Carbs 69.2g | Fiber 9.8g | Sugar 5.5g | Protein 21.3g

Roasted Carrots

Prep Time: 10 minutes
Cook Time: 20 minutes
Serves: 4
Ingredients:
- 1 ½ pounds carrots, peel and cut into slices
- ½ cup Feta cheese, crumbled
- 2 tablespoons dill, chopped
- 1 garlic clove, minced
- 2 tablespoons olive oil
- 1 teaspoon water
- 2 tablespoons honey
- Pepper
- Salt

Directions:
1. Preheat the oven to 425° F.
2. Arrange carrots onto the baking sheet.
3. Mix together honey, water, oil, garlic, dill, pepper and salt and pour over carrots.
4. Roast in preheated oven for 20-25 minutes. Stir halfway through.
Serving Suggestion: Top with Feta cheese and serve.
Variation Tip: Add 2 tablespoons of chopped basil.
Nutritional Information per Serving:
Calories 216 | Fat 11.1g | Sodium 369mg | Carbs 27.3g | Fiber 4.4g | Sugar 17.8g | Protein 4.4g

Garlicky Mashed Cauliflower

Prep Time: 10 minutes
Cook Time: 3 hours on high
Serves: 6
Ingredients:
- 1 head of cauliflower, cut into florets
- 1 small head of garlic, peeled
- 4 cups vegetable broth
- ⅓ cup sour cream
- 4 tablespoons combined fresh chopped herbs: chives, parsley, spring onions

- Salt and black pepper, to taste
Preparation:
1. Place the cauliflower and garlic in a slow cooker. Pour in the broth until the cauliflower is covered. Add more liquid, if needed.
2. Cover and cook on high for 3 hours.
3. Drain the liquid, reserving it for later.
4. Mash the vegetables with a fork or a potato masher.
5. Add the cream and mash again until smooth.
6. Add some of the reserved cooking liquid to soften the mash.
7. Mix in the chopped herbs, adding salt and fresh ground pepper. Stir to combine thoroughly.
Serving Suggestion: Serve warm with roast chicken.
Variation Tip: Switch up the vegetable broth with chicken broth.
Nutritional Information per Serving:
Calories 83 | Fat 3.8g | Sodium 531mg | Carbs 7.8g | Fiber 1.7g | Sugar 1.7g | Protein 13g

Minty Potato Bake

Prep Time: 10 minutes
Cook Time: 1 hour 20 minutes
Serves: 10
Ingredients:
- 5 pounds potato, cut into wedges
- 6 cloves garlic, minced
- ¾ cup olive oil
- 1 cup water
- ¼ cup fresh lemon juice
- Sea salt and black pepper, to taste
- 1½ tablespoons dried oregano
- 1 teaspoon fresh mint, chopped
- 8 ounces feta cheese, crumbled

Preparation:
1. Coat a casserole dish with olive oil and preheat the oven to 450°F.
2. Mix the pepper, potatoes, salt, garlic, lemon juice, water, and olive oil in a bowl, then layer everything in the prepared dish.
3. Cook in the oven for 45 minutes, then top the mix with the mint and oregano.
4. Add some water (½ cup) if the potatoes look too dry, then cook everything for 42 more minutes.
5. Add some feta to the dish before letting the contents sit for 10 minutes.
6. Enjoy!
Serving Suggestion: Serve with sour cream dip.
Variation Tip: Add chili flakes for some heat.
Nutritional Information per Serving:
Calories 379 | Fat 21.3g | Sodium 305mg | Carbs 41g | Fiber 5.8g | Sugar 3.7g | Protein 8g

Turkish Stuffed Eggplant

Prep Time: 40 minutes
Cook Time: 1 hour 15 minutes
Serves: 4
Ingredients:
- ¼ cup water
- ¼ teaspoon ground cinnamon
- ½ cup medium-grind bulgur, rinsed
- 1 onion, chopped fine
- 1-pound plum tomatoes, cored, seeded, and chopped
- 1 cup Pecorino Romano cheese, grated
- 2 tablespoons extra-virgin olive oil, divided
- 2 tablespoons fresh parsley, minced
- 2 tablespoons pine nuts, toasted
- 2 teaspoons fresh oregano, minced
- 2 teaspoons red wine vinegar
- 3 garlic cloves, minced
- 4 (10-ounce) Italian eggplants, halved along the length
- Pinch of cayenne pepper
- Salt and pepper, to taste

Preparation:
1. Preheat the oven to 400℉.
2. Line baking sheets with parchment paper. Place in the oven to preheat.
3. Scoop out the flesh of each eggplant half in a 1-inch diamond pattern, about 1-inch deep.
4. Brush the scooped sides of the eggplant halves with one tablespoon of oil and sprinkle with salt and pepper.
5. Lay the eggplant halves cut side down on the pre-heated baking sheets and roast until their flesh is tender, about 40 minutes.
6. Move the eggplant halves, cut side down, to a paper towel-lined baking sheet, and let them drain.
7. Toss the bulgur with the water in a container and allow it to sit until the grains are softened, and the liquid is fully absorbed (about 30 minutes).
8. Heat the rest of the oil in a 12-inch skillet on moderate heat until it starts to shimmer. Put in the onion and cook until tender, about 5 minutes.
9. Mix in the garlic, oregano, ½ teaspoon salt, cinnamon, and cayenne, and cook until aromatic, approximately half a minute.
10. Remove from the heat, mix in the bulgur, tomatoes, ¾ cup Pecorino, pine nuts, and vinegar, and allow to sit until heated through (approximately 1 minute). Sprinkle with salt and pepper to taste.
11. Return the eggplant halves, cut side up, to a rimmed baking sheet. Using two forks, gently push the eggplant flesh to the sides to make room for the filling.
12. Mound the bulgur mixture into the eggplant halves and pack lightly with the back of a spoon. Sprinkle with the remaining ¼ cup Pecorino.
13. Bake on the upper rack until the cheese is melted, 5 to 10 minutes.
14. Sprinkle with parsley and serve.
Serving Suggestion: Serve with hot whole-grain rice.
Variation Tip: Substitute fresh oregano with ½ teaspoon of dried oregano.
Nutritional Information per Serving:
Calories 433 | Fat 19.5g | Sodium 596mg | Carbs 56.7g | Fiber 19.7g | Sugar 25g | Protein 18.7g

Quick Zucchini Pasta Bowl

Prep Time: 10 Minutes
Cook Time: 10 Minutes
Serves: 4
Ingredients:
- ½ pound rotini pasta
- 2 tablespoons olive oil
- 6 garlic cloves, crushed
- 1 teaspoon red chili powder
- 2 scallions, finely sliced
- 3 teaspoons fresh rosemary, chopped
- 1 large zucchini, cut up in half lengthways and sliced
- 5 large portobello mushrooms, chopped
- 1 can tomatoes
- 4 tablespoons parmesan cheese, grated
- Salt and black pepper, to taste

Preparation:
1. Cook the pasta in boiling water until al dente.
2. Place a large-sized frying pan over medium heat.
3. Add the oil and allow it to heat up. Add the garlic, scallions, and chili, and sauté for a few minutes until golden.
4. Add the zucchini, rosemary, and mushroom, and sauté for a few minutes.
5. Increase the heat to medium-high and add the tinned tomatoes to the sauce until thick.
6. Drain your boiled pasta and transfer it to a serving platter. Pour the tomato mixture on top and mix using tongs.
7. Enjoy!
Serving Suggestion: Garnish with the grated parmesan cheese and freshly ground black pepper.
Variation Tip: Use two fresh tomatoes in place of the canned tomatoes.
Nutritional Information per Serving:
Calories 361| Fat 12g | Sodium 126mg | Carbs 47g | Fiber 3.7g | Sugar 3.5g | Protein 14g

Turkish Beet Greens

Prep Time: 10 minutes
Cook Time: 10 minutes
Serves: 2

Ingredients:
- 2 cups beet greens
- 7 dried Turkish figs, stemmed and quartered
- ½ cup white grape juice
- 2 cups fresh spinach
- 1 clove garlic, minced
- 2 teaspoons olive oil
- Salt, to taste
- ½-ounce parmesan cheese, grated (optional)

Preparation:
1. Cook the beet greens, white grape juice, and figs over medium heat in a pan for about seven minutes before adding the olive oil, spinach, and garlic.
2. Turn the heat down to low and cook for another three minutes before adding some salt.
3. Add the parmesan cheese on top before serving.

Serving Suggestion: Serve alongside grilled meat.
Variation Tip: Add chili flakes for some heat.
Nutritional Information per Serving:
Calories 328 | Fat 7g | Sodium 260mg | Carbs 49.4g | Fiber 10.2g | Sugar 30g | Protein 6.7g

Vegetarian Casserole

Prep Time: 10 minutes
Cook Time: 40 minutes
Serves: 4

Ingredients:
- 1 onion, finely chopped
- 1 teaspoon smoked paprika
- 1 tablespoon rapeseed oil
- 3 garlic cloves, minced
- ½ teaspoon ground cumin
- 3 medium carrots, sliced

- 1 red pepper, chopped
- 2 (14-ounce) cans tomatoes
- 2 zucchinis, thickly sliced
- 1¼ cups lentils, cooked
- 1 tablespoon dried thyme
- 2 medium sticks celery, finely sliced
- 1 yellow pepper, chopped
- 1 vegetable stock cube
- 2 sprigs fresh thyme

Preparation:
1. Heat the rapeseed oil in a heavy pan and add the onions.
2. Sauté for about 10 minutes and add the garlic cloves, smoked paprika, ground cumin, dried thyme, carrots, celery sticks, red pepper, and yellow pepper.
3. Cook for about 5 minutes and then stir in the vegetable stock, tomatoes, zucchinis, and fresh thyme.
4. Cook for about 25 minutes and then add the cooked lentils.
5. Let the mixture come to a simmer, and then remove from the heat to serve.

Serving Suggestion: Serve with wild rice.
Variation Tip: You can use yellow, green, and brown lentils.
Nutritional Information per Serving:
Calories: 340 | Fat: 5.1g | Sat Fat: 0.5g | Carbohydrates: 62.7g | Fiber: 24.5g | Sugar: 12.6g | Protein: 19.5g

Roasted Brussels Sprouts and Pecans

Prep Time: 10 minutes
Cook Time: 3 hours
Serves: 4

Ingredients:
- 1½ pounds fresh Brussels sprouts
- 4 tablespoons olive oil
- 4 cloves garlic, minced
- 3 tablespoons water
- Salt and pepper, to taste
- ½ cup pecans, chopped

Preparation:
1. Place all ingredients in an Instant Pot or pressure cooker. Stir to combine well.
2. Close the lid and ensure the steam release valve is set to vent.
3. Slow cook for 3 hours.
4. Serve with a dash of lemon juice.

Serving Suggestion: Serve with grilled meat.
Variation Tip: You can use chestnuts or walnuts instead of pecans.
Nutritional Information per Serving:
Calories 161 | Fat 13.1g | Sodium 43mg | Carbs 10.2g | Fiber 6.8g | Sugar 3.8g | Protein 4.1g

Zesty Roasted Brussels Sprouts and Parsnips

Prep Time: 15 minutes
Cook Time: 35 minutes
Serves: 6

Ingredients:
- 1-pound Brussels sprouts, trimmed and halved
- 1-pound red potatoes, unpeeled, cut into 1-inch pieces
- 1 tablespoon lemon juice, plus extra for seasoning
- 1 teaspoon fresh rosemary, minced
- 1 teaspoon sugar
- 1½ tablespoons capers, rinsed and minced
- 2 tablespoons fresh parsley, minced
- 2 teaspoons fresh thyme, minced
- 3 tablespoons extra-virgin olive oil
- 4 carrots, peeled and cut into 2-inch lengths, thick ends halved along the length
- 6 garlic cloves, peeled
- 8 shallots, peeled and halved
- Salt and pepper, to taste

Preparation:
1. Place the oven rack in the center of the oven and preheat the oven to 450℉.
2. Toss the Brussels sprouts, potatoes, shallots, and carrots with the garlic, 1 tablespoon of oil, thyme, rosemary, sugar, ¾ teaspoon salt, and ¼ teaspoon pepper.
3. Place the vegetables in a single layer on a rimmed baking sheet, arranging the Brussels sprouts cut side down in the center of the sheet.
4. Roast until the vegetables are soft and golden brown, 30 to 35 minutes, rotating the sheet halfway through roasting.
5. Whisk the parsley, capers, lemon juice, and the remaining 2 tablespoons of oil together in a large bowl. Put in the roasted vegetables and toss to combine.
6. Sprinkle with salt, pepper, and extra lemon juice to taste.
7. Serve.

Serving Suggestion: Top with chopped cilantro.
Variation Tip: Substitute the fresh herbs with dried herbs.
Nutritional Information per Serving:
Calories 204 | Fat 7.5g | Sodium 292g | Carbs 31.2g | Fiber 6.2g | Sugar 6.7g | Protein 5.8g

Zucchini Feta Fritters

Prep Time: 10 minutes
Cook Time: 6 minutes
Serves: 6

Ingredients:
- ¼ cup all-purpose flour
- 1 garlic clove, minced
- 1 pound zucchini, shredded
- 2 large eggs, lightly beaten
- 2 scallions, minced
- 2 tablespoons fresh dill, minced
- 1 cup feta cheese, crumbled
- 6 tablespoons extra-virgin olive oil
- 3 lemon wedges
- Salt and pepper, to taste

Preparation:
1. Toss the shredded zucchini with 1 teaspoon of salt and allow to drain using a fine-mesh strainer for about 10 minutes.
2. Wrap the zucchini in a clean dish towel, squeeze out excess liquid and move to a large bowl.
3. Mix in the feta, scallions, eggs, dill, garlic, and ¼ teaspoon pepper. Sprinkle the flour over the mixture and stir to incorporate.
4. Heat 3 tablespoons oil in a 12-inch non-stick frying pan on moderate heat until it starts to shimmer.
5. Drop 2-tablespoon-size portions of batter into the frying pan and use the back of a spoon to press the batter into a 2-inch-wide fritter (you should fit about six fritters in the frying pan at a time).
6. Fry until golden brown, approximately three minutes on each side.
7. Move the fritters to a paper towel-lined baking sheet and keep warm in the oven.
8. Wipe the frying pan clean using paper towels and repeat with the remaining three tablespoons of oil and remaining batter.

Serving Suggestion: Serve with the lemon wedges on the side.
Variation Tip: Substitute all-purpose flour with almond flour.
Nutritional Information per Serving:
Calories 247 | Fat 21.2g | Sodium 313mg | Carbs 9.1g | Fiber 1.4g | Sugar 2.7g | Protein 7.5g

Pumpkin Cauliflower Curry

Prep Time: 10 minutes
Cook Time: 20 minutes
Serves: 4
Ingredients:
- ½ cup pumpkin puree
- 4 cups cauliflower florets
- ½ yellow onion, chopped
- 2 cloves garlic, minced
- 2 cups coconut milk
- 2 tablespoons olive oil
- 1 teaspoon coriander
- 1 teaspoon ginger
- A handful of fresh cilantro, chopped
- Salt and black pepper, to taste
- ½ teaspoon paprika
- ½ teaspoon turmeric
- 1 teaspoon cumin
- ½ teaspoon chili powder

Preparation:
1. Heat the onions and garlic in olive oil in a skillet over medium heat until fragrant.
2. Add the ginger and sauté for 5 minutes.
3. Add the coconut milk, coriander, salt, pepper, paprika, turmeric, cumin, and chili powder to the skillet and stir until combined.
4. Add the cauliflower florets and pumpkin puree and simmer for 10 minutes. Serve.

Serving Suggestion: Top with fresh cilantro.
Variation Tip: Switch up cauliflower with broccoli.
Nutritional Information per Serving:
Calories 379 | Fat 35.8g | Sodium 58mg | Carbs 16.2g | Fiber 7.1g | Sugar 8.3g | Protein 5.3g

Zucchini and Tomato Casserole

Prep Time: 10 minutes
Cook Time: 40 minutes
Serves: 2

Ingredients:
- 4 cups zucchini, sliced
- ½ cup cherry tomatoes, halved
- 1 teaspoon garlic, minced
- 1 tablespoon olive oil
- ½ cup parmesan cheese, grated
- ¼ cup breadcrumbs
- 4 tablespoons fresh basil
- Salt and pepper, to taste

Preparation:
1. Preheat the oven to 350°F.
2. Add the olive oil to a skillet over medium heat and cook the zucchini, salt, and pepper for 10 minutes.
3. Add the garlic and cook until fragrant.
4. Put the zucchini in a baking dish along with the tomatoes and basil.
5. Top with the breadcrumbs and parmesan cheese.
6. Bake for 30 minutes.

Serving Suggestion: Garnish with fresh basil.
Variation Tip: Feel free to add your favorite herbs.
Nutritional Information per Serving:
Calories 185 | Fat 9.7g | Sodium 302mg | Carbs 20.4g | Fiber 4.2g | Sugar 6.8g | Protein 7.3g

Zucchini Pasta with Mango Sauce

Prep Time: 10 minutes
Cook Time: 20 minutes
Serves: 2

Ingredients:
- 1 teaspoon dried herbs (optional)
- ½ cup raw kale leaves, shredded
- 2 small dried figs, chopped
- 3 Medjool dates, chopped
- 4 medium kiwis, peeled and chopped
- 2 large mangoes, peeled and cut into cubes
- 2 cup zucchini, spiralized
- ¼ cup roasted cashew

Preparation:
1. Put the kale in a large salad bowl and top it with the zucchini noodles. Sprinkle with the dried herbs. Set aside.
2. In a food processor, grind the cashews into a powder.
3. Add the figs, dates, kiwis, and mango, then puree to a smooth consistency.
4. Pour the mixture over the zucchini pasta.
5. Serve and enjoy.

Serving Suggestion: Serve alongside fish.
Variation Tip: Add chili for some heat.
Nutritional Information per Serving:
Calories 530 | Fat 18.5g | Sodium 31mg | Carbs 95.4g | Fiber 15.8g | Sugar 89.5g | Protein 8.0g

Italian Garlic Mushrooms

Prep Time: 10 minutes
Cook Time: 25 minutes
Serves: 8

Ingredients:
- 1 teaspoon ground black pepper
- 4 ounces cheddar cheese, grated
- 2 tablespoons garlic, minced
- 1 tablespoon Italian seasoning
- 1 tablespoon green chives
- 1-pound mushroom, sliced
- ¼ teaspoon salt
- 1 teaspoon olive oil

Preparation:
1. Sprinkle the mushrooms with salt.
2. Combine the minced garlic with the ground black pepper and olive oil in a skillet and sauté for 1 minute.
3. Add the sliced mushrooms and cook the mixture for 15 minutes, stirring constantly. Avoid browning the ingredients.
4. Sprinkle with Italian seasoning and chives.
5. Add the grated cheese and mix carefully until the cheese melts.
6. Transfer to serving plates and serve hot.

Serving Suggestion: Top with lemon slices.
Variation Tip: Add paprika for a vibrant flavor.
Nutritional Information per Serving:
Calories 84 | Fat 6g | Sodium 166mg | Carbs 3.1g | Fiber 0.7g | Sugar 1.2g | Protein 5.5g

Cauliflower Pasta

Prep Time: 10 minutes
Cook Time: 20 minutes
Serves: 2

Ingredients:
- 2 tablespoons olive oil
- 1 head cauliflower
- ¼ teaspoons chili flakes
- 4 cloves garlic, divided
- 4 ounces pasta
- Lemon zest from 1 lemon
- ½ cup toasted walnuts, chopped
- 1 cup fresh parsley, chopped
- 2 tablespoons capers, optional

Preparation:
1. Preheat the oven to 425℉.
2. Place the cauliflower in a bowl coated with olive oil.
3. Sprinkle over pepper and salt, some chili flakes, two-thirds of the garlic, and half of the lemon zest, and toss well.
4. Spread the mixture on a parchment-lined pan in a single layer and place it in the oven.
5. Roast for 25 minutes.
6. Cook the pasta, drain it, and keep it in a bowl.
7. Drizzle over the olive oil and add the remaining garlic, lemon zest, parsley, capers, and walnuts.
8. Add the cauliflower to the bowl and toss.
9. Sprinkle with chili flakes.

Serving Suggestion: Top with fresh herbs and parmesan cheese.
Variation Tip: Omit chili flakes for a milder dish.
Nutritional Information per Serving:
Calories 386 | Fat 26g | Sodium 249mg | Carbs 38g | Fiber 6g | Sugar 3g | Protein 10g

Pasta with Tomatoes and Herbs

Prep Time: 15 minutes
Cook Time: 15 minutes
Serves: 4

Ingredients:
- 2 tablespoons olive oil
- 8 ounces angel hair pasta
- 1 tablespoon garlic, minced
- 1 tablespoon dried basil, crushed
- 2 cups cherry tomatoes, halved
- 1 tablespoon dried oregano, crushed
- 1 teaspoon dried thyme, crushed

Preparation:
1. Cook the pasta as per the packet instructions in salted boiling water until al dente.
2. Drain the pasta well and set it aside.
3. In a large skillet placed over medium heat, heat the olive oil and sauté the garlic for about 1 minute.
4. Sprinkle in the basil, oregano, and thyme, and sauté for about 1 minute.
5. Add the pasta and cook for about 3 minutes until it is thoroughly heated.
6. Fold in the tomatoes and remove the skillet from the heat.
7. Serve hot.

Serving Suggestion: Serve with cheese and cauliflower breadsticks.
Variation Tip: You can add veggies to this pasta.
Nutritional Information per Serving:
Calories: 247 | Fat: 8.6g | Sat Fat: 1.3g | Carbohydrates: 36.1g | Fiber: 1.7g | Sugar: 2.4g | Protein: 7.5g

Vegetable Curry

Prep Time: 20 minutes
Cook Time: 30 minutes
Serves: 6
Ingredients:
- 2 carrots, peeled and chopped
- 6 tablespoons olive oil, divided
- 1 sweet potato, peeled and cubed
- 1 onion, chopped
- 1 red bell pepper, seeded and chopped
- 1 tablespoon curry powder
- 1 teaspoon ground cinnamon
- ¾ tablespoon sea salt
- 1 zucchini, sliced
- ¼ cup almonds, blanched
- 10 ounces fresh spinach
- 1 medium eggplant, cubed
- 1 green bell pepper, seeded and chopped
- 3 garlic cloves, minced
- 1 teaspoon ground turmeric
- ¾ teaspoon ground cayenne pepper
- 1 (15-ounce) can low-sodium garbanzo beans, rinsed and drained
- 1 cup fresh orange juice
- 2 tablespoons golden raisins

Preparation:
1. In a large wok placed over medium heat, heat 3 tablespoons of the olive oil.
2. Add the sweet potato, carrots, eggplant, onion, and bell peppers, and sauté for about 5 minutes.
3. Meanwhile, in another frying pan placed over medium heat, heat the rest of the olive oil.
4. Add the garlic, cinnamon, curry powder, turmeric, salt, and cayenne pepper and sauté for about 3 minutes.
5. Shift the garlic mixture into the pan of the vegetables and toss to combine well.
6. Stir in the zucchini, beans, orange juice, raisins, and almonds.
7. Cover the pan and simmer for about 20 minutes.
8. Remove the lid and stir in the spinach.
9. Cook for about 5 minutes (with the lid removed) and serve hot.
Serving Suggestion: Serve over a bed of rice.
Variation Tip: You can replace the cashews with almonds.

Nutritional Information per Serving:
Calories: 517 | Fat: 21.1g | Sat Fat: 2.7g | Carbohydrates: 70.1g | Fiber: 19.8g | Sugar: 21.2g | Protein: 18.8g

Lentils Stuffed Butternut

Prep Time: 10 minutes
Cook Time: 55 minutes
Serves: 2
Ingredients:
For the squash:
- 1 butternut squash
- 1 tablespoon olive oil
- Salt and black pepper, to taste
For the stuffing:
- 2 teaspoons olive oil
- 1 clove garlic, crushed
- 1 red onion, sliced
- 1-inch ginger piece, grated
- ½ teaspoon ground cinnamon
- ½ teaspoon cumin seeds
- ½ teaspoon paprika
- ⅓ cup sultanas
- 1 cup green lentils
- 1 cup spinach, chopped

Preparation:
1. Preheat the oven to 390°F.
2. Place the squash halves in an ovenproof dish, oil them, and season with salt and fresh black pepper. Roast for around 35 minutes until cooked.
3. Heat the oil in a skillet, add the garlic and red onion, then cook, occasionally stirring, for about 5 minutes.
4. Add all the other ingredients and cook for 10 minutes on low heat until the flavors are combined, stirring frequently.
5. Add the spinach and cook for 3–4 minutes.
6. Place the stuffing mixture on top of the roasted squash, return to the oven, and bake for 10–15 minutes.
7. Serve immediately with the pan juices spooned over.
Serving Suggestion: Garnish with parsley.
Variation Tip: Substitute spinach with kale.
Nutritional Information per Serving:
Calories 254 | Fat 14.5g | Sodium 34mg | Carbs 32.8g | Fiber 5.3g | Sugar 10.7g | Protein 3.5g

Beans and Rice

Prep Time: 10 Minutes
Cook Time: 55 Minutes
Serves: 6

Ingredients:
- 1 tablespoon olive oil
- 1 yellow onion, chopped
- 2 celery stalks, chopped
- 2 garlic cloves, minced
- 2 cups brown rice
- 1½ cups canned black beans, rinsed and drained
- 4 cups water
- Salt and black pepper, to taste

Preparation:
1. Heat a pan with the oil over medium heat. Add the celery, garlic, and onion, stir and cook for 10 minutes.
2. Add the rest of the ingredients, stir, and bring to a simmer. Cook over medium heat for 45 minutes.
3. Divide between plates and serve.

Serving Suggestion: Serve alongside a salad.
Variation Tip: Substitute the black beans with red kidney beans.
Nutritional Information per Serving:
Calories 224 | Fat 8.4g | Sodium 30mg | Carbs 15.3g | Fiber 3.4g | Sugar 1.1g | Protein 6.2g

Fennel Wild Rice

Prep Time: 10 Minutes
Cook Time: 25 Minutes
Serves: 6

Ingredients:
- 1 tablespoon fresh parsley, chopped
- 2 cups cooked wild rice
- 1 cup fennel, diced
- 1 tablespoon olive oil
- ½ cup sweet onion, chopped
- ½ red bell pepper, finely diced
- ¼ teaspoon fine sea salt
- ¼ teaspoon black pepper

Preparation:
1. Place a skillet over medium-high heat.
2. Heat the olive oil and add the onion, red bell pepper, and fennel.
3. Sauté for 6 minutes. It should become tender.
4. Stir in the wild rice, and cook for 5 minutes, and then add in your parsley.
5. Season with salt and pepper before serving warm.

Serving Suggestion: Garnish with fennel.
Variation Tip: Use 1 tablespoon of orange zest for a zingy flavor.
Nutritional Information per Serving:
Calories 222 | Fat 3g | Sodium 178mg | Carbs 43g | Fiber 1.2g | Sugar 1.5g | Protein 8g

Tomato and Millet Mix

Prep Time: 10 Minutes
Cook Time: 20 Minutes
Serves: 6

Ingredients:
- 3 tablespoons olive oil
- 1 cup millet
- 2 scallions, chopped
- 2 tomatoes, chopped
- ½ cup cilantro, chopped
- 1 teaspoon chili paste
- 6 cups cold water
- ½ cup lemon juice
- Salt and black pepper, to taste

Preparation:
1. Heat a pan with the oil over medium heat, add the millet, stir, and cook for 4 minutes.
2. Add the water, salt, and pepper, stir, and bring to a simmer over medium heat. Cook for 15 minutes.
3. Add the rest of the ingredients and toss well.
4. Divide the mixture between plates and serve as a side dish.

Serving Suggestion: Serve with seared scallops.
Variation Tip: When the dish is ready, top with shaved parmesan cheese if desired
Nutritional Information per Serving:
Calories 222 | Fat 10.2g | Sodium 45mg | Carbs 14.5g | Fiber 3.4g | Sugar 1.6g | Protein 2.4g

Herbed Risotto

Prep Time: 10 Minutes
Cook Time: 15 Minutes
Serves: 4

Ingredients:
- 2 cups of rice
- 2 tablespoon parmesan cheese, grated
- 3½ ounces heavy cream
- 1 tablespoon fresh oregano, chopped
- 1 tablespoon fresh basil, chopped
- ½ tablespoon fresh sage, chopped
- 1 onion, chopped
- 2 tablespoons olive oil
- 1 teaspoon garlic, minced
- 4 cups vegetable stock
- Salt and black pepper, to taste

Preparation:
1. Add the oil to an Instant Pot and set the pot to Sauté mode.
2. Add the garlic and onion and sauté for 2–3 minutes.
3. Add the remaining ingredients except for the parmesan cheese and heavy cream and stir well.
4. Seal the pot with the lid and cook on High for 12 minutes.
5. Once done, allow to release the pressure naturally for 10 minutes. Then release the remaining pressure using quick release.
6. Remove the lid and serve.

Serving Suggestion: Stir in the cream and cheese just before serving.

Variation Tip: Use a teaspoon of paprika for a vibrant taste.

Nutritional Information per Serving:
Calories 514 | Fat 17.6g | Sodium 801mg | Carbs 79.4g | Fiber 2.4g | Sugar 2.1g | Protein 8.8g

Spinach Pesto Pasta

Prep Time: 10 Minutes
Cook Time: 10 Minutes
Serves: 4

Ingredients:

- 8 ounces whole-grain pasta
- ⅓ cup mozzarella cheese, grated
- ½ cup pesto
- 5 ounces fresh spinach
- 1¾ cups water
- 8 ounces mushrooms, chopped
- 1 tablespoon olive oil
- Salt and black pepper, to taste

Preparation:
1. Add the oil to the Instant Pot and set the pot to Sauté mode.
2. Add the mushrooms and sauté for 5 minutes.
3. Add the water and pasta and stir well.
4. Seal the pot with the lid and cook on High for 5 minutes.
5. Once done, release the pressure using quick release.
6. Remove the lid.
7. Stir in the remaining ingredients and serve.

Serving Suggestion: Serve with steak, roasted vegetables, or chicken.

Variation Tip: Flat linguine is highly recommended for this recipe.

Nutritional Information per Serving:
Calories 213 | Fat 17.3g | Sodium 239mg | Carbs 9.5g | Fiber 11.9g | Sugar 4.5g | Protein 7.4 g

Mediterranean Spiced Lentils

Prep Time: 5 minutes
Cook Time: 20 minutes
Serves: 6

Ingredients:
- 1 teaspoon dried oregano
- ¾ cup green lentils
- 1 teaspoon dried basil
- ¼ teaspoon ground sage
- 2¼ cups water
- ½ teaspoon dried parsley
- ¼ teaspoon onion powder

Preparation:
1. In a heavy saucepan placed over medium-high heat, add the lentils, water, and spices.
2. Let the ingredients come to a boil, and then cover with a lid.
3. Reduce the heat and simmer for about 20 minutes.
4. Stir well and serve hot.

Serving Suggestion: Top with fresh cilantro before serving.

Variation Tip: You can also add dried rosemary.

Nutritional Information per Serving:
Calories: 258 | Fat: 0.9g | Sat Fat: 0.1g | Carbohydrates: 44.1g | Fiber: 22.4g | Sugar: 1.6g | Protein: 18.7g

Lentils in Tomato Sauce

Prep Time: 10 Minutes
Cook Time: 30 Minutes
Serves: 4
Ingredients:
- 2½ cups water
- 1 cup green lentils
- 1 tablespoon olive oil
- 1 zucchini, cubed
- ½ large onion, diced
- 2 cloves garlic, minced
- 2 tablespoons lovage, chopped
- 1 tablespoon fresh thyme, chopped
- 2 cups tomato sauce

Preparation:
1. Add the water to a saucepan, add the lentils, and bring to a boil. Cover and simmer until the lentils are tender (about 20 minutes).
2. Heat the olive oil in a skillet over high heat. Sauté the onion, garlic, and zucchini for 5–7 minutes.
3. Add the lovage and thyme and cook until slightly wilted (about 10 seconds).
4. Add the lentils and tomato sauce.
5. Reduce the heat and cook for 3–5 minutes.
Serving Suggestion: Serve over a bed of pasta or rice.
Variation Tip: You can use brown or red lentils.
Nutritional Information per Serving:
Calories 288 | Fat 10.5g | Sodium 649mg | Carbs 39g | Fiber 10g | Sugar 8g | Protein 11g

Mediterranean White Beans

Prep Time: 10 minutes
Cook Time: 20 minutes
Serves: 4
Ingredients:
- ¼ cup extra-virgin olive oil
- 1 (24-ounce) jar white beans, drained and rinsed
- ½ cup onion, chopped
- 1 large garlic clove, minced
- 1 teaspoon salt
- ½ teaspoon dried rosemary, crushed
- ½ cup celery, chopped
- 1 (16-ounce) can diced tomatoes, with juice
- 1 teaspoon sugar
- ¼ cup fresh Italian parsley, chopped

Preparation:
1. Heat the olive oil in a skillet placed over medium-high heat and sauté the garlic and onion for about 5 minutes.
2. Add the white beans, tomatoes, rosemary, salt, and sugar, and let the mixture come to a boil.
3. Reduce the heat, cover with a lid, and simmer for about 15 minutes.
4. Stir in the parsley and serve.
Serving Suggestion: Serve as a tasty side dish for pork or chicken.
Variation Tip: Almond milk can be replaced with coconut milk.
Nutritional Information per Serving:
Calories: 346 | Fat: 8.3g | Sat Fat: 1.3g | Carbohydrates: 60.2g | Fiber: 2.1g | Sugar: 1.8g | Protein: 7.9g

Cherry Tomatoes and Black Beans

Prep Time: 10 minutes
Cook Time: 15 minutes
Serves: 2
Ingredients:
- 1 (15-ounce) can black beans, undrained
- 1 cup cherry tomatoes, halved
- 1 teaspoon salt
- 1 tablespoon dried oregano
- 1 teaspoon red pepper flakes

Preparation:
1. Pour the black beans and their liquid into a large skillet and bring to a low boil over medium-high heat.
2. Reduce the heat to low and simmer for 5 minutes.
3. Stir in the cherry tomatoes, salt, oregano, and red pepper flakes, and cook for 10 minutes.
4. Serve and enjoy.
Serving Suggestion: Serve over hot rice.
Variation Tip: Feel free to add in other spices.
Nutritional Information per Serving:
Calories 185 | Fat 1g | Sodium 987mg | Carbs 34g | Fiber 12g | Sugar 2g | Protein 12g

Quinoa, Bean, and Vegetable Stew

Prep Time: 20 minutes
Cook Time: 45 minutes
Serves: 6

Ingredients:
- 2 cups seasonal vegetables (zucchini, yellow squash, bell pepper, sweet potatoes), chopped
- 3 tablespoons olive oil, extra-virgin
- 3 carrots, peeled and chopped
- 1 medium yellow onion, chopped
- 6 garlic cloves, minced
- 1 (28-ounce) can diced tomatoes with juices (low-sodium)
- 4 cups low-sodium vegetable broth
- 2 bay leaves
- Salt and black pepper, to taste
- 1 cup fresh kale, chopped
- ¼ cup parmesan cheese, freshly grated
- 2 celery stalks, chopped
- ½ teaspoon dried thyme, crushed
- 1 cup quinoa, rinsed and drained
- 2 cups water
- 1 pinch red pepper flakes, crushed
- 1 (15-ounce) can low-sodium Great Northern beans, rinsed and drained
- 2 teaspoons fresh lemon juice

Preparation:
1. Put the olive oil, seasonal vegetables, carrots, celery, garlic, thyme, onion, and a pinch of salt in a large wok placed over medium heat. Cook for about 8 minutes, stirring occasionally.
2. Stir in the diced tomatoes with their juices and cook for about 3 minutes, stirring occasionally.
3. Add the quinoa, water, broth, red pepper flakes, bay leaves, 1 teaspoon of salt, and black pepper and stir well.
4. Increase the heat to high and let the mixture come to a boil.
5. Reduce the heat to low, cover partially, and simmer for about 25 minutes.
6. Stir in the kale and beans and simmer, uncovered, for about 5 minutes.

7. Remove from the heat and dispose of the bay leaves.
8. Squeeze in the lemon juice and serve topped with the parmesan cheese.
Serving Suggestion: Serve with brown rice.
Variation Tip: Parmesan cheese can be replaced with Pecorino cheese.
Nutritional Information per Serving:
Calories: 507 | Fat: 11.9g | Sat Fat: 2.4g | Carbohydrates: 76.9g | Fiber: 19.9g | Sugar: 8.6g | Protein: 26.9g

Greek Inspired Rice

Prep Time: 10 Minutes
Cook Time: 30 Minutes
Serves: 4

Ingredients:
- 1 yellow onion, chopped
- 1 cup fresh parsley, chopped
- 1 teaspoon dill weed
- 2 cups rice
- 1 garlic clove, minced
- 2 ounces spinach
- ½ cup orzo pasta
- 3 tablespoons olive oil
- 2 tablespoons lemon juice
- 2 cups broth
- A pinch of salt

Preparation:
1. Wash and soak the rice for 20 minutes in cold water. Drain.
2. Heat the oil in a pan over medium heat. Add the onion and garlic and cook for 3–4 minutes.
3. Add the pasta and cook until it gains some color. Now add the rice.
4. Add the spinach, lemon juice, and broth. Bring to a boil and then reduce back to medium heat.
5. Cover the pot and cook until the rice is done (around 20 minutes). All the liquid should be completely absorbed and the rice tender. Remove from the heat.
6. For better flavor, leave the pot covered, and don't stir the rice (about 10 minutes).
7. Uncover and stir in the parsley and lemon zest.
8. Serve and enjoy.
Serving Suggestion: Garnish with some slices of lemon on top.
Variation Tip: Add in other seasonings you like.
Nutritional Information per Serving:
Calories 145 | Fat 6.9g | Sodium 249mg | Carbs 18.3g | Fiber 5g | Sugar 5g | Protein 3.3g

Herbed Rice

Prep Time: 10 Minutes
Cook Time: 20 Minutes
Serves: 4
Ingredients:
- 1 teaspoon salt
- 2 tablespoons olive oil
- 1 onion, chopped
- 1 teaspoon black pepper
- 3 cups chicken broth
- 1 teaspoon garlic, minced
- ¼ cup lemon juice
- ½ cup basmati rice
- ½ teaspoon each of dried rosemary, basil, dill, parsley, oregano, and thyme

Preparation:
1. Melt the olive oil in a pan on moderate heat. Add the salt and black pepper.
2. Add the onion and cook until it has softened. Add the garlic and cook for 1 minute.
3. Add the chicken broth and lemon juice, along with the dried herbs and rice. Keep stirring until mixed.
4. Wait for the mixture to boil, then cover and lower the heat.
5. Keep cooking until the rice is well softened.
6. Serve and enjoy.
Serving Suggestion: Garnish with fresh herbs such as parsley.
Variation Tip: You can opt to use nut butters like almond butter.
Nutritional Information per Serving:
Calories 227 | Fat 0g | Sodium 1198mg | Carbs 49g | Fiber 3g | Sugar 1.8g | Protein 4g

Black-Eyed Peas

Prep Time: 10 Minutes (plus 6 hours for soaking)
Cook Time: 1 Hour 20 Minutes
Serves: 12
Ingredients:
- 2 cups dried black-eyed peas
- 5 cloves garlic, chopped
- 12 ounces smoked turkey
- 3½ cups water
- 1 onion, chopped
- A pinch cayenne pepper
- ½ teaspoon ground ginger
- 1 cup celery, diced
- ½ teaspoon dried thyme
- ½ teaspoon curry powder

Preparation:
1. Put the black-eyed peas in a large bowl. Pour the water over them. (There should be enough to cover them by about 4 inches.)
2. Cover the bowl and let the peas soak overnight (or for at least six hours).
3. Rinse the peas under cold water, then drain.
4. Add all the remaining ingredients and black-eyed peas to a large pot over high heat, and then bring to a boil.
5. Once boiling, reduce the heat to low. Cover with a lid.
6. Cook until the peas are tender, stirring occasionally (about 1 hour).
Serving Suggestion: Serve over rice and garnish with chives.
Variation Tip: Use other seasonings if desired.
Nutritional Information per Serving:
Calories 304 | Fat 24g | Sodium 211mg | Carbs 8g | Fiber 1g | Sugar 1.2g | Protein 12g

Baked Black-Eyed Peas

Prep Time: 15 minutes
Cook Time: 35 minutes
Serves: 3
Ingredients:
- 2 (15-ounce) cans black-eyed peas, drained and rinsed
- 3 tablespoons extra-virgin olive oil
- Salt, to taste
- 2 teaspoons Za'atar
- 2 teaspoons sumac
- 2 teaspoons harissa

Preparation:
1. Preheat the oven to 400°F.
2. Place the black-eyed peas on a baking sheet and drizzle with the olive oil.
3. Season with salt and toss to coat well.
4. Bake for about 35 minutes, shaking the baking pan three times during the cooking time.
5. Remove from the oven and season with the Za'atar, sumac, and harissa.
6. Serve warm.
Serving Suggestion: Serve as a snack with tea.
Variation Tip: You can use seasonings of your choice.
Nutritional Information per Serving:
Calories: 478 | Fat: 18.5g | Sat Fat: 2.3g | Carbohydrates: 66.1g | Fiber: 13.1g | Sugar: 0.9g | Protein: 14.9g

Quinoa and Lentil Casserole

Prep Time: 15 minutes
Cook Time: 50 minutes
Serves: 4

Ingredients:
- 2 tablespoons olive oil
- Olive oil cooking spray
- 1 large yellow onion, chopped
- 10 ounces fresh baby spinach
- 1½ cups brown lentils, cooked
- 2 medium eggs
- 6 ounces feta cheese, crumbled
- ½ teaspoon salt
- 3 garlic cloves, minced
- 2½ cups cooked quinoa
- 2 cups fresh cherry tomatoes, halved
- ½ cup plain, non-fat Greek yogurt
- ½ cup fresh dill, chopped
- 1 pinch black pepper

Preparation:
1. Preheat the oven to 375°F and grease a casserole dish with the olive oil cooking spray.
2. In a large skillet placed over medium heat, sauté the olive oil, onion, and garlic for about 3 minutes.
3. Stir in the spinach, cover with a lid, and cook for about 3 minutes.
4. Uncover and cook for another 3 minutes.
5. Transfer the spinach mixture onto a plate lined with paper towels to drain.
6. In a bowl, add the quinoa, tomatoes, lentils, and spinach mixture.
7. Add the yogurt, eggs, feta, dill, salt, and black pepper to another big bowl. Combine well.
8. Stir in the quinoa mixture and toss well.
9. Evenly place the mixture into the prepared casserole dish.
10. Bake for about 40 minutes until the top becomes golden brown.
11. Remove from the oven and set aside to cool.
12. Cut into the desired size slices and serve.

Serving Suggestion: Serve alongside a salad.
Variation Tip: Feta cheese can be replaced with goat's cheese.

Nutritional Information per Serving:
Calories: 479 | Fat: 17.1g | Sat Fat: 6g | Carbohydrates: 62.6g | Fiber: 8.9g | Sugar: 6.6g | Protein: 21.5g

Cannellini Beans and Farro Stew

Prep Time: 20 minutes
Cook Time: 45 minutes
Serves: 6

Ingredients:
- 1 cup carrots, peeled and chopped
- 2 tablespoons olive oil
- 1 cup celery, chopped
- 4 garlic cloves, minced
- 1 cup uncooked farro, rinsed
- 1 bay leaf
- Salt, to taste
- 4 cups fresh kale, chopped
- 1 tablespoon lemon juice, fresh
- 1 cup yellow onion, chopped
- 1 (14½-ounce) can diced tomatoes
- ½ cup fresh parsley sprigs
- 1 teaspoon dried oregano
- 5 cups low-sodium vegetable broth
- 1 (15-ounce) can low-sodium cannellini beans, rinsed and drained
- ½ cup feta cheese, crumbled

Preparation:
1. In a large pan placed over medium-high heat, heat the oil and sauté the celery, carrots, garlic, and onion for about 3 minutes.
2. Stir in the farro, tomatoes, parsley sprigs, oregano, bay leaf, broth, and salt, and let it come to a boil.
3. Reduce the heat to medium-low, cover, and simmer for about 20 minutes.
4. Discard the parsley sprigs and stir in the kale, cooking for about 15 minutes.
5. Stir in the cannellini beans and cook for about 5 minutes until thoroughly heated.
6. Discard the bay leaf and squeeze in the lemon juice.
7. Remove from the heat and serve topped with feta cheese.

Serving Suggestion: Serve with yellow rice.
Variation Tip: Kale can be replaced with spinach.

Nutritional Information per Serving:
Calories: 520 | Fat: 10.5g | Sat Fat: 3g | Carbohydrates: 79.1g | Fiber: 22.6g | Sugar: 6.5g | Protein: 30g

Rice and Veggie Jambalaya

Prep Time: 20 minutes
Cook Time: 55 minutes
Serves: 4
Ingredients:
- 2 tablespoons olive oil
- 2 celery stalks, chopped
- ½ red bell pepper, seeded and chopped
- 1 (14-ounce) can crushed tomatoes (low-sodium)
- 4 cups low-sodium vegetable broth
- 2 tablespoons low-sodium soy sauce
- 1 teaspoon dried thyme, crushed
- 1 teaspoon dried oregano, crushed
- ½ teaspoon smoked paprika
- Salt and black pepper, to taste
- 1 scallion, chopped
- 1 onion, chopped
- 4 garlic cloves, minced
- ½ green bell pepper, seeded and chopped
- 2 cups brown rice, uncooked
- 2 tablespoons Tabasco sauce
- 2 bay leaves
- 1 teaspoon dried basil, crushed
- 1 teaspoon sweet paprika
- ½ teaspoon cayenne pepper
- 3 cups canned low-sodium mixed beans (chickpeas, white beans, and kidney beans)

Preparation:
1. In a large pan placed over medium heat, sauté the olive oil, onion, and garlic for about 5 minutes.
2. Add the celery and bell peppers and sauté for about 5 minutes.
3. Stir in the crushed tomatoes, broth, rice, Tabasco sauce, bay leaves, soy sauce, dried herbs, spices, and black pepper, and let it come to a boil.
4. Reduce the heat to low, cover the pan, and simmer for about 40 minutes, stirring occasionally, until the rice is cooked.
5. Uncover the lid and stir in the beans and salt.
6. Simmer for about 3 minutes until heated through.
7. Reduce from the heat and serve garnished with the scallions.
Serving Suggestion: Top with fresh parsley before serving.
Variation Tip: More scallions can be added.
Nutritional Information per Serving:
Calories: 518 | Fat: 11.2g | Sat Fat: 1.9g | Carbohydrates: 89g | Fiber: 8.2g | Sugar: 9.4g | Protein: 16g

Freekeh Pilaf

Prep Time: 10 minutes
Cook Time: 1 hour 10 minutes
Serves: 5
Ingredients:
- 3¾ cups water
- ¼ cup fresh mint, chopped
- ¼ cup extra-virgin olive oil, plus extra for serving
- ¼ cup shelled pistachios, toasted and coarsely chopped
- ¼ teaspoon ground coriander
- ¼ teaspoon ground cumin
- 1 head cauliflower (2 pounds), cored and cut into ½-inch florets
- 1 shallot, minced
- 1½ cups whole freekeh
- 1½ tablespoons lemon juice
- 1½ teaspoons grated fresh ginger
- 3 ounces pitted dates, chopped
- Salt and pepper, to taste

Preparation:
1. Bring the water to a boil in a pot.
2. Put in the freekeh and one tablespoon of salt, return to the boil and cook until the grains are tender (30–45 minutes).
3. Drain the freekeh, return to the now-empty pot, and cover to keep warm.
4. Heat 2 tablespoons of oil in a frying pan on moderate to high heat until it starts to shimmer.
5. Put in the cauliflower, salt, and pepper, cover, and cook until the florets are softened and brown, approximately 5 minutes.
6. Remove the lid and continue to cook, stirring intermittently, until the florets turn spotty brown, about 10 minutes.
7. Put in the remaining 2 tablespoons of oil, dates, shallot, ginger, coriander, and cumin and cook, stirring often, until the dates and shallot are softened and aromatic, approximately 3 minutes.
8. Reduce the heat to low, put in the freekeh, and cook, stirring often, until heated through (about 1 minute). Remove from the heat, mix in the pistachios, mint, and lemon juice.
9. Drizzle with some extra oil.
10. Serve.
Serving Suggestion: Garnish with cilantro.
Variation Tip: Substitute lemon juice with lime juice.
Nutritional Information per Serving:
Calories 520 | Fat 14g | Sodium 45mg | Carbs 54g | Fiber 7.9g | Sugar 13.7g | Protein 36g

Fava Beans With Basmati Rice

Prep Time: 10 Minutes
Cook Time: 35 Minutes
Serves: 4
Ingredients:
- ¼ cup olive oil
- 4 cups fresh fava beans, shelled
- 4½ cups water, plus more for drizzling
- 2 cups basmati rice
- ⅛ teaspoon salt
- ⅛ teaspoon freshly ground black pepper
- 2 tablespoons pine nuts, toasted
- ½ cup fresh garlic chives or fresh chives, chopped

Preparation:
1. Fill the saucepan with the olive oil and cook over medium heat.
2. Add the fava beans and drizzle them with water to avoid them burning or sticking. Cook for 10 minutes.
3. Gently stir in the rice. Add the water, salt, and pepper. Increase the heat and bring the mixture to a boil.
4. Reduce the heat and let it simmer for 15 minutes.
5. Remove from the heat and let it rest for 10 minutes before serving. Spoon onto a serving platter

Serving Suggestion: Serve with a sprinkle of the toasted pine nuts and garlic chives or chives.
Variation Tip: Use a teaspoon of ground cardamom for a fragrant dish.
Nutritional Information per Serving:
Calories 587 | Fat 17g | Sodium 134mg | Carbs 97g | Fiber 38.9g | Sugar 8.8g | Protein 2g

Gigante Beans in Tomato Sauce

Prep Time: 10 minutes
Cook Time: 5 minutes
Serves: 2
Ingredients:
- 1 (12-ounce) jar gigante beans, undrained
- 6 ounces tomato paste
- ¾ cup water

- ½ teaspoon dried oregano

Preparation:
1. Pour the beans and their liquid into a small saucepan and bring to a boil over medium-high heat.
2. Remove the pan from the heat and drain the liquid.
3. In another small saucepan, combine the tomato paste and water and bring to a simmer to heat through.
4. Arrange the beans on a serving dish.
5. Spoon over the tomato sauce and enjoy.

Serving Suggestion: Sprinkle with the dried oregano.
Variation Tip: If you can't find gigante beans, good substitutes are corona beans or large butter beans.
Nutritional Information per Serving:
Calories 238 | Fat 1g | Sodium 616mg | Carbs 46g | Fiber 12g | Sugar 11g | Protein 15g

Mediterranean Spinach and Beans

Prep Time: 10 minutes
Cook Time: 20 minutes
Serves: 4
Ingredients:
- 1 small onion, chopped
- 1 tablespoon olive oil
- 2 garlic cloves, minced
- 2 tablespoons Worcestershire sauce
- ¼ teaspoon pepper
- 1 can (15 ounces) cannellini beans, rinsed and drained
- 8 cups fresh baby spinach
- 1 can (14½-ounces) diced no-salt-added tomatoes, undrained
- ¼ teaspoon salt
- ⅛ teaspoon red pepper flakes, crushed
- 1 can (14 ounces) water-packed artichoke hearts, rinsed, drained, and quartered

Preparation:
1. Heat the olive oil in a skillet placed over medium-high heat and sauté the garlic and onion for about 5 minutes.
2. Add the Worcestershire sauce, tomatoes, and seasonings, and let the mixture come to a boil.
3. Reduce the heat and simmer for about 8 minutes.
4. Stir in the beans, spinach, and artichoke hearts, and cook for about 5 minutes.

Serving Suggestion: Serve drizzled with additional olive oil.
Variation Tip: You can use beans of your choice.
Nutritional Information per Serving:
Calories: 241 | Fat: 4.3g | Sat Fat: 0.6g | Carbohydrates: 39.5g | Fiber: 16g | Sugar: 16g | Protein: 5.1g

Brown Rice Pilaf with Raisins

Prep Time: 10 minutes
Cook Time: 15 minutes
Serves: 6
Ingredients:
- 1 tablespoon extra-virgin olive oil
- 1 cup onion, chopped
- ½ cup carrot, shredded
- 1 teaspoon ground cumin
- ½ teaspoon ground cinnamon
- 2 cups instant brown rice
- 1¾ cups 100% orange juice
- ¼ cup water
- 1 cup golden raisins
- ½ cup shelled pistachios
- Bunch of fresh chives, chopped (optional)

Preparation:
1. In a medium saucepan over medium-high heat, heat the oil.
2. Add the onion and cook for 5 minutes, stirring frequently.
3. Add the carrot, cumin, and cinnamon, and cook for 1 minute, stirring frequently.
4. Stir in the rice, orange juice, and water.
5. Bring to a boil, cover, then lower the heat to medium-low.
6. Simmer for 7 minutes, or until the rice is cooked through and the liquid is absorbed.
7. Stir in the raisins, pistachios, and chives (if using) and serve.

Serving Suggestion: Serve with your favorite salad.
Variation Tip: Substitute pistachios with almonds.
Nutritional Information per Serving:
Calories 320 | Fat 7g | Sodium 18mg | Carbs 61g | Fiber 4.1g | Sugar 26.3g | Protein 6g

Mashed Fava Beans

Prep Time: 10 minutes
Cook Time: 10 minutes
Serves: 4
Ingredients:

- 3 pounds fava beans, removed from their pods but unpeeled
- ¼ cup water
- ¼ cup extra-virgin olive oil
- 3 garlic cloves, chopped
- 1 tablespoon fresh rosemary, finely chopped
- Salt and black pepper, to taste

Preparation:
1. Bring a large pot of water to a boil over high heat and cook the beans for 3 minutes.
2. Drain the beans and rinse under cold running water to cool. Peel the outer skin off the beans. The inner bean should pop out easily.
3. Put the beans in a food processor, add the water and salt, and puree.
4. In a skillet, heat the olive oil over low heat.
5. Add the fava bean puree, garlic, rosemary, and pepper.
6. Stir to combine and cook for about 5 minutes, until most of the water evaporates.

Serving Suggestion: Serve with your favorite greens.
Variation Tip: Substitute water with your favorite broth.
Nutritional Information per Serving:
Calories 423 | Fat 16g | Sodium 45mg | Carbs 61g | Fiber 26g | Sugar 31g | Protein 27g

Lemon Couscous

Prep Time: 10 minutes
Cook Time: 15 minutes
Serves: 4
Ingredients:
- 1 cup pearl couscous
- 1¼ cups of water
- 1 tablespoon olive oil
- ¾ teaspoon kosher salt
- 1 clove garlic, minced
- ¾ cup scallions, sliced
- ¼ teaspoon pepper
- 1 teaspoon lemon zest

Preparation:
1. Heat the water in a saucepan.
2. Add half a teaspoon of salt and the couscous, then cover and reduce the heat. Simmer for 9 minutes.
3. Heat the oil in a skillet. Add the scallions and sauté for 4 minutes.
4. Add the garlic and cook it for a minute. Stir in the lemon zest.
5. Stir the scallion mix into the couscous.
6. Season with pepper and salt.
7. Serve and enjoy.

Serving Suggestion: Serve with lemon wedges.
Variation Tip: Feel free to add in more seasoning.
Nutritional Information per Serving:
Calories 38 | Fat 4g | Sodium 243mg | Carbs 2g | Fiber 1g | Sugar 1g | Protein 1g

Kale Fried Rice

Prep Time: 10 minutes
Cook Time: 15 minutes
Serves: 2

Ingredients:
- 2 eggs, whisked together with some salt
- 2 tablespoons coconut oil
- ¾ cup green onions, chopped
- 2 garlic cloves, minced
- 1 cup vegetables, chopped (Brussels sprouts, carrot, bell pepper), optional
- 1 bunch kale
- ¾ cup unsweetened coconut flakes
- ¼ teaspoon sea salt
- 2 teaspoons low-sodium soy sauce
- 2 cups brown rice, cooked
- 1 lime, halved
- 2 teaspoons sriracha or chili garlic sauce
- Chopped fresh parsley, for garnish

Preparation:
1. Heat a wok over medium to high heat.
2. Add a teaspoon of oil. Coat the bottom of the wok.
3. Pour in the eggs and cook. Stir frequently. The eggs should be scrambled.
4. Transfer the eggs to a bowl. Add a teaspoon of oil to your wok.
5. Add the onions, garlic, and optional vegetables. Cook for 30 seconds.
6. Add the kale and cook for a minute more. Transfer the wok contents to the bowl of eggs. Add the remaining kale to your wok.
7. Now, pour in the coconut flakes. Cook while stirring for 30 seconds.
8. Add the rice. Cook for 3 minutes, stirring occasionally. Pour the bowl contents back into your wok.
9. Use a spoon or spatula to break up the scrambled egg.
10. Add the chili garlic sauce and the juice from the half lime. Combine well.
11. Divide the rice into serving bowls.

Serving Suggestion: Garnish with chopped parsley and lime wedges.

Variation Tip: Switch up the coconut oil with olive oil.

Nutritional Information per Serving:
Calories 934 | Fat 60g | Sodium 260mg | Carbs 154g | Fiber 12g | Sugar 4g | Protein 26g

Chickpeas with Garlic and Parsley

Prep Time: 10 Minutes
Cook Time: 20 Minutes
Serves: 6

Ingredients:
- ¼ cup extra-virgin olive oil
- 4 garlic cloves, thinly sliced
- ⅛ teaspoon red pepper flakes
- 1 onion, chopped
- Salt and pepper, to taste
- 2 (15-ounce) cans chickpeas, rinsed
- 1 cup chicken broth
- 2 tablespoons fresh parsley, minced
- 2 teaspoons lemon juice

Preparation:
1. Add three tablespoons of the oil to a skillet and cook the garlic and pepper flakes for 3 minutes over medium heat.
2. Stir in the onion and ¼ teaspoon of salt and cook for 5–7 minutes.
3. Mix in the chickpeas and broth and bring to a simmer.
4. Lower the heat and simmer on low for 7 minutes, covered.
5. Uncover and set the heat to high and cook for 3 minutes, or until all the liquid has evaporated.
6. Set aside and mix in the lemon juice and parsley.
7. Season with salt and pepper to taste and serve.

Serving Suggestion: Drizzle with a tablespoon of olive oil.

Variation Tip: Add more seasoning if required.

Nutritional Information per Serving:
Calories 611 | Fat 17.6g | Sodium 163mg | Carbs 89.5g | Fiber 25.2g | Sugar 16.1g | Protein 28.7g

Mediterranean Tomato Rice

Prep Time: 20 minutes
Cook Time: 20 minutes
Serves: 4
Ingredients:
- 2 garlic cloves, minced
- 1 cup onions, chopped
- 2 tablespoons olive oil
- 1 teaspoon dried thyme
- 1 cup green bell pepper, diced
- 1 tablespoon tomato paste
- 3 cups rice, cooked
- 1 cup celery, thinly sliced
- ½ teaspoon dried marjoram
- 1(15-ounce) can tomatoes, drained and liquid reserved
- Salt and black pepper, to taste

Preparation:
1. In a big skillet placed over medium heat, sauté the olive oil, onions, and garlic for about 5 minutes, frequently stirring.
2. Stir in the marjoram, celery, and thyme, and cook for 2 more minutes.
3. Add in the bell pepper and cook for 3 more minutes, stirring occasionally.
4. Stir in the drained tomatoes, tomato paste, salt, and black pepper.
5. Fold in the rice and stir well to mix thoroughly.
6. Dish out and serve warm.

Serving Suggestion: Serve with Mediterranean vegetable curry.
Variation Tip: You can add seasonings of your choice.
Nutritional Information per Serving:
Calories: 617 | Fat: 8.3g | Sat Fat: 1.3g | Carbohydrates: 122.3g | Fiber: 4.8g | Sugar: 6.5g | Protein: 11.9g

Greek Lemon Rice

Prep Time: 20 minutes
Cook Time: 25 minutes
Serves: 6
Ingredients:
- 2 cups long-grain rice, soaked for about 15 minutes and drained
- 3 tablespoons extra-virgin olive oil
- 1 medium yellow onion, chopped
- 2 cups low-sodium chicken broth
- 1 garlic clove, minced
- 1 pinch salt
- ½ cup orzo pasta
- ¼ cup fresh parsley, chopped
- 2 lemons, juice and zest
- 1 teaspoon dry dill weed

Preparation:
1. Heat the olive oil in a skillet placed over medium-high heat, and sauté the onions for about 4 minutes.
2. Add the garlic and orzo and sauté for about 3 minutes.
3. Stir in the rice and toss well.
4. Pour in the broth and lemon juice and let the mixture come to a boil.
5. Reduce the heat, cover with a lid, and simmer for about 20 minutes.
6. Remove from the heat and let it remain covered for about 10 minutes.
7. Uncover the lid and stir in the parsley, lemon zest, and dill weed to serve.

Serving Suggestion: Serve with a few slices of lemon on top.
Variation Tip: Vegetable broth can also work.
Nutritional Information per Serving:
Calories: 346 | Fat: 8.3g | Sat Fat: 1.3g | Carbohydrates: 60.2g | Fiber: 2.1g | Sugar: 1.8g | Protein: 7.9g

Ful Medames

Prep Time: 10 minutes
Cook Time: 15 minutes
Serves: 5
Ingredients:
- ½ cup water
- 2 cans plain fava beans
- Kosher salt, to taste
- 2 hot peppers, chopped
- 1 large lemon, juiced
- 1 cup parsley, chopped
- 1 teaspoon ground cumin
- 2 garlic cloves, chopped
- 3 tablespoons extra-virgin olive oil
- 1 tomato, diced

Preparation:
1. Put the fava beans, salt, cumin, and water in a saucepan placed over medium-high heat. Cover and cook for about 15 minutes.
2. Mash the fava beans with a fork.
3. Smash the garlic and hot peppers in a mortar, and mix them with the fava beans.
4. Squeeze in the lemon juice and drizzle with the olive oil.
5. Serve topped with the diced tomatoes and parsley.

Serving Suggestion: Serve with pita bread, sliced veggies, and olives.
Variation Tip: You can add more hot peppers on top.
Nutritional Information per Serving:
Calories: 218 | Fat: 9.1g | Sat Fat: 1.2g | Carbohydrates: 25.3g | Fiber: 1.2g | Sugar: 1.7g | Protein: 14.9g

Chickpea Stew

Prep Time: 15 minutes
Cook Time: 35 minutes
Serves: 3
Ingredients:
- 1 red bell pepper, seeded and julienned
- 1 tablespoon extra-virgin olive oil
- 3 scallions, thinly sliced
- 2 garlic cloves, minced
- ½ teaspoon paprika
- 1 pinch brown sugar
- ½ cup low-sodium vegetable broth
- 2 tablespoons fresh parsley, minced
- 1 jalapeño pepper, chopped
- ½ teaspoon ground cumin
- 1 (28-ounce) can whole tomatoes (low-sodium), peeled and crushed
- Salt and black pepper, to taste
- 2 cups low-sodium canned chickpeas, rinsed and drained
- 1 teaspoon fresh lemon zest, grated

Preparation:
1. Heat the oil in a pan placed over medium heat, and sauté the bell pepper, scallions, jalapeño, garlic, pan, cumin, and paprika for about 5 minutes.
2. Stir in the tomatoes, brown sugar, broth, salt, and black pepper, and let it come to a boil.
3. Reduce the heat to medium-low and simmer for about 20 minutes.
4. Stir in the chickpeas, parsley, and lemon zest and simmer for about 10 minutes.
5. Remove from the heat and serve hot.

Serving Suggestion: Serve with Mediterranean tomato rice.
Variation Tip: Jalapeño pepper can be omitted.
Nutritional Information per Serving:
Calories: 605 | Fat: 13.8g | Sat Fat: 1.7g | Carbohydrates: 97.1g | Fiber: 27.8g | Sugar: 24.1g | Protein: 29.9g

Orzo Rice Pilaf

Prep Time: 10 minutes
Cook Time: 35 minutes
Serves: 6

Ingredients:
- 3 cups parboiled brown rice
- ¼ cup olive oil, divided
- ½ cup orzo pasta
- 4 cups water
- 1 tablespoon salt
- 1 tablespoon slivered almonds
- 1 tablespoon tahini

Preparation:
1. Fill a bowl with water, place the rice into it, and let it sit for about 10 minutes.
2. Remove the rice from the water and rinse until clear.
3. In a skillet over medium heat, add two tablespoons of olive oil and mix the orzo into the oil.
4. Fry the orzo until it becomes brownish, about five minutes.
5. Mix in all the rice and continue cooking until the rice kernels are translucent.
6. Add some water and salt and get everything to a boiling point.
7. Cover the rice, turn the heat down, and let the rice cook until it becomes fluffy, about 20 minutes.
8. In another skillet, heat the remaining olive oil on medium heat.
9. Add the almonds and fry them until they are toasted (about 5 minutes).
10. Add the tahini to the almonds and stir to combine evenly.
11. Combine the almond mixture with the rice and serve.
12. Enjoy.

Serving Suggestion: Serve with a salad of your choice.
Variation Tip: Substitute water with chicken or vegetable broth.
Nutritional Information per Serving:
Calories 203 | Fat 13.4g | Sodium 641mg | Carbs 18g | Fiber 0.8g | Sugar 0.2g | Protein 2.8g

Tabouli

Prep Time: 1 hour 30 minutes
Cook Time: 10 minutes
Serves: 8

Ingredients:
- ⅔ cup water
- ⅓ cup bulgur
- Salt and pepper, to taste
- ½ cup fresh lemon juice
- ½ cup olive oil
- 4 tomatoes, chopped
- 2 onions, finely chopped
- 2 bunches fresh parsley, chopped
- 1 bunch fresh mint, chopped

Preparation:
1. Place a pot over high heat and fill it with the water.
2. Once the water boils, remove it from the heat.
3. Combine the hot water with the bulgur and place a lid over the pot.
4. Let the bulgur sit for about 20 mins, then transfer the bulgur to a serving bowl.
5. Combine the bulgur with the mint, salt, parsley, onions, lemon juice, tomatoes, and olive oil.
6. Toss the bulgur mixture and then refrigerate it for about 1 hour (until cool).
7. Plate and enjoy.

Serving Suggestion: Garnish with mint leaves.
Variation Tip: Substitute lemon juice with lime juice.
Nutritional Information per Serving:
Calories 182 | Fat 14g | Sodium 889mg | Carbs 14.1g | Fiber 3.5g | Sugar 3.3g | Protein 2.7g

Mediterranean Lentils and Rice

Prep Time: 10 minutes
Cook Time: 25 minutes
Serves: 4

Ingredients:
- 2¼ cups low-sodium vegetable broth
- ½ cup uncooked brown or green lentils
- ½ cup uncooked instant brown rice
- ½ cup diced carrots
- ½ cup diced celery
- 1 (2¼-ounce) can sliced olives, drained
- ¼ cup red onion, diced
- ¼ cup fresh curly-leaf parsley, chopped
- 1½ tablespoons extra-virgin olive oil
- 1 tablespoon freshly squeezed lemon juice
- 1 garlic clove, minced
- Salt and black pepper, to taste

Preparation:
1. In a medium saucepan over high heat, bring the broth and lentils to a boil.
2. Cover, and lower the heat to medium-low, then cook for 8 minutes.
3. Raise the heat to medium, and stir in the rice.
4. Cover the pot and cook the mixture for 15 minutes or until the liquid is absorbed.
5. While the lentils and rice are cooking, mix the carrots, celery, olives, onion, and parsley in a large serving bowl.
6. Remove the pot from the heat and let it sit, covered, for 1 minute, then stir.
7. Whisk together the oil, lemon juice, garlic, salt, and pepper in a small bowl. Set aside.
8. When the lentils and rice are cooked, add them to the serving bowl.
9. Pour the dressing on top, and mix everything.
10. Serve warm or cold, or store in a sealed container in the refrigerator for up to 7 days.

Serving Suggestion: Garnish with cilantro.
Variation Tip: Substitute vegetable broth with chicken broth.

Nutritional Information per Serving:
Calories 388 | Fat 21.9g | Sodium 256mg | Carbs 37.8g | Fiber 9.5g | Sugar 1.8g | Protein 11.2g

Herbed Farro

Prep Time: 10 minutes
Cook Time: 40 minutes
Serves: 5

Ingredients:
- 6 cups water
- ¼ cup fresh mint, chopped
- ¼ cup fresh parsley, chopped
- 1 garlic clove, minced
- 1 onion, finely chopped
- 1 tablespoon lemon juice
- 1½ cups whole farro
- 3 tablespoons extra-virgin olive oil
- Salt and pepper, to taste

Preparation:
1. Bring the water to boil in a Dutch oven.
2. Put in the farro and 1 tablespoon of salt. Return to the boil and cook until the grains are soft with a slight chew, 30 minutes.
3. Drain the farro, return it to the now-empty pot, and cover to keep warm.
4. Heat 2 tablespoons of oil in a 12-inch frying pan on moderate heat until it starts to shimmer.
5. Put in the onion, salt, and pepper and cook until tender, approximately 5 minutes.
6. Mix in the garlic and cook until aromatic, approximately half a minute.
7. Put in the residual 1 tablespoon of oil and farro and cook, stirring, until heated through, approximately 2 minutes.
8. Remove from the heat and mix in the parsley, mint, and lemon juice.
9. Serve.

Serving Suggestion: Garnish with mint leaves.
Variation Tip: Feel free to add in other spices.

Nutritional Information per Serving:
Calories 243 | Fat 14g | Sodium 38mg | Carbs 22g | Fiber 6.4g | Sugar 1g | Protein 10g

Baked Cheesy Brown Rice

Prep Time: 10 minutes
Cook Time: 1 hour 25 minutes
Serves: 6
Ingredients:
- ½ cup fresh parsley, minced
- ¾ cup jarred roasted red peppers, rinsed, patted dry, and chopped
- 1 cup chicken broth
- 1½ cups long-grain brown rice, rinsed
- 2 onions, chopped
- 2¼ cups water
- 4 teaspoons extra-virgin olive oil
- ½ cup parmesan cheese, grated
- 3 lemon wedges
- Salt and pepper, to taste

Preparation:
1. Place the oven rack in the center of the oven and preheat the oven to 375℉.
2. Heat the oil in a Dutch oven on moderate heat until it starts to shimmer.
3. Put in the onions and 1 teaspoon of salt and cook, stirring intermittently, until tender and well browned (12–14 minutes).
4. Mix in the water and broth and bring to boil. Mix in the rice, cover, and move the pot to the oven. Bake until the rice becomes soft and the liquid is absorbed (about 1 hour).
5. Remove the pot from the oven. Sprinkle the red peppers over the rice, cover, and allow to sit for about 5 minutes.
6. Put in the parsley, salt, and pepper and fluff gently with a fork to combine.
7. Serve.
Serving Suggestion: Serve garnished with the grated parmesan and lemon wedges.
Variation Tip: Substitute chicken broth with vegetable broth.
Nutritional Information per Serving:
Calories 100 | Fat 21g | Sodium 244mg | Carbs 27g | Fiber 2.9g | Sugar 2.1g | Protein 2g

Chickpea Bulgur

Prep Time: 10 minutes
Cook Time: 25 minutes
Serves: 5
Ingredients:
- ¾ cup chicken or vegetable broth
- ¾ cup water
- 1 (15-ounce) can chickpeas, rinsed
- 1 cup medium-grind bulgur, rinsed
- 1 onion, finely chopped
- 1 tablespoon lemon juice
- 2 tablespoons za'atar, divided
- 3 garlic cloves, minced
- 3 cups baby spinach, chopped
- 3 tablespoons extra-virgin olive oil
- Salt and pepper, to taste

Preparation:
1. Heat 2 tablespoons of the oil in a big saucepan on moderate heat until it starts to shimmer.
2. Put in the onion and ½ teaspoon of salt and cook until tender (approximately 5 minutes).
3. Mix in the garlic and 1 tablespoon of za'atar and cook until aromatic (approximately half a minute).
4. Mix in the bulgur, chickpeas, broth, water, salt, and pepper and bring to a simmer.
5. Reduce the heat, cover, and simmer gently until the bulgur is tender (20 minutes).
6. Remove from the heat, lay a clean dish towel underneath the lid, and let the bulgur sit for about 10 minutes.
7. Put in the spinach, lemon juice, remaining za'atar, and residual 1 tablespoon of oil and fluff gently with a fork to combine.
8. Serve.
Serving Suggestion: Garnish with tomato slices.
Variation Tip: Substitute vegetable broth with any other broth of your choice.
Nutritional Information per Serving:
Calories 319 | Fat 12g | Sodium 64mg | Carbs 43g | Fiber 21g | Sugar 10.3g | Protein 10g

Barley Pilaf

Prep Time: 10 minutes
Cook Time: 45 minutes
Serves: 5

Ingredients:
- ¼ cup fresh parsley, minced
- 1 small onion, finely chopped
- 1½ cups pearl barley, rinsed
- 1½ teaspoons lemon juice
- 1½ teaspoons fresh thyme, minced
- 2 garlic cloves, minced
- 2 tablespoons fresh chives, minced
- 2½ cups water
- 3 tablespoons extra-virgin olive oil
- Salt and pepper, to taste

Preparation:
1. Heat the oil in a big saucepan on moderate heat until it starts to shimmer.
2. Put in the onion and ½ teaspoon of salt and cook until tender (approximately 5 minutes).
3. Mix the barley, garlic, and thyme and cook, stirring often, until the barley is lightly toasted and aromatic (approximately 3 minutes).
4. Mix in the water and bring to a simmer. Decrease the heat to low, cover, and simmer until the barley becomes soft and the water is absorbed (20–40 minutes).
5. Remove from the heat, and let the pilaf sit for about 10 minutes.
6. Add the parsley, chives, lemon juice, salt, and pepper to the pilaf and fluff gently with a fork to combine.
7. Serve.

Serving Suggestion: Garnish with mint leaves.
Variation Tip: Substitute fresh thyme with ½ teaspoon dried thyme.

Nutritional Information per Serving:
Calories 860 | Fat 11.1g | Sodium 39mg | Carbs 8g | Fiber 35.2g | Sugar 2.6g | Protein 22.3g

Spicy Borlotti Beans

Prep Time: 12 hours 10 minutes
Cook Time: 1 hour 50 minutes
Serves: 8

Ingredients:
- 1-pound dried borlotti beans, soaked overnight, drained, and rinsed
- 1 teaspoon salt, divided
- 2 tablespoons extra-virgin olive oil
- 1 large onion, chopped
- ½ green bell pepper, seeded and chopped
- 1 (14.5-ounce) can diced tomatoes, undrained
- 3 garlic cloves, minced
- 1 (1-inch) piece fresh red chili, seeded and minced
- ¼ teaspoon freshly ground black pepper
- ¼ teaspoon red pepper flakes

Preparation:
1. Put the beans in a large pot, cover with water, and add ½ teaspoon of salt.
2. Bring to a boil over medium-high heat, then reduce the heat to low and simmer for 1–1½ hours, until the beans soften. Drain.
3. In a large skillet, heat the olive oil over medium heat. Cook the onion and bell pepper for about 10 minutes until softened.
4. Add the beans, tomatoes and their juices, garlic, chili, remaining ½ teaspoon of salt, black pepper, and red pepper flakes.
5. Bring to a boil, then reduce the heat and simmer for 10 minutes.

Serving Suggestion: Garnish with chopped cilantro.
Variation Tip: For a milder taste, omit the red chili.

Nutritional Information per Serving:
Calories 240 | Fat 4g | Sodium 335mg | Carbs 39g | Fiber 13g | Sugar 3g | Protein 13g

Baked Mediterranean Rice

Prep Time: 20 minutes
Cook Time: 30 minutes
Serves: 8

Ingredients:
- ½ cup sweet onion, diced
- Olive oil cooking spray
- 1½ cups arborio rice
- 2 tablespoons unsalted butter, melted
- 1 cup mozzarella cheese, shredded
- 2 tablespoons fresh basil, chopped
- 2 tablespoons fresh oregano, chopped
- 1 teaspoon salt
- ¼ cup parmesan cheese, grated
- 3 cups low-sodium chicken broth
- 1-pint cherry tomatoes, cut in half
- 8 ounces baby spinach, stem and tips removed

Preparation:
1. Preheat the oven to 375°F and grease a casserole dish with the olive oil cooking spray.
2. Mix the chicken broth with the oregano, basil, and salt, and set aside
3. Arrange the rice and onions in the casserole dish and drizzle the melted butter on top.
4. Toss to coat well and stir in the chicken broth mixture.
5. Arrange the tomato halves on top of the rice and bake for 30 minutes.
6. Remove from the oven and fold in the mozzarella cheese and baby spinach into the baked rice.
7. Top with the parsley and parmesan cheese.
8. Wrap with foil and leave for 5 minutes, then serve.

Serving Suggestion: Serve alongside Mediterranean chicken curry.

Variation Tip: You can use any combination of cheese you prefer.

Nutritional Information per Serving:
Calories: 211 | Fat: 5.3g | Sat Fat: 2.9g | Carbohydrates: 33.1g | Fiber: 2.8g | Sugar: 1.9g | Protein: 7.8g

Leek Pilaf

Prep Time: 10 minutes
Cook Time: 35 minutes
Serves: 6

Ingredients:
- 1 cup rice
- 3 medium leeks, chopped
- 1 tablespoon extra-virgin olive oil,
- 1 medium onion, chopped
- 1 tablespoon Vegeta Gourmet Seasoning
- 1 tablespoon tomato paste
- 2 cups water
- Salt and black pepper, to taste

Preparation:
1. Bring a large amount of salted water to a boil in a pot over high heat.
2. When the water boils, blanch the leeks in it for 30.
3. Drain the leeks and rinse them using cold water.
4. In a strainer, rinse the rice in water. Drain and set aside.
5. On medium-high heat, heat the oil in a large, ovenproof pot.
6. Add the rice and sauté until it browns lightly.
7. Add salt, pepper, tomato paste, onions, leeks, Vegeta, and water to the rice. Bring to a simmer, then reduce the heat to low. Simmer for 15 minutes.
8. Preheat the oven to 400℉.
9. Cover the rice and bake for about 5–10 minutes.
10. Serve it hot.

Serving Suggestion: Garnish with scallions.

Variation Tip: Switch up Vegeta with a seasoning of your choice.

Nutritional Information per Serving:
Calories 156 | Fat 2.6g | Sodium 245mg | Carbs 30g | Fiber 1.3g | Sugar 2g | Protein 2.9g

Saffron Risotto

Prep Time: 10 minutes
Cook Time: 45 minutes
Serves: 4

Ingredients:
- 3 tablespoons olive oil
- 1 pound grape or cherry tomatoes
- 1 yellow or white onion, diced
- 5 garlic cloves, chopped
- 1½ cups short-grain rice
- 1 teaspoon dried thyme
- 1½ teaspoons salt
- ½ teaspoon pepper
- Pinch of saffron
- 7 cups veggie stock
- ¼ teaspoon smoked paprika
- ¼ cup parmesan, grated
- 1 tablespoon almond butter
- 1 tablespoon ground cumin, optional

Preparation:
1. Heat oil over medium heat in a skillet. Add the tomatoes and sear for 7 minutes, stirring occasionally. Turn the heat off.
2. Heat the olive oil over medium heat in a pot, add the onions and sauté for 10 minutes.
3. Add the thyme and garlic and sauté for 2 minutes more.
4. Add the rice and sauté for a minute.
5. Pour in 2 cups of the stock, smoked paprika, and saffron. Stir well, and simmer to absorb most of the liquid.
6. Add the tomatoes and a cup of broth, and stir to absorb the liquid.
7. Stir in the parmesan and butter.
8. Season with salt and pepper.

Serving Suggestion: Garnish with lemon zest and parsley.

Variation Tip: Feel free to use any nut butter.

Nutritional Information per Serving:
Calories 435 | Fat 16g | Sodium 243mg | Carbs 73g | Fiber 3g | Sugar 7g | Protein 9g

Spicy Barley

Prep Time: 10 minutes
Cook Time: 50 minutes
Serves: 4

Ingredients:
- 1 cup dry teff
- ¼ cup dry white beans
- 1 celery, finely chopped
- 1 cup broccoli florets, destemmed
- 2 carrots, peeled and diced
- 1 cup chopped tomatoes
- 2 cups assorted bell peppers, chopped
- 2 teaspoons flax meal
- 3 cloves garlic, minced
- 1½ teaspoons paprika
- 2 teaspoons canola oil
- 3 cups water
- 1 teaspoon salt

Preparation:
1. Add oil to a medium-sized saucepan; sauté the celery for 3–4 minutes on medium heat.
2. Add the garlic and sauté for another minute.
3. Add the vegetables and broccoli to the pan.
4. Pour in half a cup of water and let the vegetables cook for 5 minutes.
5. Pour in the remaining water, and add the beans, flax meal, teff, and salt.
6. Cover with a lid and simmer for 40 minutes.
7. Serve warm with a salad or side of your choice.

Serving Suggestion: Top with chopped parsley.

Variation Tip: To turn this dish into a soup, add an extra cup of water while simmering.

Nutritional Information per Serving:
Calories 286 | Fat 4g | Sodium 644mg | Carbs 53.5g | Fiber 12.5g | Sugar 5.9g | Protein 11.7g

Black-Eyed Peas Stew

Prep Time: 10 minutes
Cook Time: 55 minutes
Serves: 6

Ingredients:
- 2 tablespoons olive oil
- 4 garlic cloves, chopped
- 30 ounces black-eyed peas
- 1 yellow onion, chopped
- 1 green bell pepper, chopped
- 15 ounces tomato, diced
- 3 carrots, chopped
- 1 tablespoon lime juice
- 2 cups water
- 1½ teaspoons ground cumin
- 1 bay leaf
- 1 teaspoon dried oregano
- Kosher salt, to taste
- ½ teaspoon red pepper flakes
- ½ teaspoon paprika
- Black pepper, to taste
- 1 cup fresh parsley, chopped

Preparation:
1. Sauté the garlic and onions in the oil in a heated Dutch oven over medium flame for 5 minutes, constantly stirring.
2. Stir in the tomatoes, pepper, water, spices, bay leaf, and salt. Let it simmer.
3. Mix in the black-eyed peas and cook for 5 more minutes.
4. Cover and reduce the flame. Simmer for 30 more minutes.
5. Squeeze in the lime juice and mix.
6. Serve and enjoy.

Serving Suggestion: Garnish with parsley.
Variation Tip: Substitute water with vegetable broth.

Nutritional Information per Serving:
Calories 197 | Fat 6.3 g | Sodium 92mg | Carbs 30.4g | Fiber 7.7g | Sugar 5.4g | Protein 8.9g

Cauliflower Rice

Prep Time: 10 minutes
Cook Time: 35 minutes
Serves: 4

Ingredients:
- 1 cup pumpkin, grated
- 2 cups cauliflower, grated
- 4 tablespoons olive oil
- 1 small white onion, chopped
- 1 teaspoon ginger paste
- ¼ teaspoon turmeric powder
- 1 teaspoon curry powder
- 1 teaspoon red chili powder
- $^1/_3$ cup vegetable broth
- ½ cup snow peas
- ½ cup coconut milk

Preparation:
1. In a large non-stick skillet, heat the olive oil.
2. Add the onions and sauté for a few minutes.
3. Add the ginger and cook until fragrant.
4. Next, add the peas along with the vegetable broth. Cover the skillet and simmer for 10 minutes on medium flame.
5. Remove the lid and add the pumpkin and cook for about 10 minutes.
6. Pour in the coconut milk.
7. Add the curry powder, turmeric powder, and chili powder. Next, add the grated cauliflower. Cover the skillet with a lid and cook for 12 minutes.
8. Serve warm.

Serving Suggestion: Top with chopped green onions.
Variation Tip: Omit red chili powder for a milder taste.

Nutritional Information per Serving:
Calories 247 | Fat 21.8g | Sodium 95mg | Carbs 13.5g | Fiber 5.1g | Sugar 5.9g | Protein 3.8g

Cheesy Cucumber Rice

Prep Time: 10 minutes
Cook Time: 55 minutes
Serves: 8
Ingredients:
- 3 garlic cloves, minced
- 1 pound heirloom tomatoes
- 8 ounces feta cheese
- 1 cup parsley leaves
- 7 tablespoons olive oil
- Kosher salt, to taste
- Black pepper, to taste
- 1½ cups brown rice
- 1 onion, chopped
- 3 cucumbers, chopped
- 3 tablespoons sherry vinegar
- 1 cup mint leaves

Preparation:
1. Add 2 tablespoons of oil to a heated skillet.
2. Add the garlic, onion, and salt, and cook for 2 minutes. Transfer the mixture to a large bowl.
3. In another heated skillet, add 1 tablespoon of oil and the rice. Cook for 3 minutes while stirring until it turns golden and nutty.
4. Add water, decrease the heat to low, and then cover it.
5. Cook until the rice is tender and the water has been absorbed. Remove it from the stove and let it cool for 5 minutes.
6. Put the rice in the bowl with the onion mixture and let it cool for 20 minutes.
7. Mix in the cucumbers, tomatoes, vinegar, and remaining oil, then season with sea salt and black pepper.
8. Finally, cover with the cheese, parsley, and mint.

Serving Suggestion: Garnish with thyme sprigs.
Variation Tip: Substitute sherry vinegar with red wine vinegar.
Nutritional Information per Serving:
Calories 359 | Fat 20.9g | Sodium 375mg | Carbs 36.5g | Fiber 3.2g | Sugar 3.7g | Protein 8.9g

Sweet Red Lentils

Prep Time: 10 minutes
Cook Time: 15 minutes
Serves: 4
Ingredients:
For the sauce:
- 2 cups water
- 2 tablespoons brown sugar
- ¼ cup coconut aminos
- 2 garlic cloves, chopped
- ½ teaspoon crushed red pepper
- 1 tablespoon fresh ginger, minced
- 1 teaspoon olive oil
For the lentils:
- 1 tablespoon olive oil
- ½ yellow onion, chopped
- 1 cup red lentils
- 2 green onions, sliced, for serving

Preparation:
1. In a jar, mix all the sauce ingredients.
2. Pour the oil into a large pot over medium-high heat.
3. Add the onion and sauté for about 3 minutes.
4. Once the onion begins to brown and becomes soft, add the sauce and lentils and bring to a gentle boil. Simmer, cover, and cook for about 8–10 minutes.
5. Wait until the lentils are tender and the liquid is absorbed (mostly).
6. Serve hot.

Serving Suggestion: Garnish with parsley and green onions.
Variation Tip: Omit crushed red pepper for a milder taste.
Nutritional Information per Serving:
Calories 277 | Fat 7.7g | Sodium 27mg | Carbs 39.7g | Fiber 15.4g | Sugar 6.2g | Protein 12.9g

Cumin Beef Rice

Prep Time: 10 minutes
Cook Time: 18 minutes
Serves: 4

Ingredients:
*   1 green onion, chopped
*   2 cloves garlic, minced
*   ½-pound ground beef
*   1 tablespoon ground cumin
*   2 eggs
*   1 tablespoon ginger, minced
*   3 cups brown rice
*   Salt, to taste
*   3 tablespoons olive oil

Preparation:
1. In a large skillet on medium heat, add the olive oil.
2. Once the oil is hot, add the cumin and allow it to toast.
3. Add in the ground beef and break up the meat. Stir and cook until it's cooked through.
4. Add the salt, ginger, and garlic and cook for another few minutes before adding the eggs.
5. Swirl the yolk around so it mixes with the beef. Add the rice.
6. Break up the bigger rice pieces until the rice is spread out evenly with the meat and egg.
7. Remove from the heat and serve.

Serving Suggestion: Garnish with chopped parsley.
Variation Tip: Substitute ground beef with ground lamb.

Nutritional Information per Serving:
Calories 756 | Fat 20.5g | Sodium 116mg | Carbs 111.1g | Fiber 5.3g | Sugar 0.4g | Protein 31.2g

Kidney Beans Meal

Prep Time: 10 Minutes
Cook Time: 0 Minutes
Serves: 6

Ingredients:
*   1 can (15 ounces) kidney beans, drained and rinsed
*   ½ English cucumber, chopped
*   1 medium heirloom tomato, chopped
*   1 bunch fresh cilantro, stems removed and chopped
*   1 red onion, chopped
*   1 large lime, juiced
*   3 tablespoons extra-virgin olive oil
*   1 teaspoon Dijon mustard
*   ½ teaspoon fresh garlic paste
*   1 teaspoon sumac
*   Salt and pepper, to taste

Preparation:
1. In a medium-sized bowl, add the kidney beans, chopped veggies, and cilantro.
2. Take a small bowl and make the vinaigrette by adding the lime juice, oil, garlic paste, pepper, mustard, and sumac.
3. Pour the vinaigrette over the salad and give it a gentle stir.
4. Add some salt and pepper. Cover the bowl and allow it to chill for half an hour.
5. Serve and enjoy!

Serving Suggestion: Drizzle with some balsamic vinegar.
Variation Tip: You can use garbanzo, white, or black beans.

Nutritional Information per Serving:
Calories 74 | Fat 0.7g | Sodium 313mg | Carbs 16g | Fiber 5.8g | Sugar 3.6g | Protein 5.5g

Pumpkin Rice

Prep Time: 10 minutes
Cook Time: 20 minutes
Serves: 3

Ingredients:
- 2 cups pumpkin, cubed
- 1 cup cauliflower rice
- Salt and black pepper, to taste
- 4 tablespoons olive oil
- 2 cups vegetable broth
- 1 cup brown rice, presoaked
- 2 cloves garlic, minced
- ¼ teaspoon fresh ginger, minced
- 1 green onion, chopped

Preparation:
1. Put an Instant Pot on sauté mode.
2. Add the oil and sauté the green onions for 1 minute.
3. Add the ginger and garlic and cook until fragrant.
4. Add the cauliflower and pumpkin cubes.
5. Sauté for a few minutes and then add salt, black pepper, and vegetable broth.
6. Add the brown rice and lock the lid.
7. Cook it at high pressure for 15 minutes. Once the timer beeps, release the steam naturally.
8. The rice should be fluffy, and the vegetables should be tender.
9. Serve and enjoy.

Serving Suggestion: Garnish with basil leaves.
Variation Tip: Substitute vegetable broth with chicken broth.

Nutritional Information per Serving:
Calories 470 | Fat 20.9g | Sodium 397mg | Carbs 66.3g | Fiber 8.4g | Sugar 7.5g | Protein 7.5g

Tomato Lentil Bowl

Prep Time: 10 minutes
Cook Time: 30 minutes
Serves: 6

Ingredients:
- 2 onions, chopped
- 1 tablespoon olive oil
- 2 cups dried brown lentils, rinsed
- 4 cloves garlic, minced
- ½ teaspoon ground ginger
- 1 teaspoon salt
- ¼ teaspoon pepper
- ½ teaspoon paprika
- ¼ cup lemon juice
- 3 cups water
- ¾ cup fat-free plain Greek yogurt
- 3 tablespoons tomato paste
- Fresh cilantro, minced, optional
- Tomatoes, chopped, optional

Preparation:
1. Heat the oil over medium to high heat in a saucepan.
2. Sauté the onions for 2 minutes. Add the garlic and cook for a minute.
3. Stir in the seasonings, water, and lentils and bring to a boil. Reduce the heat.
4. Keep the saucepan covered and simmer for 25 minutes. Stir in the tomato paste and lemon juice. Heat through.
5. Serve.

Serving Suggestion: Serve with the yogurt, cilantro, and tomatoes.
Variation Tip: Substitute Greek yogurt with soy yogurt.

Nutritional Information per Serving:
Calories 294 | Fat 3g | Sodium 219mg | Carbs 49g | Fiber 8g | Sugar 5g | Protein 21g

Chickpea Curry

Prep Time: 10 minutes
Cook Time: 35 minutes
Serves: 6

Ingredients:
- 1 onion, chopped
- 1 tablespoon olive oil
- 1 tablespoon curry powder
- 2 cloves garlic, minced
- 2 cans garbanzo beans or chickpeas, rinsed and drained
- 2 cans diced tomatoes
- 1 cup light coconut milk
- 2 cups sweet potato, cubed and peeled
- ¼ teaspoon red pepper flakes, crushed
- 2 teaspoons sugar
- 1½ cups frozen peas
- 1 cup whole-wheat pearl couscous
- ¼ teaspoon salt
- A handful of fresh parsley, chopped

Preparation:
1. Heat the oil over medium heat in a skillet. Sauté the garlic and onion with the curry powder for 3–4 minutes.
2. Stir in the garbanzo beans, tomatoes, coconut milk, sweet potato, sugar, and pepper flakes, and then boil.
3. Reduce the heat and let the mixture simmer uncovered for about 30 minutes.
4. The potatoes should become tender, and the mixture should be thickened. Stir occasionally.
5. Prepare the peas and couscous separately as per the package instructions.
6. Stir the salt into the peas.
7. Divide your couscous among six bowls.

Serving Suggestion: Top with the peas, chickpea mixture, and parsley.

Variation Tip: Add in more seasoning if needed.

Nutritional Information per Serving:
Calories 390 | Fat 10g | Sodium 361mg | Carbs 68g | Fiber 13g | Sugar 14g | Protein 13g

Tuna and Couscous

Prep Time: 10 Minutes
Cook Time: 0 Minutes
Serves: 4
Ingredients:
- 1 cup chicken stock
- 1¼ cups couscous
- A pinch of salt and black pepper
- 10 ounces canned tuna, drained and flaked
- 1-pint cherry tomatoes, halved
- ½ cup pepperoncini, sliced
- ⅓ cup parsley, chopped
- 1 tablespoon olive oil
- ¼ cup capers, drained
- ½ lemon, juiced

Preparation:
1. Put the stock in a pan and bring to a boil over medium-high heat.
2. Add the couscous, stir, take off the heat, cover, and set aside for 10 minutes. Fluff with a fork and transfer to a bowl.
3. Add the tuna and the rest of the ingredients, toss and serve right away.

Serving Suggestion: Serve over lettuce and with a garnish of parsley.
Variation Tip: You can substitute couscous with cooked quinoa.
Nutritional Information per Serving:
Calories 253 | Fat 11.5g | Sodium 494mg | Carbs 16.5g | Fiber 3.4g | Sugar 2.6g | Protein 23.2g

Cod and Brussels Sprouts

Prep Time: 10 Minutes
Cook Time: 20 Minutes
Serves: 4
Ingredients:
- 1 teaspoon garlic powder
- 1 teaspoon smoked paprika
- 2 tablespoons olive oil
- 2 pounds Brussels sprouts, trimmed and halved
- 4 boneless cod fillets
- ½ cup tomato sauce

- 1 teaspoon Italian seasoning
- 1 tablespoon chives, chopped

Preparation:
1. In a roasting pan, combine the sprouts with the garlic powder and the other ingredients except for the cod, and then toss.
2. Put the cod on top, cover the pan with tin foil and bake at 450°F for 20 minutes.
3. Divide between plates and serve.

Serving Suggestion: Garnish with fresh parsley.
Variation Tip: You can use artichokes in place of Brussels sprouts.
Nutritional Information per Serving:
Calories 188 | Fat 12.8g | Sodium 144mg | Carbs 22.2g | Fiber 9.2g | Sugar 3.2g | Protein 16.8g

Herb-Crusted Halibut

Prep Time: 10 Minutes
Cook Time: 15 Minutes
Serves: 4
Ingredients:
- ⅓ cup fresh parsley
- ¼ cup fresh dill
- ¼ cup fresh chives
- 1 teaspoon lemon zest
- ¾ cup panko breadcrumbs
- 1 tablespoon olive oil
- ¼ teaspoon freshly cracked black pepper
- 1 teaspoon sea salt
- 4–6 ounces halibut fillets

Preparation:
1. Chop the fresh dill, chives, and parsley.
2. Line a baking tray with foil. Set the oven to 400°F.
3. Combine the salt, pepper, lemon zest, olive oil, chives, dill, parsley, and breadcrumbs in a mixing bowl.
4. Rinse the halibut thoroughly. Use paper towels to dry it before baking. Arrange the fish on the baking sheet.
5. Spoon the crumbs over the fish and press them into each of the fillets.
6. Bake until the top is browned and easily flaked (about 10–15 minutes).

Serving Suggestion: Serve with savory potatoes and peas.
Variation Tip: You can use other fresh herbs of your liking.
Nutritional Information per Serving:
Calories 273 | Fat 7g | Sodium 593mg | Carbs 5.1g | Fiber 1.1g | Sugar 0.2g | Protein 38g

Broiled Blackened Tilapia

Prep Time: 10 Minutes
Cook Time: 10 Minutes
Serves: 3
Ingredients:
- 4 fillets tilapia
Seasoning
- 2 teaspoons smoked paprika
- 1 teaspoon dried oregano
- 1 teaspoon garlic powder
- ¾ teaspoon cumin
- ½ teaspoon cayenne pepper
- 2 tablespoons olive oil
Preparation:
1. Put the broiler on moderate heat and lightly oil a baking pan.
2. Wash and then pat the fish dry.
3. Mix all of the seasonings and coat the fish with the mixture. Place the fish in the baking pan.
4. Broil the fish for 3–5 minutes on each side or until the flesh flakes easily.
5. Serve and enjoy.
Serving Suggestion: Garnish with fresh parsley and lemon slices.
Variation Tip: You can also use lemon pepper to further season the fillets.
Nutritional Information per Serving:
Calories 154 | Fat 5g | Sodium 314mg | Carbs 4g | Fiber 1g | Sugar 2.1g | Protein 23g

Buttered Thyme Scallops

Prep Time: 10 Minutes
Cook Time: 5 Minutes
Serves: 2
Ingredients:
- ¾ pound sea scallops
- ½ tablespoon fresh thyme, minced
- Salt and freshly cracked black pepper, to taste

- 1 tablespoon unsalted butter, melted
- 1 tablespoon olive oil
Preparation:
1. Preheat the oven to 390°F.
2. In a large bowl, add all the ingredients and toss until well coated.
3. Grease a baking dish with oil. Add the prepared scallop mixture to it and bake for 5 minutes until thoroughly cooked.
4. When done, take out the baking dish, then allow the scallops to cool for 5 minutes before serving.
Serving Suggestion: Serve with a creamy lemon sauce.
Variation Tip: You can also use dried thyme.
Nutritional Information per Serving:
Calories 202 | Fat 7.1g | Sodium 315mg | Carbs 4.4g | Fiber 0.1g | Sugar 0g | Protein 28.7g

Shrimp Alfredo

Prep Time: 10 Minutes
Cook Time: 4 Minutes
Serves: 4
Ingredients:
- 12 shrimps, shells removed
- 1 tablespoon garlic, minced
- ¼ cup parmesan cheese, grated
- 2 cups whole-wheat fettuccini pasta
- 1 cup fish broth
- 15 ounces alfredo sauce
- 1 onion, chopped
- Salt and black pepper, to taste
Preparation:
1. Add all ingredients except the parmesan cheese to the Instant Pot. Stir well.
2. Seal the pot with the lid and cook on High for 4 minutes.
3. Once done, release the pressure using quick release
4. Remove the lid and serve.
Serving Suggestion: Stir in the parmesan cheese just before serving.
Variation Tip: You can substitute the fish broth with vegetable broth.
Nutritional Information per Serving:
Calories 669 | Fat 23.1g | Sodium 174mg | Carbs 76g | Fiber 1.4g | Sugar 2.4g | Protein 37.8g

Grilled Swordfish

Prep Time: 10 Minutes
Cook Time: 8 Minutes
Serves: 4
Ingredients:
- 10 garlic cloves
- 2 tablespoons lemon juice
- ⅓ cupolive oil
- 1teaspoon Spanish paprika
- ¾ teaspoon cumin
- ¾ teaspoon salt
- 4 swordfish steaks
- ½ teaspoon black pepper
- Crushed red pepper, to taste
- 2 teaspoons fresh parsley, chopped, for garnish.

Preparation:
1. Blend the olive oil, pepper, garlic, salt, cumin, paprika, and lemon juice in a blender to obtain a smooth mixture.
2. Coat the swordfish with the blended mixture and set it aside for 15 minutes.
3. Heat a skillet with some oil on high heat. Add the fish and cook for five minutes on each side.
4. Sprinkle with the lemon juice and crushed red pepper and serve.

Serving Suggestion: Garnish with the chopped parsley.
Variation Tip: Use chili for hotter steaks.
Nutritional Information per Serving:
Calories 398 | Fat 30.7g | Sodium 348mg | Carbs 3.1g | Fiber 0.6g | Sugar 0.9g | Protein 28.4g

Halibut Parcel with Olives and Capers

Prep Time: 15 minutes
Cook Time: 40 minutes
Serves: 4
Ingredients:
- 1 large tomato, chopped
- 1 onion, chopped
- 1 (5-ounce) jar pitted Kalamata olives
- ¼ cup olive oil, extra-virgin
- Salt and black pepper, to taste
- 1 tablespoon Greek seasoning
- ¼ cup capers
- 1 tablespoon fresh lemon juice
- 4 (6-ounce) halibut fillets

Preparation:
1. Preheat the oven to 350°F.
2. Mix the tomato, onion, olives, capers, oil, lemon juice, salt, and black pepper in a bowl.
3. Season the halibut fillets evenly with the Greek seasoning.
4. Arrange the halibut fillets onto a large piece of foil and top with the tomato mixture.
5. Fold all the edges carefully to create a large parcel.
6. Place the parcel onto a baking sheet and bake for about 40 minutes.
7. Remove from the oven and serve hot.

Serving Suggestion: Serve with stir-fried vegetables.
Variation Tip: You can also add jalapeños.
Nutritional Information per Serving:
Calories: 365 | Fat: 20.7g | Sat Fat: 2.9g | Carbohydrates: 8.2g | Fiber: 2.6g | Sugar: 2.5g | Protein: 37.2g

Pan-Seared Shrimp

Prep Time: 10 Minutes
Cook Time: 10 Minutes
Serves: 6
Ingredients:
- 1 tablespoon olive oil
- 6 tablespoons lemon juice
- 1 cup orange juice
- 1 orange, sliced
- 5garlic cloves, minced
- 1tablespoon fresh parsley, chopped
- 1 tablespoon red onion, chopped
- A pinchof red pepper flakes
- Kosher salt and black pepper, to taste
- 3 pounds shrimp
- 1 lemon, cut into wedges, for garnish

Preparation:
1. Mix the parsley, red pepper flakes, orange juice, oil, garlic, lemon juice, and onions in a large bowl.
2. Transfer the mixture to a skillet and cook over medium heat for 8 minutes.
3. Add the salt, pepper, and shrimp and cook for 5 minutes (or until the shrimp is done).
4. Serve and enjoy.

Serving Suggestion: Garnish with the lemon wedges.
Variation Tip: You can remove or leave the tails on the shrimps.
Nutritional Information per Serving:
Calories 291 | Fat 6g | Sodium 555mg | Carbs 11g | Fiber 1g | Sugar 9.3g | Protein 47g

Salmon with Fennel and Couscous

Prep Time: 20 minutes
Cook Time: 22 minutes
Serves: 4
Ingredients:
- ¼ teaspoon salt
- 1¼ pounds salmon, boneless, skinless, and cut into 4 equal-sized pieces
- ¼ teaspoon black pepper
- 2 tablespoons extra-virgin olive oil, divided
- 1 cup whole-wheat couscous
- ¼ cup green olives, pitted and sliced
- 2 garlic cloves, sliced
- 1½ cups low-sodium chicken broth
- 4 tablespoons sun-dried tomato pesto, divided
- 2 fennel bulbs, cut into ½-inch wedges, fronds reserved
- 3 scallions, thinly sliced
- 2 tablespoons pine nuts, toasted
- 2 teaspoons lemon zest, finely grated
- 1 lemon, cut into 8 slices

Preparation:
1. Season the salmon pieces with the salt and black pepper.
2. Gently spread 1½ teaspoons of the pesto on each salmon piece.
3. In a large skillet placed over medium-high heat, heat 1 tablespoon of the olive oil and cook half of the fennel for about 3 minutes.
4. Transfer the fennel onto a plate and repeat with the remaining olive oil and fennel.
5. In the same skillet placed over medium heat, add the couscous and scallions and cook for about 2 minutes, stirring frequently.
6. Fold in the pine nuts, olives, garlic, remaining 2 tablespoons of the pesto, lemon zest, and broth, and stir well.
7. Place the cooked salmon and fennel on top and press gently into the couscous mixture.
8. Top with the lemon slices evenly.
9. Reduce the heat to medium-low, cover, and cook for about 14 minutes.
10. Remove from the heat and serve hot with the topping of reserved fennel fronds.
Serving Suggestion: Serve with roasted garlic on the side.
Variation Tip: Cod can be used instead of salmon.

Nutritional Information per Serving:
Calories: 519 | Fat: 21.2g | Sat Fat: 2.7g | Carbohydrates: 46.7g | Fiber: 6.7g | Sugar: 1.4g | Protein: 38.3g

Grilled Lemon Salmon

Prep Time: 15 minutes
Cook Time: 12 minutes
Serves: 4
Ingredients:
- 3 garlic cloves, minced
- ½ cup plain Greek yogurt
- 2 tablespoons fresh dill, minced
- 1 tablespoon olive oil, extra-virgin
- 1½ teaspoons ground cumin
- 4 (6-ounce) salmon fillets, skinless
- 2 tablespoons fresh basil leaves
- 2 tablespoons fresh lemon juice
- 1½ teaspoons ground cilantro
- Salt and black pepper, to taste
- Olive oil cooking spray

Preparation:
1. Mix all the ingredients, except the salmon and basil, in a large bowl.
2. Move half of the mixture into another bowl and place it in the refrigerator.
3. In the large bowl of the remaining yogurt mixture, add the salmon fillets and coat well.
4. Refrigerate for about 30 minutes, flipping once halfway.
5. Preheat the broiler to medium-high heat and lightly grease a baking pan with the cooking spray.
6. Remove the salmon fillets from the bowl and discard the excess yogurt mixture.
7. Arrange the salmon fillets onto the baking pan and cook for about 6 minutes per side.
8. Remove from the broiler and place onto the serving plates.
9. Serve garnished with the basil and topped with the reserved yogurt mixture.
Serving Suggestion: Serve with roasted veggies.
Variation Tip: You can use parsley leaves instead of basil.
Nutritional Information per Serving:
Calories: 284 | Fat: 14.3g | Sat Fat: 2.1g | Carbohydrates: 3g | Fiber: 0.4g | Sugar: 1g | Protein: 36.7g

Lemon Basil Halibut

Prep Time: 10 minutes
Cook Time: 8 minutes
Serves: 4
Ingredients:
- 24 ounces halibut fillets
- 2 garlic cloves, crushed
- 2 tablespoons olive oil
- 2 teaspoons capers, drained
- 3 tablespoons fresh basil, sliced
- 2 ½ tablespoons fresh lemon juice

Directions:
1. In a small bowl, mix together garlic, lemon juice, olive oil, 2 tablespoons of basil, pepper and salt.
2. Preheat the grill over medium-high heat.
3. Season fish fillets with pepper and salt and brush with garlic mixture.
4. Place fish fillets onto the grill and cook for 4 minutes on each side.
Serving Suggestion: Transfer fish fillets to a serving plate and top with remaining garlic mixture and basil.
Variation Tip: Add your choice of seasonings.
Nutritional Information per Serving:
Calories 254 | Fat 11.1g | Sodium 134mg | Carbs 0.8g | Fiber 0.2g | Sugar 0.2g | Protein 36.1g

Greek Tilapia

Prep Time: 10 minutes
Cook Time: 18 minutes
Serves: 4
Ingredients:
- 4 tilapia fillets
- ½ cup Feta cheese, crumbled
- 2 tablespoons olive oil
- 4 tomatoes, chopped
- ½ cup parsley, chopped
- 1 tablespoon garlic, minced

- Pepper
- Salt

Directions:
1. Preheat the oven to 400° F.
2. Place fish fillets into the baking dish.
3. Drizzle with oil and season with pepper and salt.
4. Add cheese, garlic, and tomatoes on top of fish fillets.
5. Bake for 15-18 minutes.
Serving Suggestion: Garnish with parsley and serve.
Variation tip: You can also use crumbled Goat cheese instead of Feta cheese.
Nutritional Information per Serving:
Calories 231 | Fat 12.3g | Sodium 299mg | Carbs 6.7g | Fiber 1.8g | Sugar 4.1g | Protein 25.1g

Zesty Garlic Salmon

Prep Time: 10 Minutes
Cook Time: 18 Minutes
Serves: 6
Ingredients:
Salmon
- 2 pounds salmon fillet
- 2 tablespoons parsley, chopped, for garnish
- Olive oil
- Kosher salt, to taste
- ½ lemon, sliced, for garnish

Lemon-garlic sauce
- Zest of one lemon
- 3 tablespoons olive oil
- 3 tablespoons lemon juice
- 5 garlic cloves, chopped
- 1 teaspoon sweet paprika
- ½ teaspoon dry oregano
- ½ teaspoon black pepper

Preparation:
1. Preheat the oven to 375°F.
2. In a bowl, whisk the olive oil, pepper, garlic, lemon zest and juice, oregano, and paprika in a mixing bowl and set aside. The lemon-garlic sauce is ready!
3. Line a baking tray with foil and brush it with oil.
4. Season the salmon with salt and place it on the baking tray. Pour the lemon-garlic sauce over the salmon.
5. Bake in the preheated oven for 20 minutes.
6. Broil the baked salmon for 3 minutes and serve.
Serving Suggestion: Serve garnished with the fresh parsley and lemon slices.
Variation Tip: You can substitute the olive oil in the lemon-garlic sauce with butter.
Nutritional Information per Serving:
Calories 338 | Fat 25.8g | Sodium 341mg | Carbs 11.8g | Fiber 3g | Sugar 2.9g | Protein 33.1g

Crab Patties

Prep Time: 10 minutes
Cook Time: 10 minutes
Serves: 4

Ingredients:
- 2 eggs, lightly beaten
- 18 ounces can crab meat, drained
- 2 ½ tablespoons mayonnaise
- ¼ cup almond flour
- 1 teaspoon dried parsley
- 1 teaspoon Italian seasoning
- 1 ½ tablespoons Dijon mustard
- Pepper
- Salt

Directions:
1. Add crab meat and remaining ingredients into the bowl and mix well.
2. Make patties from crab mixture and place them into the air fryer basket.
3. Cook at 320° F for 10 minutes. Turn patties halfway through.

Serving Suggestion: Serve with your favorite dip.
Variation Tip: Add 1 teaspoon of dill.
Nutritional Information per Serving:
Calories 159 | Fat 6.7 | Sodium 989mg | Carbs 5.4g | Fiber 0.4g | Sugar 3.1g | Protein 20.5g

Parmesan Salmon

Prep Time: 10 minutes
Cook Time: 20 minutes
Serves: 2

Ingredients:
- 2 salmon fillets
- 2 tablespoons Parmesan cheese, grated

- 1 tablespoons olive oil
- 1 tomato, sliced
- 1 tablespoon dried basil

Directions:
1. Preheat the oven to 375° F.
2. Place fish fillets onto the baking sheet. Sprinkle basil on top.
3. Arrange tomato slices on top of fish fillets.
4. Drizzle with oil. Sprinkle cheese on top of salmon.
5. Bake for 20 minutes.

Serving Suggestion: Garnish with basil and serve.
Variation Tip: Season salmon fillets with Italian seasonings.
Nutritional Information per Serving:
Calories 340 | Fat 20.6g | Sodium 191mg | Carbs 1.7g | Fiber 0.4g | Sugar 0.8g | Protein 38.7g

Tilapia with Capers

Prep Time: 15 minutes
Cook Time: 15 minutes
Serves: 4

Ingredients:
- 1½ teaspoons paprika
- 1½ teaspoons ground cumin
- 2 shallots, finely chopped
- 2 tablespoons fresh lemon juice
- 1 pound tilapia, cut into 8 pieces
- Salt and black pepper, to taste
- 3 garlic cloves, minced
- 1½ tablespoons unsalted butter, melted
- ¼ cup capers

Preparation:
1. Preheat the oven to 375°F and line a baking sheet with parchment paper.
2. Combine the paprika, cumin, salt, and black pepper in a small bowl and toss well.
3. Mix the butter, garlic, shallots, butter, and lemon juice in another small bowl and mix well.
4. Dust the tilapia fillets evenly with the spice mixture and coat generously with the butter mixture.
5. Arrange the tilapia fillets in a single layer onto the baking sheet and top with the capers.
6. Bake for about 15 minutes and serve hot.

Serving Suggestion: Serve over a bed of basmati rice.
Variation Tip: Tilapia can be replaced with halibut.
Nutritional Information per Serving:
Calories: 151 | Fat: 5.8g | Sat Fat: 3.3g | Carbohydrates: 3.8g | Fiber: 0.8g | Sugar: 0.3g | Protein: 22.2g

Shrimp Stir Fry

Prep Time: 10 minutes
Cook Time: 10 minutes
Serves: 2
Ingredients:
- ½ pound shrimp, peeled and deveined
- 2 tablespoons olive oil
- 1 cup tomatoes, diced
- 1 tablespoons garlic, minced
- ⅓ cup olives
- 1 cup mushrooms, sliced
- 1 small onion, chopped
- Pepper
- Salt

Directions:
1. Heat oil in a pan over high heat.
2. Add onion, mushrooms and garlic and sauté until onion soften.
3. Add shrimp and tomatoes and stir until shrimp is cooked through.
4. Add olives and stir well. Season with pepper and salt.
Serving Suggestion: Top with green onion and serve
Variation Tip: Add ¼ teaspoon of chili powder.
Nutritional Information per Serving:
Calories 325 | Fat 18.7g | Sodium 558mg | Carbs 12.5g | Fiber 3g | Sugar 4.5g | Protein 28.6g

Easy Shrimp Skewers

Prep Time: 10 minutes
Cook Time: 10 minutes
Serves: 6
Ingredients:

- 1 ½ pound shrimp, deveined
- 1 teaspoon sweet paprika
- 2 fresh lemon juice
- 2 teaspoon garlic paste
- ¼ cup olive oil
- ½ tablespoon dried oregano
- Pepper
- Salt

Directions:
1. Add shrimp and remaining ingredients into the bowl and toss well.
2. Cover and place in the refrigerator for 2 hours.
3. Thread marinated shrimp onto the soaked wooden skewers.
4. Grill shrimp for 5-7 minutes. Turn halfway through.
Serving Suggestion: Garnish with chopped parsley and serve.
Variation Tip: Add ¼ teaspoon of smoked paprika for more spicy flavor.
Nutritional Information per Serving:
Calories 214 | Fat 10.5g | Sodium 307mg | Carbs 2.8g | Fiber 0.4g | Sugar 0.4g | Protein 26.1g

Healthy Shrimp Egg Salad

Prep Time: 10 minutes
Cook Time: 10 minutes
Serves: 4
Ingredients:
- 2 eggs, hard-boiled and chopped
- 1 pound medium shrimp, peeled, deveined, and cooked
- 4 tablespoons mayonnaise
- ½ green bell pepper, chopped
- 2 celery stalks, diced
- ½ onion, diced
- 2 tablespoons fresh lime juice
- 1 Jalapeno pepper, chopped
- 2 radishes, diced
- Salt

Directions:
1. Add shrimp and remaining ingredients into the bowl and mix well.
Serving Suggestion: Garnish with parsley and serve.
Variation Tip: Add your choice of salad dressing.
Nutritional Information per Serving:
Calories 215 | Fat 8.5g | Sodium 440mg | Carbs 8.5g | Fiber 0.9g | Sugar 3.1g | Protein 27.7g

Halibut With Kale

Prep Time: 10 minutes
Cook Time: 15 minutes
Serves: 4

Ingredients:
- 3 tablespoons olive oil, divided
- 3 cups kale, coarsely chopped
- 2 cups cherry tomatoes, halved
- 4 (4-ounce) boneless, skinless halibut fillets
- Juice and zest of 1 lemon
- Sea salt and black pepper, to taste
- 1 tablespoon fresh basil, chopped

Preparation:
1. Preheat the oven to 375°F.
2. Lightly grease an 8-inch x 8-inch baking dish with two teaspoons of olive oil.
3. Arrange the kale in the bottom of the baking dish and top with the cherry tomatoes and the halibut.
4. Drizzle over the remaining olive oil and the lemon juice, lemon zest, basil, salt, and pepper.
5. Bake until the fish flakes easily and the greens are wilted (about 15 minutes).
6. Serve and enjoy.

Serving Suggestion: Garnish with cilantro.
Variation Tip: You can also cook the fish and vegetables in individual foil packets on a baking sheet instead of in a baking dish for easy serving.
Nutritional Information per Serving:
Calories 228 | Fat 10g | Sodium 284mg | Carbs 9g | Fiber 2g | Sugar 2g | Protein 28g

Tuna Patties

Prep Time: 10 minutes
Cook Time: 10 minutes
Serves: 6

Ingredients:
- 1 egg, lightly beaten
- 10 ounces can tuna, drained
- 3 tablespoons flax meal

- ½ cup Feta cheese, crumbled
- ½ teaspoon lemon zest
- 1 teaspoon dried oregano
- 2 tablespoons fresh mint, chopped
- 3 tablespoons olive oil
- 1 garlic clove, minced
- 1 tablespoon lemon juice
- 2 tablespoons green onion, minced

Directions:
1. Add all ingredients except oil into the mixing bowl and mix until well combined.
2. Make small patties from the tuna mixture and set them aside.
3. Heat oil in a pan over medium heat.
4. Place patties onto the hot pan and cook for 10 minutes.
5. Turn patties halfway through.

Serving Suggestion: Serve tuna patties with your favorite dip.
Variation Tip: You can use crumbled Goat cheese instead of Feta cheese.
Nutritional Information per Serving:
Calories 177 | Fat 121g | Sodium 53mg | Carbs 2.3g | Fiber 1.3g | Sugar 0.7g | Protein 15.7g

Zesty Scallops

Prep Time: 10 minutes
Cook Time: 5 minutes
Serves: 4

Ingredients:
- 1-pound sea scallops
- Sea salt and black pepper, to taste
- 2 tablespoons olive oil
- Juice of 1 lime
- Pinch of red pepper flakes
- 1 tablespoon fresh cilantro, chopped

Preparation:
1. Season the scallops lightly with salt and pepper.
2. In a large skillet, heat the olive oil over medium-high heat.
3. Add the scallops to the skillet, making sure they don't touch one another.
4. Sear on both sides, turning once, for a total of about 3 minutes.
5. Add the lime juice and red pepper flakes to the skillet and toss the scallops in the juice.
6. Serve.

Serving Suggestion: Top with the fresh cilantro.
Variation Tip: Look for dried scallops not stored in a milky liquid called sodium triphosphate. This additive causes the scallops to soak up water, and your scallops will have less flavor.
Nutritional Information per Serving:
Calories 160 | Fat 8g | Sodium 241mg | Carbs 3g | Fiber 0.1g | Sugar 0.2g | Protein 19g

Baked Trout With Dill

Prep Time: 10 minutes
Cook Time: 20 minutes
Serves: 4
Ingredients:
- 3 teaspoons olive oil, divided
- 2 (8-ounce) whole trout, cleaned
- Sea salt and black pepper, to taste
- 1 lemon, thinly sliced into about 6 pieces
- 1 tablespoon fresh dill, finely chopped
- 1 tablespoon fresh parsley, chopped
- ½ cup low-sodium fish stock

Preparation:
1. Preheat the oven to 400°F.
2. Lightly grease a 9-inch x 13-inch baking dish with one teaspoon of olive oil.
3. Rinse the trout, pat dry with paper towels, and coat with the remaining two teaspoons of olive oil. Season with salt and pepper.
4. Stuff the interior of the trout with the lemon slices, dill, and parsley and place it into the prepared baking dish.
5. Bake the fish for 10 minutes, then add the fish stock to the dish.
6. Continue to bake until the fish flakes easily with a fork, about 10 minutes.
7. Serve.

Serving Suggestion: Garnish with fresh dill and lemon slices.
Variation Tip: Substitute fish stock with chicken stock.
Nutritional Information per Serving:
Calories 194 | Fat 10g | Sodium 128mg | Carbs 1g | Fiber 0g | Sugar 0g | Protein 25g

Clams Toscano

Prep Time: 10 minutes
Cook Time: 15 minutes
Serves: 6

Ingredients:
- 36 clams in the shell, scrubbed
- 3 tablespoons olive oil
- 5 cloves garlic, minced
- 2 cups fish broth
- 1 tablespoon dried oregano
- 1 tablespoon dried parsley
- 1 teaspoon crushed red pepper flakes (optional)

Preparation:
1. Stir fry your garlic in olive oil for a minute, then add the pepper flakes, broth, parsley, and oregano.
2. Add in the clams and stir the mix.
3. Place a lid on the pan and let everything cook until the clams open.
4. Divide the mix between serving bowls.
5. Enjoy.

Serving Suggestion: Garnish with cilantro.
Variation Tip: Substitute fish stock with chicken stock.
Nutritional Information per Serving:
Calories 227 | Fat 15.7 g | Sodium 126 mg | Carbs 4.4g | Fiber 0.5g | Sugar 0.3g | Protein 3.2 g

Grilled Squid

Prep Time: 10 minutes
Cook Time: 6 minutes
Serves: 6

Ingredients:
- 2 pounds squid, cleaned
- 1 lemon, sliced
- Chopped parsley, for garnish

For the marinade:
- 1 cup olive oil
- 4 cloves garlic, pounded into a paste
- Salt and pepper, to taste
- 1 tablespoon fresh sage, chopped

Preparation:
1. Combine the ingredients for the marinade and place it in a dish.
2. Pat the squid dry with paper towels.
3. Marinate the squid for 20 minutes in the marinade.
4. Preheat an oiled grill pan over high heat.
5. Sear the squid to brown quickly (about 3 minutes on each side). Overcooking will make the squid rubbery.
6. Serve.

Serving Suggestion: Serve with a simple salad and lemon slices.
Variation Tip: Substitute lemon with lime.
Nutritional Information per Serving:
Calories 243 | Fat 27g | Sodium 570mg | Carbs 1g | Fiber 0.5g | Sugar 0.3g | Protein 0.2g

Greek Stuffed Squid

Prep Time: 10 minutes
Cook Time: 1 hour 15 minutes
Serves: 4

Ingredients:
- ¼ cup golden raisins
- ¼ cup pine nuts, toasted
- ½ cup red wine
- ½ cup plain dried breadcrumbs
- 1 (15-ounce) can tomato sauce
- 1 garlic clove, minced
- 1 tablespoon dried mint
- 16 medium squid bodies, plus 6 ounces tentacles, chopped
- 2 tablespoons extra-virgin olive oil
- 3 onions, finely chopped
- 4 anchovy fillets, rinsed and minced
- 5 tablespoons fresh parsley, minced
- Salt and pepper, to taste

Preparation:
1. Heat 1 tablespoon of oil in a 12-inch non-stick frying pan on moderate to high heat until it starts to shimmer.
2. Put in two-thirds of the onions and cook until they become tender (approximately 5 minutes). Mix in squid tentacles and cook until no longer translucent, 1–2 minutes.
3. Mix in the pine nuts, mint, and ¼ teaspoon pepper and cook until aromatic, approximately 1 minute.
4. Move the mixture to a large bowl and mix in the breadcrumbs, ¼ cup parsley, raisins, and anchovies.
5. Sprinkle with salt and pepper to taste and allow to cool slightly.
6. Using a small soup spoon, portion 2 tablespoons of filling into each squid body, pressing on the filling gently to create a 1-inch space at the top.
7. Thread a toothpick through the opening of each squid to close securely.
8. Heat the residual 1 tablespoon of oil in the now-empty frying pan on moderate to high heat until it starts to shimmer.
9. Put in the remaining onions and cook until they become tender (approximately 5 minutes).
10. Mix in the garlic, ¼ teaspoon salt, and ¼ teaspoon pepper and cook until aromatic, approximately half a minute.
11. Mix in the wine, tomato sauce, salt, and pepper and bring to simmer.
12. Add the squid into the sauce.
13. Reduce the heat to low, cover, and simmer gently until the sauce has thickened slightly and the squid is easily pierced with a paring knife, about 1 hour, turning the squid halfway through cooking.
14. Season the sauce with salt and pepper to taste.

15. Remove the toothpicks from the squid and garnish with the remaining 1 tablespoon of parsley.
16. Serve.
Serving Suggestion: Garnish with basil leaves.
Variation Tip: Add chili for a kick.
Nutritional Information per Serving:
Calories 733 | Fat 22.3g | Sodium 1012mg | Carbs 44.9g | Fiber 4.9g | Sugar 14.8g | Protein 55g

Classic Calamari Stew

Prep Time: 10 minutes
Cook Time: 45 minutes
Serves: 6

Ingredients:
- ¼ cup extra-virgin olive oil, plus extra for serving
- ¼ teaspoon red pepper flakes
- ⅓ cup pitted brine-cured green olives, coarsely chopped
- ½ cup red wine
- 1 tablespoon capers, rinsed
- 2 celery ribs, thinly sliced
- 2 onions, finely chopped
- 2 pounds small squid, bodies sliced crosswise into 1-inch-thick rings, tentacles halved
- 3 (28-ounce) cans whole peeled tomatoes, drained and chopped coarsely
- 3 tablespoons fresh parsley, minced
- 8 garlic cloves, minced
- Salt and pepper, to taste

Preparation:
1. Heat the oil in a Dutch oven on moderate to high heat until it starts to shimmer.
2. Put in the onions and celery and cook until they become tender (approximately 5 minutes).
3. Mix in the garlic and pepper flakes and cook until aromatic, approximately half a minute.
4. Mix in the wine, and cook until nearly evaporated (approximately 1 minute).
5. Pat the squid dry using paper towels and sprinkle with salt and pepper. Stir the squid into the pot.
6. Reduce the heat to moderate to low, cover, and simmer gently until the squid has released its liquid (about 15 minutes).
7. Mix in the tomatoes, olives, and capers, cover, and continue cooking until the squid is very tender (30 minutes).
8. Remove from the heat, mix in the parsley and sprinkle with salt and pepper to taste.
Serving Suggestion: Serve, drizzling individual portions with extra oil.
Variation Tip: Add chili for a hotter flavor.
Nutritional Information per Serving:
Calories 480 | Fat 13.3g | Sodium 217mg | Carbs 32g | Fiber 3.8g | Sugar 1.9g | Protein 26.7g

Octopus Braised in Red Wine

Prep Time: 10 minutes
Cook Time: 2 hours
Serves: 4

Ingredients:
- 1 (4-pound) octopus, rinsed
- 1 cup dry red wine
- 1 sprig of fresh rosemary
- 1 tablespoon extra-virgin olive oil
- 2 bay leaves
- 2 tablespoons red wine vinegar
- 2 tablespoons tomato paste
- 2 tablespoons unflavored gelatin
- 2 teaspoons fresh parsley, chopped
- 4 garlic cloves, peeled and smashed
- Salt and black pepper, to taste
- Pinch of ground cinnamon
- Pinch of ground nutmeg

Preparation:
1. Using a sharp knife, separate the octopus mantle (large sac) and body (lower section with tentacles) from the head (midsection containing eyes); discard the head.
2. Place the octopus in a large pot, cover with water by 2 inches, and bring to a simmer on high heat.
3. Reduce the heat, cover, and simmer gently, flipping the octopus occasionally, until the skin between the tentacle joints tears easily when pulled (45 minutes to 1¼ hours).
4. Move the octopus to a slicing board and allow it to cool slightly.
5. Measure out and reserve 3 cups of the octopus cooking liquid; discard the remaining liquid and wipe the pot dry using paper towels.
6. While the octopus is still warm, use a paring knife to cut the mantle into quarters, trimming and scraping away skin and interior fibers. Transfer it to a bowl. Using your fingers, remove the skin from the body, being careful not to remove the suction cups from the tentacles. Cut the tentacles from around the core of the body in three sections; discard the core.
7. Separate the tentacles and cut them into 2-inch lengths; move to a bowl.
8. Heat the oil in the now-empty pot on moderate to high heat until it starts to shimmer.
9. Put in the tomato paste and cook, stirring continuously, until starting to darken, approximately 1 minute.
10. Mix in the garlic, rosemary sprig, bay leaves, ½ teaspoon pepper, cinnamon, and nutmeg, and cook until aromatic, approximately half a minute.
11. Mix in the reserved octopus cooking liquid, wine, vinegar, and gelatin, scraping up any browned bits. Bring to a boil and cook, stirring intermittently, for 20 minutes.
12. Mix in the octopus and any accumulated juices and bring to a simmer.
13. Cook, stirring intermittently, until the octopus becomes soft and the sauce has thickened slightly and coats the back of a spoon (20 minutes to half an hour).
14. Remove from the heat and discard the rosemary sprig and bay leaves.
15. Serve.

Serving Suggestion: Mix in parsley and season with pepper to taste.

Variation Tip: Add a tablespoon of paprika for a more vibrant dish.

Nutritional Information per Serving:
Calories 457 | Fat 7.9g | Sodium 22mg | Carbs 5.2g | Fiber 0.8g | Sugar 1.5g | Protein 75g

Salmon with Rigatoni

Prep Time: 20 minutes
Cook Time: 20 minutes
Serves: 8

Ingredients:
- 1-pound boneless salmon fillets
- 16 ounces whole-wheat rigatoni, uncooked
- Olive oil cooking spray
- Salt and black pepper, to taste
- ½ cup fresh basil leaves, finely chopped
- 1 teaspoon garlic, minced
- 2 tablespoons fresh lemon juice
- ¼ cup parmesan cheese, grated
- 2 teaspoons capers
- 2 teaspoons fresh lemon zest, finely grated
- 2 tablespoons extra-virgin olive oil

Preparation:
1. Preheat the oven to 350°F and grease a baking sheet lightly with the cooking spray.
2. Season the salmon fillets with salt and black pepper.
3. Arrange the salmon fillets on the prepared baking sheet and bake for about 20 minutes.
4. Remove the salmon from the oven and cut it into bite-sized pieces with a fork.
5. In the meantime, in a heavy pan of salted water, add the rigatoni and cook for about 10 minutes until al dente.
6. Drain the rigatoni and transfer it to a bowl.
7. Add the remaining ingredients, except the parmesan, and toss to coat well.
8. Add the salmon and gently toss to coat well.
9. Serve immediately garnished with the parmesan cheese.

Serving Suggestion: Serve with asparagus.

Variation Tip: You can use cheese of your choice.

Nutritional Information per Serving:
Calories: 298 | Fat: 9.3g | Sat Fat: 1.5g | Carbohydrates: 35.3g | Fiber: 6.1g | Sugar: 1.1g | Protein: 19.2g

Citrus Clams

Prep Time: 10 minutes with at least 2 hours soaking time
Cook Time: 15 minutes
Serves: 4

Ingredients:
- 2¼ pounds clams
- ½ cup olive oil
- 4 cloves garlic, minced
- 1 cup fresh parsley, chopped
- ¾ cup cilantro, chopped
- 2 tablespoons lemon juice
- Salt and pepper, to taste

Preparation:
1. Soak the clams in water for 2 hours. Rinse well and drain.
2. Heat the oil in a skillet over medium heat and sauté the garlic until slightly browned (about 2 minutes).
3. Add the clams and the rest of the ingredients. Cook until the clams are done or until they open (about 10 minutes). Discard any unopened clams.

Serving Suggestion: Top with parsley and serve with lemon wedges.
Variation Tip: Substitute lemon with lime juice.
Nutritional Information per Serving:
Calories 514 | Fat 26.6g | Sodium 2167mg | Carbs 67.4g | Fiber 3.1g | Sugar 20.1g | Protein 4.3g

Garlicky Octopus

Prep Time: 10 minutes
Cook Time: 1 hour 5 minutes
Serves: 4

Ingredients:
- 2 pieces whole octopus (about 3 pounds), washed and cleaned
- 1 large onion
- 2 pounds baby potatoes, scrubbed and washed

- Salt, to taste
- 4 bay leaves
- 1 bunch fresh parsley, chopped
- 6 cloves garlic, crushed
- 1½ teaspoons balsamic vinegar
- ½ cup olive oil (or more, to cover octopus)

Preparation:
1. Preheat the oven to 400°F.
2. Place the octopus in a pressure cooker with the (unsliced) onion and pressure cook for 15 minutes. Remove from the pot and transfer to a baking dish.
3. Place the potatoes in another baking dish and sprinkle with salt. Drizzle with olive oil.
4. Sprinkle the garlic, bay leaves, parsley, and vinegar over the octopus.
5. Pour in enough olive oil to almost cover the octopus.
6. Bake both the octopus and potatoes until tender (about 15–20 minutes), spooning the oil over the octopus occasionally to prevent it from drying.
7. Remove from the oven.
8. Cut the octopus into large pieces and mix with the potatoes.
9. Arrange on a serving platter and drizzle with the hot olive oil sauce.

Serving Suggestion: Serve over brown rice.
Variation Tip: Substitute balsamic vinegar with lemon juice.
Nutritional Information per Serving:
Calories 733 | Fat 38.5g | Sodium 58mg | Carbs 50.5g | Fiber 3.4g | Sugar 0.8g | Protein 48g

Baked Mackerel

Prep Time: 10 minutes
Cook Time: 20 minutes
Serves: 6

Ingredients:
- 2 tablespoons lemon juice
- 2 pounds mackerel fillets
- 1 teaspoon salt
- 3 tablespoons olive oil
- ⅛ teaspoon paprika
- ⅛ teaspoon black pepper

Preparation:
1. Preheat the oven to 350°F.
2. Mix all the items in a bowl except the fillets.
3. Coat the fillets with the mixture, place them in a baking dish, and bake for 25 minutes.

Serving Suggestion: Serve with baked potatoes.
Variation Tip: Substitute mackerel fillets with herring fillets.
Nutritional Information per Serving:
Calories 399 | Fat 31g | Sodium 514mg | Carbs 0.5g | Fiber 0.2g | Sugar 0.2g | Protein 28.8g

Mahi-Mahi and Mushrooms

Prep Time: 10 minutes
Cook Time: 25 minutes
Serves: 4
Ingredients:
- 3 tablespoons olive oil, divided
- ¼ cup lemon juice
- ¼ cup fresh chives, minced
- ¼ cup pine nuts or nuts of your choice
- 1 large onion, chopped
- 5 pounds portobello mushrooms, chopped
- Salt and black pepper, to taste
- ¾ cup bell pepper, chopped
- 4 (6 ounces) mahi-mahi fillets

Preparation:
1. In a large skillet on medium heat, lightly fry the fish for 8 minutes in olive oil until the fish begins to flake. Remove from the heat.
2. Add the bell peppers, onions, lemon juice, and mushrooms into the remaining oil. Season with salt and pepper. Cook until the peppers are tender.
3. Add the fish on top and season the fillets with salt and black pepper.
4. Cook for a bit longer until the fish is cooked through.
Serving Suggestion: Garnish with toasted pine nuts and chives before serving.
Variation Tip: You can substitute mahi-mahi with salmon.
Nutritional Information per Serving:
Calories 444 | Fat 16.6g | Sodium 148mg | Carbs 27g | Fiber 8.3g | Sugar 3.4g | Protein 53.9g

Citrus Scallops

Prep Time: 10 minutes
Cook Time: 18 minutes
Serves: 4
Ingredients:
- 1 sweet pepper, sliced
- 1 pound sea scallops
- 5 green onions, chopped
- Salt and black pepper, to taste
- 3 tablespoons olive oil
- ¼ teaspoon red pepper flakes
- 4 medium oranges, peeled and sectioned
- 2 teaspoons fresh cilantro or parsley, diced

- 3 tablespoons lime juice
- 4 cloves garlic, minced

Preparation:
1. In a large skillet, lightly fry the onions, garlic, and pepper in olive oil until the vegetables are soft.
2. Add the scallops and sprinkle with pepper, black pepper, and salt. Cook until the scallops are cooked through. Add the lime juice.
3. Reduce the heat before adding the orange slices and fresh cilantro.
4. Cook until the scallops are lightly golden.
5. Remove from the heat and serve.
Serving Suggestion: Garnish with parsley.
Variation Tip: Switch up oranges with clementine or grapefruit.
Nutritional Information per Serving:
Calories 275 | Fat 11.7g | Sodium 187mg | Carbs 23.7g | Fiber 4.2g | Sugar 14.4g | Protein 21.1g

Almond-Crusted Tilapia

Prep Time: 15 minutes
Cook Time: 10 minutes
Serves: 4
Ingredients:
- ¼ cup ground flax seeds
- 1 cup almonds, finely chopped and divided
- 4 (6-ounce) tilapia fillets
- 2 tablespoons olive oil
- Salt and black pepper, to taste

Preparation:
1. Mix half a cup of the almonds with the ground flax seeds in a large shallow dish.
2. Season the tilapia fillets with salt and black pepper.
3. Rub the tilapia fillets in the almond mixture and coat evenly.
4. In a heavy skillet placed over medium heat, heat the oil and cook the tilapia fillets for about 4 minutes per side.
5. Put the tilapia fillets onto a serving plate.
6. In the same heavy skillet, add the remaining almonds and cook for about 1 minute, frequently stirring.
7. Remove the almonds from the heat and sprinkle over the fish.
8. Serve warm.
Serving Suggestion: Top with sprigs of rosemary and lemon wedges.
Variation Tip: You can also add peanuts.
Nutritional Information per Serving:
Calories: 374 | Fat: 22.6g | Sat Fat: 2.9g | Carbohydrates: 7.1g | Fiber: 4.9g | Sugar: 1.1g | Protein: 38g

Shrimp Salad

Prep Time: 10 minutes
Cook Time: 5 minutes
Serves: 2
Ingredients:
- ½ pound cooked shrimp
- ⅓ cup Greek yogurt
- ½ teaspoons lemon juice
- 1 garlic clove, minced
- 2 tablespoons Feta cheese, crumbled
- ½ teaspoon dill
- Pepper
- Salt

Directions:
1. Add shrimp and remaining ingredients into the bowl and mix well.
Serving Suggestion: Garnish with dill and serve.
Variation Tip: Add 1 small chopped onion.
Nutritional Information per Serving:
Calories 188 | Fat 4.6g | Sodium 471mg | Carbs 4.1g | Fiber 0.1g | Sugar 1.8g | Protein 30.7g

Cheesy Tilapia

Prep Time: 10 minutes
Cook Time: 15 minutes
Serves: 7
Ingredients:
- ¼ cup flour
- 1 tablespoon olive oil
- 1 teaspoon dried dill
- 2 pounds tilapia fillet
- 7 ounces parmesan cheese, grated
- 1 tablespoon paprika
- 1 teaspoon dried oregano

Preparation:
1. Combine the paprika, dried dill, dried oregano, and flour. Mix well.
2. Pour the olive oil into a skillet and heat over medium heat.
3. Rub the tilapia fillets with the oregano mixture.

4. Sear the tilapia for 10 minutes in the skillet on both sides.
5. Sprinkle the grated cheese over the fish and cover it with a lid.
6. Cook the tilapia for 2 minutes more.
7. Serve hot!
Serving Suggestion: Serve with your favorite greens.
Variation Tip: Add in chili for a hotter taste.
Nutritional Information per Serving:
Calories 235 | Fat 9.4g | Sodium 310mg | Carbs 5.2g | Fiber 0.6g | Sugar 0.1g | Protein 33.9g

Baked Fish with Tomatoes and Capers

Prep Time: 15 minutes
Cook Time: 38 minutes
Serves: 6
Ingredients:
- 1 small red onion, finely chopped
- ⅓ cup extra-virgin olive oil
- 2 large tomatoes, chopped
- 10 garlic cloves, chopped
- 1½ teaspoons ground cilantro
- 1 teaspoon sweet Spanish paprika
- Salt and black pepper, to taste
- 1 tablespoon fresh lemon juice
- ⅓ cup golden raisins
- 1½ tablespoons capers
- 1 teaspoon ground cumin
- ½ teaspoon ground cayenne pepper
- 1½ pounds white fish fillets
- 1 teaspoon fresh lemon zest, finely grated

Preparation:
1. Preheat the oven to 400°F and grease a 9½ x 13-inch baking dish.
2. Heat the olive oil in a medium pan placed over medium-high heat, and sauté the onion for about 3 minutes.
3. Add the raisins, tomatoes, garlic, spices, capers, a pinch of salt, and black pepper, and let the mixture come to a boil.
4. Reduce the heat to medium-low and simmer for about 15 minutes.
5. In the meantime, season the fish fillets with the salt and black pepper.
6. Remove the pan from the heat. Evenly spread about half of the cooked tomato sauce in the baking dish.
7. Arrange the fish fillets over the tomato sauce and top with the remaining tomato sauce, lemon juice, and lemon zest.
8. Bake for about 18 minutes and dish out into a platter.
9. Serve garnished with parsley.
Serving Suggestion: Serve along with fried rice.
Variation Tip: You can add spices of your choice.
Nutritional Information per Serving:
Calories: 341 | Fat: 20.1g | Sat Fat: 3g | Carbohydrates: 12g | Fiber: 1.6g | Sugar: 7g | Protein: 29.1g

Grilled Salmon

Prep Time: 10 minutes
Cook Time: 27 minutes
Serves: 6
Ingredients:
- 1½ pounds salmon fillet
- 1 tablespoon garlic powder
- ⅓ cup soy sauce
- ⅓ cup brown sugar
- ⅓ cup water
- ¼ cup olive oil
- Salt and pepper, to taste
- 1 lemon, juiced

Preparation:
1. Season the salmon fillets with lemon, pepper, salt, and garlic powder.
2. Mix the soy sauce, brown sugar, water, and olive oil in a small bowl until the sugar is dissolved.
3. Place the fish in a big resealable plastic bag with the soy sauce mixture, seal, and let marinate for at least 2 hours.
4. Preheat the broiler on medium heat. Lightly oil a griddle pan.
5. Set the salmon on the pan and discard the marinade.
6. Broil the salmon for 7 minutes per side or until the fish flakes easily with a fork.
Serving Suggestion: Serve with some greens.
Variation Tip: Add chili for extra heat.
Nutritional Information per Serving:
Calories 318| Fat 20.1g | Sodium 987mg | Carbs 13.2g | Fiber 3g | Sugar 1.9g | Protein 20.5g

Zesty Shrimp

Prep Time: 10 minutes
Cook Time: 10 minutes
Serves: 4
Ingredients:
- 40 shrimp, deveined and peeled
- 6 garlic cloves, minced
- Salt and black pepper, to taste
- 3 tablespoons olive oil

- ¼ teaspoon sweet paprika
- A pinch of red pepper flakes, crushed
- ¼ teaspoon lemon zest, grated
- 3 tablespoons sherry
- 1½ tablespoons chives, sliced
- 1 lemon, juiced

Preparation:
1. Put a pan on medium-high heat.
2. Add the oil and shrimp, sprinkle with salt and pepper, and cook for 1 minute.
3. Add the paprika, garlic, and pepper flakes; stir and cook for 1 minute.
4. Gently stir in the sherry and allow the mixture to cook for an extra minute.
5. Take the shrimp off the heat, add the chives and lemon zest, stir and transfer the shrimp to serving plates.
6. Pour over the lemon juice and serve.
Serving Suggestion: Garnish with chopped parsley.
Variation Tip: Feel free to use any other wine.
Nutritional Information per Serving:
Calories 140 | Fat 1g | Sodium 200mg | Carbs 1g | Fiber 0g | Sugar 0g | Protein 18g

Italian Pesto Trout

Prep Time: 10 minutes
Cook Time: 10 minutes
Serves: 8
Ingredients:
- 1 teaspoon garlic, minced
- 1 teaspoon dried basil
- 1 teaspoon olive oil
- 2 pounds trout fillets
- 3 tablespoons pesto
- 1 teaspoon mustard

Preparation:
1. Combine the garlic, dried basil, mustard, and pesto in a bowl.
2. Rub the trout fillets with the pesto mixture and leave them for 10 minutes to marinate.
3. Pour the olive oil into a skillet, heat it up, and add the fillets.
4. Sear for 2 minutes on each side and then place in a baking dish.
5. Preheat the oven to 354℉.
6. Put the baking dish in the oven and cook for 8 minutes.
7. Serve hot.
Serving Suggestion: Serve with baked potatoes.
Variation Tip: Substitute trout fillet with flounder fillet.
Nutritional Information per Serving:
Calories 248 | Fat 12.8g | Sodium 112mg | Carbs 2.2g | Fiber 0.2g | Sugar 0.4g | Protein 30.9g

Salmon with White Sauce

Prep Time: 10 minutes
Cook Time: 25 minutes
Serves: 7

Ingredients:
- 1 teaspoon ground black pepper
- 1 tablespoon olive oil
- 1 teaspoon oregano
- 1 white onion, chopped
- 1 cup milk
- 3 garlic cloves, crushed
- 1 tablespoon pistachio, crushed
- 1 teaspoon salt
- 3 pounds salmon fillets
- 3 bay leaves
- 3 tablespoons flour
- 3 tablespoons almond butter

Preparation:
1. Rub the salmon fillets with salt, ground black pepper, and oregano, and leave for some time to marinate.
2. Meanwhile, boil the milk in a saucepan.
3. Add the chopped onion and let it simmer for 5 minutes.
4. Add the garlic cloves and bay leaf, then simmer for 4 minutes on low heat.
5. After this, remove the bay leaf from the milk, add the flour, and pulse the mixture with a blender.
6. Add the butter and leave it to get warm in the sauce. Stir the sauce from time to time to get it well-blended.
7. Pour the olive oil into a skillet and add the marinated salmon. (You may need to cook in batches, depending on the size of your skillet and the fillets.)
8. Sear the fillets on both sides for 2 minutes on high heat.
9. Add the crushed pistachio to the white sauce.
10. Take a dish, put the roasted salmon with a drizzle of the white sauce, and transfer it to the oven.
11. Cook the salmon for 15 minutes in a preheated oven at 360℉.
12. When the salmon is cooked, drizzle it with the remaining white sauce.

Serving Suggestion: Top with chopped parsley.
Variation Tip: Substitute salmon with trout.
Nutritional Information per Serving:
Calories 359 | Fat 18.9g | Sodium 440mg | Carbs 8.1g | Fiber 1.4g | Sugar 2.6g | Protein 41.1g

Octopus in Honey Sauce

Prep Time: 20 minutes
Cook Time: 1 hour 25 minutes
Serves: 8

Ingredients:
- 1 bay leaf
- 2¼ pounds fresh octopus, washed
- ⅓ cup water
- 2 onions, finely chopped
- 1 garlic clove, finely chopped
- 1 (14-ounce) can diced low-sodium tomatoes
- ¾ cup red wine
- ¼ cup fresh basil leaves, chopped
- 4 tablespoons olive oil
- 1 pinch saffron thread, crushed
- 1 tablespoon tomato paste
- 1 tablespoon honey
- Salt and black pepper, to taste

Preparation:
1. Prepare and clean the head of the octopus.
2. In a heavy-bottomed pan placed over medium heat, add the octopus, bay leaf, and water, and cook for about 20 minutes.
3. Stir in the wine and simmer for about 50 minutes.
4. For the sauce: In a skillet placed over medium heat, heat the olive oil and sauté the onions and saffron for about 4 minutes.
5. Stir in the tomato paste and garlic and sauté for about 2 minutes.
6. Stir in the tomatoes and honey and simmer for about 10 minutes.
7. Transfer the sauce into the pan with the octopus and cook for about 15 minutes.
8. Serve hot garnished with the basil.

Serving Suggestion: Serve with egg noodles on the side.
Variation Tip: Saffron threads can be omitted if not available.
Nutritional Information per Serving:
Calories: 319 | Fat: 10.2g | Sat Fat: 1g | Carbohydrates: 13.9g | Fiber: 1.3g | Sugar: 5g | Protein: 38.4g

Pork and Peas

Prep Time: 10 Minutes
Cook Time: 20 Minutes
Serves: 4

Ingredients:
- 4 ounces snow peas
- 2 tablespoons avocado oil
- 1-pound boneless pork loin, cubed
- ¾ cup beef stock
- ½ cup red onion, chopped
- Salt and white pepper, to taste

Preparation:
1. Heat a pan with the oil over medium-high heat. Add the pork and brown for 5 minutes.
2. Add the peas and the rest of the ingredients, toss, bring to a simmer and cook over medium heat for 15 minutes.
3. Divide between plates and serve right away.

Serving Suggestion: Serve with mashed potatoes.
Variation Tip: You can use green onions instead.

Nutritional Information per Serving:
Calories 332 | Fat 16.5g | Sodium 219mg | Carbs 20.7g | Fiber 10.3g | Sugar 1.8g | Protein 26.5g

Cumin Pork

Prep Time: 10 Minutes
Cook Time: 45 Minutes
Serves: 4

Ingredients:
- 1 red onion, chopped
- 1 tablespoon olive oil
- 1½ teaspoons fresh ginger, grated
- 3 garlic cloves, chopped
- Salt and black pepper, to taste
- 2 teaspoons ground cumin

- 1½ pounds pork meat, roughly cubed
- 2 cups chicken stock
- 2 tablespoons lime juice

Preparation:
1. Heat a pot with the oil over medium heat. Add the meat and brown for 5 minutes.
2. Add the onion and garlic and cook for 5 minutes more.
3. Add the rest of the ingredients, bring to a simmer and cook over medium heat for 35 minutes.
4. Divide between plates and serve.

Serving Suggestion: Serve over hot rice and with a garnish of fresh parsley.
Variation Tip: Add in more spices and dried herbs if desired.

Nutritional Information per Serving:
Calories 292 | Fat 16.5g | Sodium 695mg | Carbs 10.7g | Fiber 9.3g | Sugar 1.2g | Protein 14.5g

Beef Chili Verde

Prep Time: 10 Minutes
Cook Time: 23 Minutes
Serves: 2

Ingredients:
- ½ pound beef stew meat, cut into cubes
- ¼ teaspoon chili powder
- 1 tablespoon olive oil
- 1 cup chicken broth
- 1 serrano pepper, chopped
- 1 teaspoon garlic, minced
- 1 small onion, chopped
- ¼ cup grape tomatoes, chopped
- ¼ cup tomatillos, chopped
- Salt and black pepper, to taste

Preparation:
1. Add the oil to an Instant Pot and set the pot on Sauté mode.
2. Add the garlic and onion and sauté for 3 minutes.
3. Add the remaining ingredients and stir well. Seal the pot with the lid and cook on High for 20 minutes.
4. Once done, allow to release the pressure naturally. Remove the lid.
5. Stir well and serve.

Serving Suggestion: Serve with some pinto beans.
Variation Tip: For a twist, add in 1 (15-ounce) can of rinsed pinto or kidney beans until well cooked through.

Nutritional Information per Serving:
Calories 317 | Fat 15.1g | Sodium 460mg | Carbs 6.4g | Fiber 1.6g | Sugar 2.6g | Protein 37.8g

Lamb Chops with Veggies

Prep Time: 20 minutes (plus 3 hours for marinating)
Cook Time: 27 minutes
Serves: 4

Ingredients:
- ½ cup fresh basil leaves
- 8 (4-ounce) lamb loin chops
- ½ cup fresh mint leaves
- 2 garlic cloves
- 2 zucchinis, sliced
- 1 eggplant, sliced
- 8 ounces fresh cherry tomatoes
- 1 tablespoon fresh rosemary leaves
- 3 tablespoons olive oil
- 1 red bell pepper, seeded and chunked
- 1¾ ounces feta cheese, crumbled

Preparation:
1. Preheat the oven to 390°F and lightly grease a large baking sheet.
2. Process the fresh herbs, garlic, and 2 tablespoons of the olive oil in a food processor until smooth.
3. Transfer the herb mixture to a large bowl.
4. Add the lamb chops to the bowl and coat generously with the herb mixture.
5. Refrigerate to marinate for about 3 hours.
6. Arrange the zucchini, eggplant, and bell pepper on a baking sheet and drizzle with the remaining olive oil.
7. Top with the lamb chops in a single layer and bake for about 20 minutes.
8. Remove the chops and place them on a platter. Wrap the chops with foil to keep them warm.
9. Top the veggies on the baking sheet with the feta cheese.
10. Bake for another 7 minutes and transfer to a platter for serving.

Serving Suggestion: Serve with a dip of your choice.
Variation Tip: Parsley leaves can be added.
Nutritional Information per Serving:
Calories: 619 | Fat: 30.6g | Sat Fat: 9.4g | Carbohydrates: 17.1g | Fiber: 7.4g | Sugar: 8.7g | Protein: 69.2 g

Beef and Prune Stew

Prep Time: 20 minutes
Cook Time: 1 hour 35 minutes
Serves: 8

Ingredients:
- 1 tablespoon olive oil
- 1 (14½-ounce) can low-sodium diced tomatoes with juice
- 1 tablespoon organic honey
- ¼ teaspoon garlic powder
- ¼ cup red wine vinegar
- 3 cups sweet potato, peeled and cubed
- 2 cups prunes, pitted
- 2 pounds beef chuck roast, boneless and cut into ¾-inch cubes
- ¼ cup quick-cooking tapioca
- 2 teaspoons ground cinnamon
- Salt and black pepper, to taste
- 2 cups low-sodium beef broth
- 2 yellow onions, thinly chopped into wedges

Preparation:
1. Heat 1 tablespoon of the olive oil in a heavy bottom pan placed over medium-high heat. Sear the beef cubes in two batches for about 5 minutes until browned.
2. In the same pan, stir in the tapioca, tomatoes, honey, garlic powder, cinnamon, black pepper, broth, and vinegar, and let the mixture come to a boil.
3. Reduce the heat to low, cover, and simmer for about 1 hour, stirring occasionally.
4. Stir in the onions and sweet potato and simmer for about another 30 minutes.
5. Fold in the prunes and cook for about 5 minutes.
6. Remove from the heat and serve hot.

Serving Suggestion: Top with fresh cilantro before serving.
Variation Tip: You can also use cranberries instead of prunes.
Nutritional Information per Serving:
Calories: 665 | Fat: 34.1g | Sat Fat: 13g | Carbohydrates: 54.5g | Fiber: 7.1 g| Sugar: 26.2g | Protein: 34.1g

Pork Skewers

Prep Time: 10 minutes
Cook Time: 8 minutes
Serves: 6
Ingredients:
- 2 pounds pork tenderloin, cut into 1-inch cubes
- ½ cup olive oil
- ½ cup vinegar
- 3 tablespoons fresh parsley, chopped
- 1 tablespoon garlic, chopped
- 1 onion, chopped
- Pepper
- Salt

Directions:
1. Add meat and remaining ingredients into the zip-lock bag, seal bag and place in refrigerator for overnight.
2. Thread marinated meat pieces onto soaked wooden skewers.
3. Preheat the grill.
4. Place meat skewers onto the grill and cook for 4 minutes on each side.
Serving Suggestion: Garnish with parsley and serve.
Variation Tip: Add your choice of seasonings.
Nutritional Information per Serving:
Calories 375 | Fat 22.2g | Sodium 116mg | Carbs 2.5g | Fiber 0.5g | Sugar 0.9g | Protein 39.9g

Lamb Stew

Prep Time: 10 minutes
Cook Time: 30 minutes
Serves: 4
Ingredients:

- 2 pounds lamb, cut into chunks
- 1 teaspoon dried oregano
- 1 tablespoon olive oil
- 1 tablespoon garlic, minced
- 1 cup tomatoes, chopped
- 1 cup olives, pitted and sliced
- 1 onion, chopped
- ½ cup cilantro, chopped
- Pepper
- Salt

Directions:
1. Add oil into the instant pot and set pot on sauté mode.
2. Add onion, garlic and oregano and cook for 5 minutes.
3. Add meat and sauté for 5 minutes.
4. Add remaining ingredients and stir well.
5. Cover and cook on high for 20 minutes.
6. Once done, allow to release pressure naturally. Remove the lid.
Serving Suggestion: Garnish with cilantro and serve.
Variation Tip: Top with crumbled cheese.
Nutritional Information per Serving:
Calories 514 | Fat 23.9g | Sodium 204mg | Carbs 7.4g | Fiber 2.5g | Sugar 2.4g | Protein 64.9g

Roasted Pepper Artichoke Beef

Prep Time: 10 minutes
Cook Time: 6 hours
Serves: 6
Ingredients:
- 2 pounds stew beef, cut into 1-inch cubes
- 12 ounces roasted red peppers, drained and sliced
- 12 ounces artichoke hearts, drained
- 1 teaspoon dried basil
- 1 teaspoon dried oregano
- 1 onion, diced
- 1 ½ cups Marinara sauce

Directions:
1. Add all meat and remaining ingredients into the slow cooker and stir well.
2. Cover and cook on low for 6 hours.
Serving Suggestion: Allow to cool slightly and serve.
Variation Tip: Add ¼ cup of freshly chopped parsley.
Nutritional Information per Serving:
Calories 325 | Fat 11g | Sodium 445mg | Carbs 19.9g | Fiber 5.9g | Sugar 9.4g | Protein 37g

Feta Stuffed Pork Chops

Prep Time: 10 minutes
Cook Time: 30 minutes
Serves: 4
Ingredients:
- 4 pork chops
- 1 teaspoon dried oregano
- 1 teaspoon dried basil
- 2 tablespoons fresh dill, chopped
- 1 tablespoon parsley, chopped
- 4 ounces feta cheese, crumbled
- 1 pinch chili flakes

Preparation:
1. Season the pork chops with oregano and basil, then cut a small pocket into each of them.
2. Mix the dill, parsley, feta, and chili in a bowl.
3. Stuff the pork chops with the feta mixture.
4. Heat a grill pan over medium heat and place the pork chops in it.
5. Cook on each side for 13 minutes.
6. Serve immediately.

Serving Suggestion: Garnish with cilantro.
Variation Tip: For a milder taste, omit the chili flakes.
Nutritional Information per Serving:
Calories 336 | Fat 26g | Sodium 208mg | Carbs 2.3g | Fiber 0.7g | Sugar 2g | Protein 22.4g

Roasted Pork Tenderloin

Prep Time: 1 hour 10 minutes
Cook Time: 20 minutes
Serves: 4
Ingredients:
- ¼ cup olive oil
- ¼ cup fresh rosemary, chopped
- Juice of 1 lemon
- Juice and zest of 1 lime
- 1 teaspoon garlic, minced

- 1 teaspoon ground cumin
- Sea salt, to taste
- 12 ounces boneless pork tenderloin

Preparation:
1. Whisk the salt, olive oil, rosemary, lemon juice, lime juice, lime zest, garlic, and cumin in a medium bowl.
2. Add the pork tenderloin to the bowl, and coat thoroughly. Cover and refrigerate for 1 hour.
3. Preheat a grill to medium-high heat.
4. Grill the tenderloin, turning several times and basting with the remaining marinade until it is cooked through (internal temperature: 140°F), 20 minutes.
5. Remove the tenderloin from the grill, cover it with foil, and let rest for 10 minutes.
6. Serve.

Serving Suggestion: Garnish with cilantro sprigs.
Variation Tip: Alternatively, roast the tenderloin on a baking sheet in a 400°F oven until cooked through, 25–30 minutes.
Nutritional Information per Serving:
Calories 201 | Fat 15g | Sodium 81mg | Carbs 1g | Fiber 0.1 g | Sugar 0.2g | Protein 20g

Sriracha Lamb Chops

Prep Time: 10 minutes
Cook Time: 10 minutes
Serves: 4
Ingredients:
- 4 (4-ounce) loin lamb chops with bones, trimmed
- Sea salt and black pepper, to taste
- 1 tablespoon olive oil
- 2 tablespoons sriracha sauce
- 1 tablespoon fresh cilantro, chopped

Preparation:
1. Preheat the oven to 450°F.
2. Lightly season the lamb chops with salt and pepper.
3. In a large ovenproof skillet, heat the olive oil over medium-high heat.
4. Brown the chops on both sides, about 2 minutes per side, and then spread the chops with sriracha.
5. Place the skillet in the oven and roast until the desired doneness, 4–5 minutes for medium.
6. Serve.

Serving Suggestion: Top with cilantro.
Variation Tip: Use pork tenderloin or chicken instead of lamb, in the same amount.
Nutritional Information per Serving:
Calories 223 | Fat 14g | Sodium 116mg | Carbs 1g | Fiber 0g | Sugar 1g | Protein 23g

Thyme Lamb

Prep Time: 10 minutes
Cook Time: 20 minutes
Serves: 2

Ingredients:
- 8 ounces lamb shanks
- 1 tablespoon thyme
- 1 teaspoon garlic, minced
- 1 tablespoon balsamic vinegar
- Salt and black pepper, to taste
- 1 tablespoon olive oil
- ½ cup water
- 1 tablespoon fresh dill, chopped

Preparation:
1. Rub the lamb shanks with thyme, minced garlic, balsamic vinegar, salt, and ground black pepper.
2. Sprinkle the meat with olive oil and leave for 15 minutes to marinate.
3. Transfer the marinated lamb to an Instant Pot or pressure cooker and add the fresh dill.
4. Add the water and close the lid.
5. Cook for 20 minutes on high pressure.
6. Do a natural pressure release and transfer the meat to a platter.
7. Serve and enjoy!

Serving Suggestion: Garnish with fresh rosemary.
Variation Tip: Switch up lamb shanks with lamb shoulder.

Nutritional Information per Serving:
Calories 284 | Fat 15.5g | Sodium 93mg | Carbs 2.6g | Fiber 0.9g | Sugar 0.1g | Protein 32.4g

Chili Beef Stew

Prep Time: 10 minutes
Cook Time: 6 hours on high plus 2 hours on low
Serves: 6

Ingredients:
- 3 pounds stewing beef
- 2 cans Italian diced tomatoes
- 1 cup beef broth
- 4 tablespoons olive oil
- 1 teaspoon cayenne pepper
- 1 tablespoon Worcestershire sauce
- 1 teaspoon dried oregano
- 1 teaspoon dried thyme
- Salt and pepper, to taste

Preparation:
1. Add all the ingredients to an Instant Pot or pressure cooker and mix well.
2. Cover and cook on high pressure for 6 hours.
3. Break up the beef with a fork, pulling it apart in the pot.
4. Taste and adjust the seasoning, if needed.
5. Re-cover and cook for an additional 2 hours on low.
6. Serve and enjoy.

Serving Suggestion: Serve with cucumber slices sprinkled with fresh chopped dill.
Variation Tip: Substitute beef broth with vegetable broth.

Nutritional Information per Serving:
Calories 521 | Fat 25g | Sodium 334mg | Carbs 10g | Fiber 0.3g | Sugar 2.2g | Protein 62g

Easy Beef Roast

Prep Time: 10 minutes
Cook Time: 35 minutes
Serves: 2

Ingredients:
- 1½ teaspoons rosemary
- ½ teaspoon garlic, minced
- 2 pounds roast beef
- ⅓ cup soy sauce
- Salt, to taste

Preparation:
1. Combine the soy sauce, salt, rosemary, and garlic in a mixing bowl.
2. Place the roast in an Instant Pot or pressure cooker. Pour enough water to cover it, and then add the soy sauce mixture on top; gently stir to mix well and seal the lid.
3. Cook on high pressure for 35 minutes.
4. Allow for natural pressure release. Carefully open the lid, and shred the meat.
5. Serve warm.

Serving Suggestion: Serve with a simple salad.
Variation Tip: Add chili for heat.

Nutritional Information per Serving:
Calories 423 | Fat 14g | Sodium 884mg | Carbs 12g | Fiber 0.7g | Sugar 0.7g | Protein 21g

Beef Chuck Roast

Prep Time: 10 minutes
Cook Time: 10 hours
Serves: 6
Ingredients:
- 2 pounds beef chuck roast
- ¼ cup olives, sliced
- 1 teaspoon Italian seasoning
- 2 tablespoons Balsamic vinegar
- ½ cup beef broth
- ¼ cup sun-dried tomatoes, chopped
- 15 garlic cloves, peeled

Directions:
1. Place meat into the slow cooker.
2. Pour remaining ingredients over meat.
3. Cover and cook on low for 10 hours.
4. Shred the meat using the fork.

Serving Suggestion: Garnish with cilantro and serve.
Variation Tip: Top with crumbled Feta cheese.
Nutritional Information per Serving:
Calories 574 | Fat 43.1g | Sodium 211mg | Carbs 3.3g | Fiber 0.4g | Sugar 0.4g | Protein 40.6g

Baked Lamb Patties

Prep Time: 10 minutes
Cook Time: 15 minutes
Serves: 4
Ingredients:
- 1 pound ground lamb
- 1 teaspoon cinnamon
- 1 teaspoon coriander
- 1 tablespoon garlic, minced
- ¼ teaspoon pepper

- 1 teaspoon ground cumin
- ¼ cup fresh parsley, chopped
- ¼ cup onion, minced
- ¼ teaspoon Cayenne
- ½ teaspoon allspice
- 1 teaspoon Kosher salt

Directions:
1. Preheat the oven to 450° F.
2. Add ground meat and remaining ingredients into the bowl and mix until well combined.
3. Make patties from the meat mixture and place onto the baking sheet.
4. Bake for 12-15 minutes.

Serving Suggestion: Serve with your choice of dip.
Variation Tip: Add your choice of seasonings.
Nutritional Information per Serving:
Calories 223 | Fat 8.5g | Sodium 672mg | Carbs 2.6g | Fiber 0.8g | Sugar 0.4g | Protein 32.3g

Lamb Kofta

Prep Time: 20 minutes
Cook Time: 10 minutes
Serves: 6
Ingredients:
- 2 tablespoons fat-free plain Greek yogurt
- 1 pound ground lamb
- 2 tablespoons onion, grated
- 2 tablespoons fresh cilantro, minced
- 1 teaspoon ground cumin
- Salt and black pepper, to taste
- 2 teaspoons garlic, minced
- 1 teaspoon ground cilantro
- 1 teaspoon ground turmeric
- 1 tablespoon olive oil

Preparation:
1. Combine all the ingredients in a large bowl and mix well.
2. Make 12 equal-sized oblong patties out of the mixture.
3. Heat the olive oil in a large non-stick skillet placed over medium-high heat.
4. Add the patties and cook for about 10 minutes until browned on both sides, flipping occasionally.
5. Dish out and serve.

Serving Suggestion: Serve the koftas with yogurt sauce.
Variation Tip: You can add red chili powder for spice.
Nutritional Information per Serving:
Calories: 169 | Fat: 8g | Sat Fat: 2.3g | Carbohydrates: 1.2g | Fiber: 0.2g | Sugar: 0.3g | Protein: 21.9g

Herb Pork Chops

Prep Time: 10 minutes
Cook Time: 8 minutes
Serves: 4
Ingredients:
- 4 pork chops, bone-in
- 1 teaspoon fennel seed, crushed
- 1 teaspoon dried thyme
- 2 teaspoon dried rosemary, crumbled
- ⅓ cup olive oil
- 1 bay leaf, crushed
- 2 teaspoon dried sage, crumbled
- 1 ½ teaspoon salt

Directions:
1. In a bowl, mix together sage, oil, bay leaf, thyme, rosemary, fennel seed and salt.
2. Add herb mixture and pork chops into the zip-lock bag, seal bag, and place in refrigerator for overnight.
3. Preheat the grill.
4. Place marinated pork chops on the grill and cook for 4 minutes on each side or until cooked.

Serving Suggestion: Garnish with parsley and serve.
Variation Tip: Add 1 teaspoon of minced garlic.
Nutritional Information per Serving:
Calories 406 | Fat 36.9g | Sodium 929mg | Carbs 1.1g | Fiber 0.7g | Sugar 0g | Protein 18.2g

Easy Beef Bourguignon

Prep Time: 10 Minutes
Cook Time: 20 Minutes
Serves: 4
Ingredients:
- 1½ pounds beef chuck roast, cut into chunks
- ⅔ cup beef stock
- 2 tablespoons fresh thyme
- 1 bay leaf
- 1 teaspoon garlic, minced
- 8 ounces mushroom, sliced

- 2 tablespoons tomato paste
- ⅔ cup dry red wine
- 1 onion, sliced
- 4 carrots, cut into chunks
- 1 tablespoon olive oil
- Salt and pepper, to taste

Preparation:
1. Add the oil to an Instant Pot and set the pot on Sauté mode.
2. Add the meat and sauté until brown. Add the onion and sauté until softened.
3. Add the remaining ingredients and stir well.
4. Seal the pot with the lid and cook on High for 12 minutes.
5. Once done, allow to release the pressure naturally. Remove the lid.
6. Stir well and serve.

Serving Suggestion: Garnish with sprigs of rosemary.
Variation Tip: You can also use sirloin steak.
Nutritional Information per Serving:
Calories 744 | Fat 51.3g | Sodium 296mg | Carbs 14.5g | Fiber 3.5g | Sugar 6.5g | Protein 48.1g

Garlic Veal

Prep Time: 10 minutes
Cook Time: 50 minutes
Serves: 6
Ingredients:
- 6 garlic cloves, crushed
- 3 pounds veal, cubed
- 1 cup of broth
- 1 glass of wine
- A handful of chives and parsley
- Sea salt, to taste
- Ground black pepper, to taste
- 3 tablespoons sour cream
- 4 tablespoons olive oil

Preparation:
1. Sear the veal cubes for several minutes in olive oil while constantly stirring until brown.
2. Add some chives and parsley, then sauté for several minutes.
3. Add salt and pepper as desired.
4. Add the cup of broth.
5. Slowly cook until the meat becomes tender. Add more broth as needed.
6. When the meat is tender and cooked through, add the sour cream and a glass of wine, then cook for 5 more minutes.
7. Serve.

Serving Suggestion: Garnish with basil.
Variation Tip: You can use vegetable, beef, or chicken broth.
Nutritional Information per Serving:
Calories 508 | Fat 27.9g | Sodium 399mg | Carbs 1.9g | Fiber 0.1g | Sugar 0.3g | Protein 56.4g

Parmesan Pork Chops

Prep Time: 10 minutes
Cook Time: 15 minutes
Serves: 6

Ingredients:
- 1 tablespoon salt
- 1 teaspoon ground black pepper
- 1 teaspoon chili flakes
- 2 pounds pork loin
- 1 cup breadcrumbs
- 2 tablespoons Italian seasoning
- 3 tablespoons olive oil
- 5 ounces parmesan, grated

Preparation:
1. Slice the pork loin into the serving chops. Then rub the pork chops with salt and ground black pepper.
2. Add chili flakes.
3. Combine the breadcrumbs with the Italian seasoning and stir the mixture with the help of the fork. Add the grated parmesan and stir.
4. Pour the olive oil into a skillet and heat it over medium heat.
5. Coat the pork chops in the breadcrumb mixture carefully.
6. Fry the pork chops in the preheated olive oil for 10 minutes on both sides.
7. Chill the cooked pork chops.

Serving Suggestion: Serve with lemon wedges.
Variation Tip: Add paprika for more flavor.
Nutritional Information per Serving:
Calories 574 | Fat 34.1g | Sodium 1608mg | Carbs 14.1g | Fiber 1g | Sugar 1.1g | Protein 51.3g

Almond-Crusted Rack of Lamb

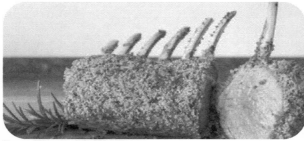

Prep Time: 10 Minutes
Cook Time: 35 Minutes
Serves: 2

Ingredients:
- 2 garlic cloves, minced
- ½ tablespoon olive oil
- Salt and black pepper, to taste
- ¾ pound rack of lamb
- 1 small organic egg
- 1 tablespoon breadcrumbs
- 2 ounces almonds, finely chopped

- ½ tablespoon fresh rosemary, chopped

Preparation:
1. Preheat the oven to 350°F.
2. Meanwhile, take a baking tray, grease it with oil, and set it aside.
3. Mix the garlic, oil, salt, and freshly cracked black pepper in a bowl. Coat the rack of lamb with this mixture, rubbing it on all sides.
4. Crack the egg in a bowl, whisk it until blended, and set aside until required.
5. Place the breadcrumbs in another dish, add the almonds and rosemary and stir until mixed.
6. Dip the seasoned rack of lamb into the egg, dredge with the breadcrumbs mixture until evenly coated on all sides, and then place it onto the prepared baking tray.
7. Cook in the preheated oven for 35 minutes until thoroughly cooked.
8. When done, transfer the rack of lamb onto a dish, and serve straight away.

Serving Suggestion: Serve with a side of asparagus.
Variation Tip: Add chili if desired.
Nutritional Information per Serving:
Calories 471 | Fat 31.6g | Sodium 145mg | Carbs 8.5g | Fiber 3.1g | Sugar 1.5g | Protein 39g

Grilled Paprika Lamb Chops

Prep Time: 10 minutes
Cook Time: 15 minutes
Serves: 4

Ingredients:
- 2 lamb racks, cut into chops
- Salt and black pepper, to taste
- 3 tablespoons paprika
- ¾ cup cumin powder
- 1 teaspoon chili powder

Preparation:
1. Combine the paprika, cumin, chili, salt, pepper in a bowl.
2. Add the lamb chops and rub the mixture over them.
3. Heat a grill pan over medium heat, add the lamb chops, cook for 5 minutes.
4. Flip and cook for 5 minutes more; flip again.
5. Cook for 2 minutes, flip and cook for 2 minutes more.
6. Serve and enjoy.

Serving Suggestion: Serve with rosemary sprigs.
Variation Tip: For a milder taste, omit the chili powder.
Nutritional Information per Serving:
Calories 392 | Fat 17g | Sodium 164mg | Carbs 11.6g | Fiber 4.2g | Sugar 1g | Protein 32.1g

Braciole Beef

Prep Time: 10 minutes
Cook Time: 1 hour 30 minutes
Serves: 8

Ingredients:
- 1 teaspoon ground black pepper
- 1 tablespoon fresh parsley
- 1 teaspoon paprika
- 1-pound beef steak
- 4 tablespoons tomato sauce
- ½ cup red wine
- 4 tablespoon olive oil
- 1 white onion, chopped
- ⅓ cup Italian breadcrumbs
- 2 ounces garlic clove, minced
- 6 ounces Romano cheese, grated
- 1 tablespoon garlic, minced
- ½ cup carrot, chopped
- 1 bay leaf

Preparation:
1. Put the Italian breadcrumbs, 1 tablespoon minced garlic, grated Romano cheese, ground black pepper, fresh parsley, and paprika in a big bowl. Mix the mixture up.
2. Sprinkle the beef steak with the breadcrumb mixture carefully.
3. Roll the beefsteak and secure the beef steak roll with the toothpicks.
4. Sprinkle the beef roll with olive oil and place it in a baking dish.
5. Preheat the oven to 365°F. Cook the beef for 35 minutes.
6. Meanwhile, make the sauce for the dish: Combine the tomato sauce and red wine.
7. Add two tablespoons of olive oil and chopped onion to the tomato sauce mixture.
8. After this, add the 2 ounces of minced garlic and chopped carrot.
9. Sprinkle the mixture with ground black pepper.
10. Toss two tablespoons of olive oil in the big saucepan.
11. Melt the mixture and add the tomato sauce.
12. Add the bay leaf and simmer the sauce for 15 minutes on medium heat.
13. When the rolled meat is cooked, place it in the sauce mixture and sauté it for 35 minutes.
14. Transfer the cooked beef to a plate and slice it.
15. Drizzle the dish with the remaining sauce.

Serving Suggestion: Serve with pasta.
Variation Tip: Add chili for a spicier dish.
Nutritional Information per Serving:
Calories 284 | Fat 17.4g | Sodium 373mg | Carbs 11.77g | Fiber 2g | Sugar 1.9g | Protein 20g

Steak with Yogurt Sauce

Prep Time: 20 minutes
Cook Time: 15 minutes
Serves: 6

Ingredients:
For the steak
- Olive oil cooking spray
- 2 tablespoons fresh rosemary, chopped
- 2 pounds flank steak, trimmed
- 3 garlic cloves, minced
- Salt and black pepper, to taste

For the sauce
- 1 cucumber, peeled, seeded, and finely chopped
- 1½ cups plain fat-free Greek yogurt
- 1 cup fresh parsley, chopped
- 1 teaspoon fresh lemon zest, finely grated
- Salt and black pepper, to taste
- 1 garlic clove, minced
- ⅛ teaspoon ground cayenne pepper

Preparation:
1. Preheat the broiler to medium-high heat and grease a baking pan lightly with the cooking spray.
2. For the steak: In a large bowl, combine all the ingredients except the steak and mix well.
3. Coat the steak generously with the mixture and set it aside for about 20 minutes.
4. Put the steak in the baking pan and cook for about 15 minutes, flipping after every 3 minutes.
5. Remove the steak from the broiler and place it onto a cutting board.
6. For the sauce: Put all the sauce ingredients in a bowl and mix well.
7. Carve the steak into the desired-size slices with a sharp knife.
8. Serve the steak slices topped with the yogurt sauce.

Serving Suggestion: Serve with grilled vegetables.
Variation Tip: You can use skirt steak too.
Nutritional Information per Serving:
Calories: 326 | Fat: 12.9g | Sat Fat: 5.3g | Carbohydrates: 5g | Fiber: 1.1g | Sugar: 1.7g | Protein: 45.4g

Easy Lamb Roast

Prep Time: 10 minutes plus 12 hours marinating time
Cook Time: 2 hours 10 minutes
Serves: 5

Ingredients:
- 3 pounds roast leg of lamb
- 1 medium onion, sliced thickly
- ¾ cup red wine
- 1½ tablespoons tomato paste
- 2 bay leaves
- 1 tablespoon fresh parsley, chopped
- 1 pound baby potatoes, scrubbed and cut into quarters
- Salt and pepper, to taste
- Herbs of your choice, for garnish

For the marinade:
- 1 medium onion, diced
- 4 cloves garlic, minced
- ¼ cup olive oil
- 1 teaspoon paprika
- 1 tablespoon fresh mint leaves, chopped
- 1 tablespoon Piri-Piri sauce, or to taste
- ½ cup red wine
- Salt and pepper, to taste

Preparation:
1. Dry the lamb using paper towels and cut slits, about ¼ to ½ inch deep, on the surface.
2. Combine the ingredients for the marinade well and rub over the lamb. Place in a container with a lid and refrigerate. Let marinate overnight.
3. Preheat the oven to 350°F.
4. Remove the marinated lamb from the refrigerator and allow it to warm up to room temperature.
5. Place the onion slices over the bottom of a baking dish.
6. Bake until the onions brown (about 10 minutes).
7. Meanwhile, dissolve the tomato paste in the wine and add the bay leaves and parsley. Place the lamb in the baking dish over the onions. Add the potatoes.
8. Pour the wine-tomato-paste mixture over the lamb and potatoes. As needed, season with salt and pepper.
9. Bake until the lamb is done (when its internal temperature reaches 170°F or when it can be shredded easily with a fork, about 2–2½ hours).
10. Scoop some of the sauce over the lamb and potatoes occasionally to prevent them from drying out.
11. Let sit for 15 minutes before serving.

Serving Suggestion: Garnish with fresh herbs.
Variation Tip: Omit Piri-Piri sauce for a milder taste.
Nutritional Information per Serving:
Calories 623 | Fat 26.7g | Sodium 823mg | Carbs 18.9g | Fiber 4.3g | Sugar 4.5g | Protein 68.7g

Beef Kebabs

Prep Time: 10 minutes plus 12 hours marinating time
Cook Time: 15 minutes
Serves: 10

Ingredients:
- 4 pounds beef sirloin, cut into cubes
- 2 onions, quartered
- 1 large bell pepper, cut into large cubes
- 5 small tomatoes, halved
- 1 tablespoon olive oil
- Salt and pepper, to taste

To serve:
- Slices of thick, crusty bread (optional)

For the marinade:
- 8 cloves garlic, minced or pounded into a paste
- 4 bay leaves, crumbled
- ¾ cup red wine of choice
- 3 tablespoons olive oil

Preparation:
1. Combine the marinade ingredients and pour into a shallow dish or Ziploc bag. Add the beef cubes and let marinate overnight.
2. Skewer the beef, alternating with the onion, bell pepper, and tomato. If using bamboo skewers, soak them in water for 1 hour before using.
3. Brush with olive oil and season with salt and pepper.
4. Cook on a grill pan (at medium heat) or broil. Cooking time depends on desired doneness (about 8 to 15 minutes).
5. Serve.

Serving Suggestion: Lay on slices of bread.
Variation Tip: Substitute beef with lamb.
Nutritional Information per Serving:
Calories 451 | Fat 19.6g | Sodium 370mg | Carbs 5.1g | Fiber 1.2g | Sugar 2.7g | Protein 55.4g

Pork Chops with Balsamic Peach Glaze

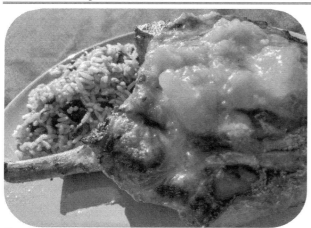

Prep Time: 15 minutes
Cook Time: 23 minutes
Serves: 2
Ingredients:
- 2 pork chops, bone-in
- 2 tablespoons extra-virgin olive oil
- Salt and black pepper, to taste
- ½ cup balsamic vinegar
- 1 tablespoon fresh oregano, chopped
- 6 ounces feta cheese, crumbled
- 1 teaspoon red pepper flakes, to taste
- 1 tablespoon honey
- 2 peaches, pitted and sliced
- ½ cup fresh basil, chopped

Preparation:
1. Preheat the broiler to high.
2. Season the pork chops with salt and black pepper.
3. In an ovenproof skillet placed over medium-high heat, heat the olive oil and sear the pork chops for about 4 minutes on each side.
4. Reduce the heat to medium and cook for another 8 minutes.
5. Stir in the balsamic vinegar, oregano, and honey, and cook for about 2 minutes.
6. Remove from the heat and fold in the peaches.
7. Shift the skillet to the broiler and broil for about 5 minutes until the peaches are lightly charred.
8. Remove from the broiler and serve hot with the topping of chili flakes, basil, and feta cheese.

Serving Suggestion: Serve with boiled jasmine rice.
Variation Tip: You can replace oregano with mixed herbs.

Nutritional Information per Serving:
Calories: 659 | Fat: 45.9g | Sat Fat: 28.8g | Carbohydrates: 28.8g | Fiber: 3.6g | Sugar: 26.5g | Protein: 34.1g

Herbed Lamb Cutlets

Prep Time: 10 Minutes
Cook Time: 45 Minutes
Serves: 6
Ingredients:
- 2 red bell peppers, seeded and cut into chunks
- 1 large sweet potato, peeled and cut into chunks
- 2 zucchinis, sliced into chunks
- 1 red onion, cut into wedges
- 1 tablespoon olive oil
- 8 lean lamb cutlets, fat trimmed
- 1 tablespoon fresh thyme, chopped
- 2 tablespoons mint leaves, chopped
- Ground black pepper, to taste

Preparation:
1. Preheat the oven to 392°F.
2. Take a large-sized baking dish and add the bell peppers, zucchinis, sweet potatoes, and onion. Drizzle the oil all over them and season with some ground pepper.
3. Roast in the preheated oven for about 25 minutes.
4. Mix the herbs with a few more twists of ground black pepper and pat the mixture all over the cutlets.
5. Take the veggies out of the oven and put them to one side of the dish using a spatula.
6. Place the lamb cutlets on the other side of the dish and roast for 10 minutes.
7. Turn the cutlets over and cook for another 10 minutes until the veggies are ready (lightly charred and tender).
8. Mix everything on the tray and enjoy!

Serving Suggestion: Serve with some roasted Brussels sprouts.
Variation Tip: Roast for a few more minutes until the desired doneness.

Nutritional Information per Serving:
Calories 429 | Fat 29g | Sodium 320mg | Carbs 23g | Fiber1.3g | Sugar 2.1g | Protein 19g

Spiced Lamb Chops

Prep Time: 15 minutes (plus 6 hours for marinating)
Cook Time: 8 minutes
Serves: 8

Ingredients:
- 1 teaspoon garlic paste
- 1 tablespoon fresh mint leaves, chopped
- 1 teaspoon ground allspice
- ½ teaspoon ground green cardamom
- Salt and black pepper, to taste
- 2 tablespoons fresh lemon juice
- 2 tablespoons unsalted butter
- ½ teaspoon ground nutmeg
- ¼ teaspoon hot paprika
- 4 tablespoons olive oil
- 2 racks of lamb, trimmed and separated into 16 chops
- 4½ cups fresh cherry tomatoes

Preparation:
1. Put all the ingredients except the chops, tomatoes, and butter in a big bowl and mix well.
2. Add the lamb chops and coat generously with the mixture.
3. Refrigerate to marinate for about 6 hours.
4. Preheat the broiler to high heat and lightly grease a baking pan.
5. Put the lamb chops on the baking pan and cook for about 8 minutes, flipping once halfway.
6. In the meantime, place a skillet over medium heat. Melt the butter and cook the tomatoes with some salt for about 2 minutes, frequently stirring.
7. Remove the lamb chops from the broiler and divide them onto the serving plates.

Serving Suggestion: Serve alongside the tomatoes.
Variation Tip: You can use pork chops instead.
Nutritional Information per Serving:
Calories: 427 | Fat: 36.2g | Sat Fat: 13.9g | Carbohydrates: 4.6g | Fiber: 1.4g | Sugar: 2.8g | Protein: 20g

Manicotti Pork

Prep Time: 10 minutes
Cook Time: 35 minutes
Serves: 8

Ingredients:
- 12 manicotti pasta tubes
- 1 cup milk
- 1 cup ricotta
- 7 ounces mozzarella, grated
- 7 ounces parmesan, grated
- 1 tablespoon fresh basil
- 1 teaspoon cilantro
- 1 teaspoon thyme
- 4 ounces white onion, diced
- 1 tablespoon olive oil
- 9 ounces ground pork
- 1 teaspoon ground black pepper
- 1 teaspoon salt
- 1 teaspoon garlic, minced
- 3 tablespoons tomato sauce
- 4 tablespoons almond butter

Preparation:
1. Cook the pasta as per the package instructions.
2. Meanwhile, combine the ground pork and olive oil in a saucepan over medium heat.
3. Add ground black pepper, salt, fresh basil, cilantro, thyme, minced garlic, and tomato sauce.
4. Add the diced onion to the ground pork mixture.
5. Add the almond butter and simmer the ground beef mixture for 15 minutes.
6. After this, combine the ricotta and milk and whisk the mixture.
7. Add the cheeses to the whisked milk mixture.
8. Chill the manicotti well and arrange them in a baking dish.
9. Sprinkle it with the cooked ground beef mixture.
10. After this, pour the milk mixture over.
11. Transfer the pan to the oven and cook it for 25 minutes in a preheated oven at 350°F.

Serving Suggestion: Garnish with basil leaves.
Variation Tip: Add chili for a spicier result.
Nutritional Information per Serving:
Calories 567 | Fat 33.3g | Sodium 773mg | Carbs 47.32g | Fiber 3g | Sugar 5.7g | Protein 54g

Chicken Breasts with Balsamic Fig Sauce

Prep Time: 15 minutes
Cook Time: 20 minutes
Serves: 4

Ingredients:
- 1½ tablespoons fresh thyme leaves, chopped and divided
- 4 (6-ounce) chicken breast halves, skinless and boneless
- ½ teaspoon salt, divided
- 2 tablespoons olive oil, divided
- ½ cup dried figs, finely chopped
- ¼ cup balsamic vinegar
- ¼ teaspoon black pepper
- ¾ cup onion, chopped
- ½ cup low-fat and low-sodium chicken broth
- 2 teaspoons low-sodium soy sauce

Preparation:
1. Put 1½ teaspoons of thyme, ¼ teaspoon of salt, and black pepper in a large bowl and mix well.
2. Dredge the chicken breast halves in the thyme mixture to evenly coat them.
3. In a large non-stick skillet placed over medium-high heat, heat 1 tablespoon of the olive oil and cook the chicken for about 6 minutes on each side.
4. Move the chicken breasts onto a plate and wrap them in foil.
5. Put the remaining olive oil and onions in the same skillet and sauté for about 3 minutes over medium-high heat.
6. Stir in the broth, figs, soy sauce, and vinegar to make the fig sauce. Let the sauce simmer for about 3 minutes.
7. Stir in the remaining thyme and salt and remove from the heat.
8. Diagonally cut the chicken breast halves into slices.
9. Serve the chicken slices topped with the fig sauce.
Serving Suggestion: Serve over a bed of rice.
Variation Tip: You can also add some oregano as a seasoning.
Nutritional Information per Serving:
Calories: 479 | Fat: 20.1g | Sat Fat: 4.6g | Carbohydrates: 20.9g | Fiber: 3.5g | Sugar: 13.5g | Protein: 52.6g

Bruschetta Chicken Breasts

Prep Time: 15 minutes
Cook Time: 40 minutes
Serves: 4

Ingredients:
- 4 (6-ounce) chicken breasts
- Olive oil cooking spray
- Salt and black pepper, to taste
- ¼ cup fresh basil leaves, chopped
- 1 teaspoon balsamic vinegar
- 5 small tomatoes, chopped
- 1 garlic clove, minced
- 1 teaspoon olive oil

Preparation:
1. Preheat the oven to 375°F and grease a baking dish with the olive oil cooking spray.
2. Season the chicken breasts with the salt and black pepper.
3. Arrange the chicken breasts in a single layer in the baking dish.
4. Cover the baking dish and bake for about 40 minutes.
5. In the meantime, in a bowl, add the tomatoes, garlic, basil, vinegar, oil, and salt.
6. Mix well and refrigerate until using.
7. Remove the chicken breasts from the oven and transfer them to serving plates.
8. Serve topped with the tomato mixture.
Serving Suggestion: Serve with your favorite pasta.
Variation Tip: You can use any variety of tomatoes that you like.
Nutritional Information per Serving:
Calories: 355 | Fat: 14g | Sat Fat: 3.7g | Carbohydrates: 4.7g | Fiber: 1.4g | Sugar: 3g | Protein: 50.3g

Roasted Whole Chicken

Prep Time: 15 minutes (plus overnight for marinating)
Cook Time: 1 hour 35 minutes
Serves: 4
Ingredients:
- 3 garlic cloves, minced
- ¼ cup extra-virgin olive oil
- 2 teaspoons fresh lemon zest, finely grated
- 1 teaspoon paprika
- 1 teaspoon ground cumin
- Salt and black pepper, to taste
- 2 teaspoons dried oregano, crushed
- 1 teaspoon ground cayenne pepper
- ½ teaspoon ground fennel seeds
- 1 (3-pound) frying chicken, neck and giblets removed

Preparation:
1. Place all the ingredients except the chicken into a large bowl and stir well.
2. Add the chicken and coat generously with the mixture.
3. Refrigerate to marinate overnight, turning the chicken occasionally.
4. Preheat the oven to 425°F.
5. Remove the chicken from the bowl and place it in a roasting pan.
6. Coat the chicken with the marinade.
7. With kitchen string, tuck the wings back under the body and tie the legs.
8. Roast for about 10 minutes.
9. Reduce the oven's temperature to 350°F and roast for about 1 hour and 30 minutes.
10. Remove from the oven and move the chicken onto a cutting board.
11. With a sharp knife, cut the chicken into desired-size pieces to serve.

Serving Suggestion: Serve with grilled vegetables.
Variation Tip: You can add spices of your choice.
Nutritional Information per Serving:
Calories: 767 | Fat: 38.2g | Sat Fat: 8.8g | Carbohydrates: 2.4g | Fiber: 0.9g | Sugar: 0.2g | Protein: 98.9g

Braised Chicken with Artichokes

Prep Time: 20 minutes
Cook Time: 1 hour 15 minutes
Serves: 4
Ingredients:
- 4 chicken leg quarters
- 1 tablespoon olive oil
- 1 yellow onion, chopped
- 1 teaspoon salt
- ½ teaspoon red pepper flakes, crushed
- 10 canned artichoke hearts, drained and halved
- 8 fresh thyme sprigs
- 1 (16-ounce) can low-sodium butter beans, rinsed and drained
- 4 garlic cloves, chopped
- 1 tablespoon black pepper
- 4 cups low-sodium chicken broth
- 2 cups cherry peppers
- 4 tablespoons fresh lemon juice

Preparation:
1. Preheat the oven to 375°F.
2. In a heavy, oven-proof wok placed over high heat, heat the oil and sear the chicken for about 5 minutes per side.
3. Put the chicken onto a warm plate.
4. In the same wok, add the garlic, onion, salt, black pepper, and red pepper flakes and sauté for about 1 minute.
5. Stir in the broth and let it come to a boil.
6. Remove the wok from the heat and stir in the cooked chicken, cherry peppers, artichoke hearts, thyme sprigs, and lemon juice.
7. Cover the pan and transfer it to the oven.
8. Bake for about 1 hour and then add the beans. Stir to combine.
9. Divide chicken leg quarters into the serving bowls and top with the artichoke mixture.
10. Serve immediately.

Serving Suggestion: Serve alongside your favorite soup.
Variation Tip: You can also use chicken wings.
Nutritional Information per Serving:
Calories: 611 | Fat: 19.8g | Sat Fat: 4.8g | Carbohydrates: 74.4g | Fiber: 29.3g | Sugar: 9.1g | Protein: 45.8g

Marinated Grill Chicken

Prep Time: 10 minutes
Cook Time: 14 minutes
Serves: 4
Ingredients:
- 2 pounds chicken breasts, skinless and boneless
- ½ teaspoon red pepper flakes
- 1 teaspoon dried oregano
- 2 tablespoons fresh lemon juice
- 1 tablespoon garlic, minced
- 3 tablespoon olive oil
- 1 tablespoon Balsamic vinegar
- ½ teaspoon onion powder
- ½ teaspoon pepper
- ½ tsp Kosher salt

Directions:
1. Add chicken and remaining ingredients into the zip-lock bag. Seal bag and place in refrigerator for overnight.
2. Preheat the grill.
3. Place marinated chicken onto the grill and cook for 5-7 minutes on each side.
Serving Suggestion: Allow to cool completely then serve.
Variation Tip: Add your choice of seasonings.
Nutritional Information per Serving:
Calories 530 | Fat 27.5g | Sodium 488mg | Carbs 1.7g | Fiber 0.4g | Sugar 0.4g | Protein 65.9g

Healthy Chicken Salad

Prep Time: 10 minutes
Cook Time: 5 minutes
Serves: 4
Ingredients:

- 8 ounces chicken, cooked and diced
- 2 ounces walnuts, chopped
- 2 tablespoons green onion, chopped
For Dressing:
- 1 tablespoon lemon juice
- 2 tablespoons fresh cilantro, chopped
- ⅛ teaspoon Cayenne
- ½ cup mayonnaise
- 1 teaspoon curry powder
- ¼ teaspoon pepper
- ¼ teaspoon salt

Directions:
1. In a small bowl, mix together all dressing ingredients and set aside.
2. Add chicken, walnuts, and green onion into the bowl and mix well.
3. Pour dressing over salad and toss well.
Serving Suggestion: Mix well and serve.
Variation Tip: You can also add chopped pecans instead of walnuts.
Nutritional Information per Serving:
Calories 292 | Fat 20g | Sodium 394mg | Carbs 9.1g | Fiber 1.3g | Sugar 2.2g | Protein 20.3g

Oregano Grilled Chicken

Prep Time: 10 minutes
Cook Time: 20 minutes
Serves: 4
Ingredients:
- ½ cup lemon juice
- ½ cup extra-virgin olive oil
- 3 tablespoons garlic, minced
- 2 teaspoons dried oregano
- 1 teaspoon red pepper flakes
- 1 teaspoon salt
- 2 pounds boneless, skinless chicken breasts

Preparation:
1. Combine the garlic, lemon juice, olive oil, oregano, red pepper flakes, and salt in a medium bowl.
2. Divide a chicken breast horizontally to get two thin pieces. Repeat this process with the rest of the chicken breasts.
3. Put the chicken in the bowl with the marinade and let it sit for at least 10 minutes before cooking.
4. Place a skillet on high heat and add some oil.
5. Cook each side of the breasts for 10 minutes, turning regularly.
6. Serve warm.
Serving Suggestion: Serve with lemon wedges.
Variation Tip: Omit red pepper flakes for a milder taste.
Nutritional Information per Serving:
Calories 479 | Fat 32g | Sodium 943mg | Carbs 5g | Fiber 1g | Sugar 1g | Protein 47g

Chicken with Artichoke

Prep Time: 10 minutes
Cook Time: 8 hours
Serves: 6
Ingredients:
- 6 chicken thighs, skinless and boneless
- 1 teaspoon dried basil
- 1 teaspoon dried oregano
- 14 olives, pitted
- 10 ounces frozen artichoke hearts
- 14 ounces can tomatoes, diced
- ½ teaspoon garlic powder
- 3 tablespoons fresh lemon juice
- Pepper
- Salt

Directions:
1. Season chicken with pepper and salt and place into the slow cooker.
2. Pour remaining ingredients over the chicken.
3. Cover and cook on low for 8 hours.
Serving Suggestion: Allow to cool completely then serve.
Variation Tip: Add 1 small sliced onion.
Nutritional Information per Serving:
Calories 329 | Fat 12.1g | Sodium 429mg | Carbs 9.5g | Fiber 4.2g | Sugar 3g | Protein 44.6g

Buttered Creamy Chicken

Prep Time: 10 minutes
Cook Time: 20 minutes
Serves: 4
Ingredients:
- ½ cup heavy whipping cream
- 1 tablespoon salt
- ½ cup bone broth
- Salt and black pepper, to taste
- 4 tablespoons cashew butter
- 4 chicken breast halves

Preparation:
1. Place a pan with one tablespoon of the cashew butter on medium heat.
2. Once the cashew butter is warm and melted, place the chicken in and cook for 7 minutes on each side.
3. Once the chicken is cooked through and golden, place it on a plate.
4. Add the bone broth, heavy whipping cream, salt, and pepper into the warm pan, and let the sauce simmer.
5. In about 5 minutes, the sauce should thicken up.
6. Add the rest of the cashew butter and the chicken back into the pan.
7. Spoon the sauce over the chicken and cover it completely.
8. Serve and enjoy!
Serving Suggestion: Top with chopped fresh parsley.
Variation Tip: Switch up cashew butter with any other nut butter.
Nutritional Information per Serving:
Calories 350 | Fat 25g | Sodium 394mg | Carbs 17g | Fiber 10g | Sugar 2g | Protein 25g

Turkey Meatballs

Prep Time: 10 minutes
Cook Time: 25 minutes
Serves: 2
Ingredients:
- 1 yellow onion, diced
- 14 ounces artichoke hearts, diced
- 1-pound ground turkey
- 1 teaspoon dried parsley
- 1 teaspoon olive oil
- 4 tablespoons basil, chopped
- Salt and pepper, to taste

Preparation:
1. Preheat the oven to 350℉. Grease a baking sheet.
2. Place the artichokes in a pan, add the oil, and sauté with the diced onions over medium heat for 5 minutes or until the onions are soft.
3. Meanwhile, mix the parsley, basil, and ground turkey with your hands in a big bowl. Season to taste.
4. Once the onion mixture has cooled, add it into the bowl and mix thoroughly.
5. With an ice cream scooper, scoop the ground turkey mixture and form balls.
6. Place the balls on the prepared baking sheet, pop in the oven, and bake until cooked (around 17 minutes).
7. Serve and enjoy.
Serving Suggestion: Serve over hot rice.
Variation Tip: Substitute turkey with chicken.
Nutritional Information per Serving:
Calories 283 | Fat 12g | Sodium 232mg | Carbs 30g | Fiber 12g | Sugar 4.3g | Protein 12g

Greek Roasted Pepper Chicken

Prep Time: 10 minutes
Cook Time: 4 hours
Serves: 6
Ingredients:
- 2 pounds chicken thighs, skinless and boneless
- ½ cup chicken stock
- ¾ cup olives
- 1 teaspoon oregano
- 1 cup roasted red peppers, chopped
- 1 tablespoon garlic, minced
- 1 tablespoon capers
- 1 teaspoon rosemary
- 1 teaspoon dried thyme
- 1 tablespoon olive oil
- ½ cup onion, sliced
- Pepper
- Salt

Directions:
1. Heat oil in a pan over medium-high heat.
2. Add chicken and cook until browned.
3. Add garlic and onion and cook for 5 minutes.
4. Transfer the chicken mixture into the slow cooker along with the remaining ingredients.
5. Cover and cook on low for 4 hours.
Serving Suggestion: Allow to cool completely then serve.
Variation Tip: Add your choice of seasonings.
Nutritional Information per Serving:
Calories 344 | Fat 15.5g | Sodium 484mg | Carbs 4.8g | Fiber 1.5g | Sugar 1.9g | Protein 44.5g

Grill Lemon Chicken

Prep Time: 10 minutes
Cook Time: 12 minutes
Serves: 4
Ingredients:
- 2 pounds chicken breasts, halves
- 1 teaspoon paprika
- 4 garlic cloves, minced

- 1 ½ teaspoon dried oregano
- 6 tablespoons olive oil
- 6 tablespoons fresh lemon juice
- 6 tablespoons fresh parsley, minced
- Pepper
- Salt

Directions:
1. Season chicken with pepper and salt.
2. Add chicken and remaining ingredients into the zip-lock bag. Seal bag and place in refrigerator for 1 hour.
3. Preheat the grill.
4. Place marinated chicken on the grill and cook for 5-6 minutes on each side.
Serving Suggestion: Allow to cool completely and serve.
Variation Tip: Add 1 teaspoon of Italian seasonings.
Nutritional Information per Serving:
Calories 626 | Fat 38.2g | Sodium 242mg | Carbs 2.5g | Fiber 0.8g | Sugar 0.6g | Protein 66.3g

Grilled Harissa Chicken

Prep Time: 10 minutes
Cook Time: 12 minutes
Serves: 2
Ingredients:
- Juice of 1 lemon
- 1 red onion, sliced
- 1½ teaspoons ground coriander
- 1½ teaspoons smoked paprika
- 1 teaspoon cumin
- 2 teaspoons cayenne pepper
- 3 tablespoons olive oil
- Kosher salt, to taste
- 8 boneless chicken thighs
- 2 tablespoons harissa paste

Preparation:
1. In a large bowl, add the chicken, olive oil, salt, onion, garlic, coriander, cumin, cayenne, lemon juice, and harissa paste, then mix well until the chicken is fully coated.
2. Place the oven rack 4 inches from the heat source. Preheat the broiler. Place the chicken on a broiler pan.
3. Broil each side of the chicken for about 7 minutes. The thickest part of the cooked chicken's temperature should read as 165℉ on a thermometer.
Serving Suggestion: Serve with a salad of your choice.
Variation Tip: For a milder taste, omit the cayenne pepper.
Nutritional Information per Serving:
Calories 142.5| Fat 4.7g | Sodium 102mg | Carbs 1.7g | Fiber 2.5g | Sugar 5.6g | Protein 22.1g

Chicken with Yogurt-Mint Sauce

Prep Time: 25 minutes
Cook Time: 25minutes
Serves: 4

Ingredients:
- 1 cup low-fat plain Greek yogurt
- 1 onion, finely chopped
- 1 tablespoon fresh mint, chopped
- 1 teaspoon fresh dill, chopped
- 1 teaspoon garlic, minced
- 1 teaspoon ground cumin
- Pinch of red pepper flakes
- 4 (3-ounce) boneless, skinless chicken breasts

Preparation:
1. In a medium bowl, whisk together the yogurt, onion, mint, dill, garlic, cumin, and red pepper flakes until blended.
2. Transfer ½ cup of the yogurt to a small bowl. Set aside, covered, in the refrigerator.
3. Add the chicken to the remaining yogurt mixture, turning to coat.
4. Cover and place the chicken in the refrigerator to marinate for 3 hours.
5. Preheat the oven to 400°F.
6. Transfer the chicken breasts to a baking sheet and roast until the chicken is cooked through, 25 minutes.
7. Serve with the reserved yogurt-mint sauce.

Serving Suggestion: Garnish with rosemary sprigs.
Variation Tip: Substitute the chicken breast with turkey breast.
Nutritional Information per Serving:
Calories 136 | Fat 7.6g | Sodium 82mg | Carbs 5.7g | Fiber 1g | Sugar 3g | Protein 26g

Feta Turkey Meatballs

Prep Time: 10 minutes
Cook Time: 20 minutes
Serves: 6

Ingredients:
- 1 egg, lightly beaten
- 2 pounds ground turkey
- 4 ounces Feta cheese, crumbled
- 1 tablespoon fresh mint, chopped

- ¼ teaspoon cumin
- ½ teaspoon onion powder
- ½ cup almond flour
- ¼ cup fresh parsley, chopped
- 1 cup spinach, chopped
- ½ teaspoon oregano
- ½ teaspoon pepper
- Salt

Directions:
1. Preheat the oven to 450° F.
2. Add ground turkey and remaining ingredients into the large bowl and mix until well combined.
3. Make small balls from the meat mixture and place onto the baking sheet.
4. Bake for 20 minutes.

Serving Suggestion: Allow to cool completely and serve.
Variation Tip: You can use crumbled Goat cheese instead of Feta cheese.
Nutritional Information per Serving:
Calories 373 | Fat 22.6g | Sodium 417mg | Carbs 2.2g | Fiber 0.6g | Sugar 1g | Protein 45.8g

Caprese Chicken

Prep Time: 10 Minutes
Cook Time: 20 Minutes
Serves: 4

Ingredients:
- 2 boneless chicken breasts, sliced
- Salt and black pepper, to taste
- 1 tablespoon olive oil
- 1 tablespoon extra-virgin olive oil
- 6 ounces pesto
- 8 tomatoes, chopped
- 6mozzarella cheese, grated
- Balsamic glaze, as needed
- Kosher salt, to taste
- Fresh basil, as required

Preparation:
1. Preheat the oven to 400°F.
2. Mix the salt, sliced chicken, and pepper in a bowl. Set aside for 10 minutes.
3. Melt the olive oil in a skillet over medium heat.
4. Cook the chicken pieces in the melted olive oil for 5 minutes on each side. Remove from the heat.
5. Spread the pesto over the chicken and place the mozzarella cheese and tomatoes on top.
6. Bake in the preheated oven for 12 minutes.
7. Serve and enjoy.

Serving Suggestion: Garnish with balsamic glaze and basil.
Variation Tip: Chicken breasts can be substituted with chicken legs.
Nutritional Information per Serving:
Calories 232 | Fat 15g | Sodium 254mg | Carbs 5g | Fiber 1g | Sugar 5.7g | Protein 18g

Turkey Casserole

Prep Time: 10 minutes
Cook Time: 40 minutes
Serves: 8
Ingredients:
- 9 ounces mozzarella cheese, sliced
- 1 teaspoon salt
- 1 teaspoon chili flakes
- 1 cup tomato juice
- 1 teaspoon oregano
- 4 sweet potatoes, peeled and spiralized
- 1-pound turkey fillet, chopped
- 4 teaspoons olive oil
- 1 tablespoon garlic, minced
- 1 cup tomatoes, sliced
- 1 cup Italian parsley, chopped
- 2 tablespoons heavy cream
- 1 tablespoon almond butter

Preparation:
1. Preheat the oven to 365°F.
2. Sprinkle the turkey with salt, chili flakes, and oregano and mix well.
3. Melt the butter in a skillet and add the turkey. Cook the turkey for 6 minutes, stirring it frequently.
4. Take a big square casserole dish and coat it with olive oil. Add the cooked turkey.
5. Add a layer of sliced tomatoes on top.
6. Combine the heavy cream with the minced garlic and tomato juice and whisk the mixture.
7. Then put the spiralized sweet potato in the dish and flatten it.
8. Pour in the tomato juice mixture and sprinkle over the chopped parsley.
9. Bake in the oven for 20 minutes.
10. Put the sliced mozzarella over the cooked casserole and bake the dish for 10 minutes more.
11. Remove the casserole from the oven and let it cool briefly before serving.

Serving Suggestion: Top with chopped parsley.
Variation Tip: Substitute turkey fillet with chicken fillet.
Nutritional Information per Serving:
Calories 433 | Fat 11g | Sodium 710mg | Carbs 23g | Fiber 30.6g | Sugar 3.8g | Protein 17.15g

Mediterranean Chicken Stir Fry

Prep Time: 10 minutes
Cook Time: 25 minutes
Serves: 4
Ingredients:
- ½ cup pitted green olives, sliced
- 2 small tomatoes, chopped
- 1 onion, chopped
- 1 zucchini, chopped
- ¼ teaspoon red pepper flakes
- 3 cloves garlic, minced
- 1 cup brown rice
- 2 teaspoons olive oil
- 1 teaspoon dried oregano
- 1 teaspoon dried basil
- 3 cups water
- 1-pound boneless chicken breasts, cubed
- Salt and pepper, to taste

Preparation:
1. In a medium pot on the stove, bring the water to a boil. Add the rice and cook as per the package instructions. Remove from the heat.
2. Add the olive oil to a skillet.
3. Lightly fry the chicken until it's fully cooked. Remove from the heat.
4. Add the onion to the same skillet. Add the garlic, red pepper, basil, zucchini, and oregano.
5. Stir fry until the vegetables become softer, then season with salt and pepper.
6. Add the cooked chicken, cooked rice, and tomatoes, and olives.

Serving Suggestion: Garnish with chopped green onions.
Variation Tip: Substitute water with chicken broth.
Nutritional Information per Serving:
Calories 401 | Fat 13.3g | Sodium 248mg | Carbs 44.1g | Fiber 3.9g | Sugar 3.3g | Protein 38g

Italian Baked Chicken Breast

Prep Time: 10 Minutes
Cook Time: 18 Minutes
Serves: 6
Ingredients:
- 2 pounds boneless chicken breast
- Salt and pepper, to taste
- 1 teaspoon thyme
- 1 red onion, sliced
- 1 teaspoon dried oregano
- 1 teaspoon sweet paprika
- 1 tablespoon olive oil
- 2 garlic cloves, minced
- 1 tablespoon lemon juice
- Campari tomatoes, to taste
- Handful fresh parsley, chopped, for garnish

Preparation:
1. Preheat the oven to 425°F.
2. Place the chicken pieces in a Ziploc bag. Flatten the pieces using a meat mallet.
3. Place the chicken into a bowl and rub the pieces with black pepper and salt.
4. Add the lemon juice, garlic, oil, and spices and mix well to coat the chicken thoroughly.
5. Place the onions in an oiled baking tray followed by the chicken and tomatoes. Cover the tray with foil.
6. Bake in the preheated oven for 10 minutes.
7. After 10 minutes, uncover and bake again for 8 more minutes.

Serving Suggestion: Serve with a sprinkling of parsley over the baked chicken.
Variation Tip: Omit the olive oil and use butter.
Nutritional Information per Serving:
Calories 290 | Fat 11.5g | Sodium 138mg | Carbs 11g | Fiber 0.8g | Sugar 2.1g | Protein 35.9g

Chicken Cacciatore

Prep Time: 10 Minutes
Cook Time: 39 Minutes
Serves: 8
Ingredients:
- 2 tablespoons extra-virgin olive oil
- 1 medium onion, chopped
- 3 tablespoons garlic, chopped
- 1 whole sized chicken, cut into 8 pieces
- 1 medium carrot, cubed
- 1 medium potato, cubed
- 1 medium red bell pepper, thinly sliced
- 2 cups stewed tomatoes
- 1 cup tomato sauce
- ½ cup green peas
- 1 teaspoon dried thyme
- Salt and black pepper, as needed

Preparation:
1. Place a large saucepan over medium-high heat.
2. Add the oil and allow it to heat up.
3. Stir in the garlic and onion and cook for 2 minutes.
4. Add the chicken and cook for 7 minutes, stirring throughout.
5. Add the carrots, red bell pepper, potato, stewed tomatoes, tomato sauce, green peas, thyme, and mix well.
6. Reduce the heat to low and simmer for 30 minutes. Season with salt and pepper.
7. Transfer to a serving dish and enjoy!

Serving Suggestion: Serve on a bed of rice or mashed potatoes.
Variation Tip: Add chili for a spicier dish.
Nutritional Information per Serving:
Calories 281 | Fat 8g | Sodium 413mg | Carbs 14g | Fiber 3.3g | Sugar 9.6g | Protein 39g

Italian Chicken Meatballs

Prep Time: 10 minutes
Cook Time: 32 minutes
Serves: 20 meatballs

Ingredients:
- 3 tomatoes, chopped
- Kosher salt and black pepper, to taste
- ½ cup fresh parsley, chopped
- 1 teaspoon dried oregano
- ½ teaspoon fresh thyme
- ¼ teaspoon sweet paprika
- 1 red onion, thinly chopped
- 1-pound ground chicken
- ½ teaspoon garlic cloves, minced
- 1 raw egg
- ¼ cup parmesan cheese, grated
- 2 tablespoons extra-virgin olive oil.

Preparation:
1. Preheat the oven to 375℉.
2. Coat a skillet with some of the extra-virgin olive oil and set it aside.
3. In a large bowl, mix the tomatoes with kosher salt and the onions.
4. Add half of your fresh thyme and sprinkle a little extra-virgin olive oil on it again.
5. Transfer this mixture to your skillet and use a spoon to spread it evenly.
6. Add the ground chicken to a mixing bowl, and add the egg, parmesan cheese, a little amount of extra-virgin olive oil, oregano, paprika, garlic, the remaining thyme, chopped parsley, and black pepper.
7. Mix the mixture well and form about 1½-inch chicken meatballs.
8. Arrange the meatballs in the prepared skillet.
9. Bake in the preheated oven for about 30 minutes.
10. Your meatballs should turn golden brown when ready.
11. Serve and enjoy.

Serving Suggestion: Serve with tomato sauce.
Variation Tip: Add a pinch of chili for spice.
Nutritional Information per Serving:
Calories 79 | Fat 4.6g | Sodium 74.7mg | Carbs 4.1g | Fiber 0.4g | Sugar 1.4g | Protein 7.8g

Garlic Chicken Thighs

Prep Time: 10 minutes plus 12 hours marinating time
Cook Time: 30 minutes
Serves: 4

Ingredients:
- 8 skinless chicken thighs
- ¼ cup olive oil
- 8 cloves garlic, smashed
- 1½ teaspoons dried thyme
- 2 bay leaves
- ½ cup wine (like sherry, marsala, or port)
- ½ cup chicken broth
- 2 teaspoons Spanish smoked paprika
- Salt and black pepper, to taste
- Fresh parsley, chopped, for garnish

Preparation:
1. Coat the chicken evenly with the smoked paprika, then refrigerate overnight.
2. Heat the oil in a large skillet over medium heat. Sear the chicken for five minutes until browned but not cooked through.
3. Add the smashed garlic and cook until fragrant and slightly browned.
4. Season with salt and pepper to taste.
5. Add the rest of the ingredients except for the parsley. Bring to a boil.
6. Let simmer until the sauce is reduced and the chicken is done (about 20 minutes).
7. Remove the bay leaves and serve.

Serving Suggestion: Garnish with the chopped parsley.
Variation Tip: You could also use breasts or legs if preferred.
Nutritional Information per Serving:
Calories 290 | Fat 8g | Sodium 368mg | Carbs 11g | Fiber 0.9g | Sugar 0.2g | Protein 28g

Chicken Liver Stew

Prep Time: 10 minutes
Cook Time: 15 minutes
Serves: 5

Ingredients:
- 1 cup brandy
- 1 pound chicken livers, rinsed
- 1 cup sherry
- Kosher salt, to taste
- ½ cup sour cream
- 3 tablespoons olive oil
- 1 tablespoon fennel, chopped
- 1 tablespoon chives, chopped
- 1 tablespoon parsley, chopped

Preparation:
1. Salt the livers, place them in a dish, cover the dish, and keep them in the refrigerator until the next day.
2. Remove the livers from the fridge and rinse the salt off.
3. Place the olive oil in a skillet.
4. Heat the oil and add the fennel and chives, stirring well. Cover the skillet and slowly cook for 7 minutes.
5. Increase the heat to high. Put in the livers, constantly stirring as you heat them for a few minutes.
6. Add the brandy quickly. Ignite it with a lit match. Cover the pan and add the sherry.
7. Add ¼ cup of the sour cream. Stir until the mixture is blended well.
8. Bring close to boiling, but don't boil.
9. Remove from the heat. Stir in the remaining sour cream.
10. Serve.

Serving Suggestion: Garnish with chopped parsley and serve with rice.
Variation Tip: Feel free to use other herbs.
Nutritional Information per Serving:
Calories 307 | Fat 19.1g | Sodium 113mg | Carbs 2g | Fiber 0.1g | Sugar 0.1g | Protein 23g

Turkey Cutlets

Prep Time: 10 minutes
Cook Time: 10 minutes
Serves: 7

Ingredients:
- 1 teaspoon chili flakes
- 2 pounds ground turkey
- 1 teaspoon salt
- 1 teaspoon ground black pepper
- 1 teaspoon fresh ginger
- ¼ cup spinach
- ¼ cup Italian parsley
- 1 tablespoon oregano
- 2 tablespoons garlic, minced
- 3 tablespoons olive oil
- 1 cup breadcrumbs

Preparation:
1. Wash the spinach and Italian parsley carefully, chop them roughly, and put them in a blender.
2. Add the oregano, minced garlic, chili flakes, salt, ground black pepper, and fresh ginger. Pulse the mixture for 3 minutes. Place the mixture in a large bowl.
3. Add the ground turkey and mix it up.
4. Make cutlets from the meat mixture and coat every cutlet in the breadcrumbs.
5. Pour the olive oil into a skillet and make it shimmer.
6. Put the cutlets into the prepared pan and cook them for 2 minutes on each side on medium heat.
7. When all the cutlets are cooked, dry them with the help of a paper towel.
8. Serve the cooked dish with garlic sauce.

Serving Suggestion: Serve with a salad.
Variation Tip: For a milder taste, omit the chili flakes.
Nutritional Information per Serving:
Calories 374 | Fat 21.2g | Sodium 588mg | Carbs 12.9g | Fiber 1.2g | Sugar 1.1g | Protein 37.9g

Honey Chicken Strips

Prep Time: 10 minutes
Cook Time: 20 minutes
Serves: 8

Ingredients:
- 1 teaspoon paprika
- 1 teaspoon chili flakes
- 3 tablespoons olive oil
- 1 teaspoon onion powder
- ½ cup flour
- 2 tablespoons honey
- 1 teaspoon thyme
- ½ teaspoon basil
- 1 teaspoon oregano
- 14 ounces chicken fillet
- 1 cup ricotta

Preparation:
1. Put the thyme, basil, oregano, paprika, chili flakes, and onion powder in a big bowl.
2. Add the flour and stir the mixture. After this, cut the chicken fillet into the strips.
3. Coat the chicken strips with the flour-herb mixture.
4. Pour the olive oil into a skillet and heat it.
5. Toss the chicken strips in the preheated oil and cook them for 10 minutes on medium heat.
6. Add the ricotta cheese and simmer the chicken for 3 minutes more.
7. Pour the honey into a separate pan and melt it.
8. Add the chicken strips to the honey and stir the dish.
9. Remove the chicken strips from the heat and leave them for 7 minutes.
10. Serve and enjoy.

Serving Suggestion: Serve with a simple salad.
Variation Tip: Substitute honey with maple syrup.
Nutritional Information per Serving:
Calories 229 | Fat 11.5g | Sodium 82mg | Carbs 12.5g | Fiber 0.5g | Sugar 4.6g | Protein 18.8g

Turkey Tomato Ragù

Prep Time: 10 Minutes
Cook Time: 30 Minutes
Serves: 4

Ingredients:
- 1 tablespoon olive oil
- 12 ounces lean ground turkey
- 3 celery stalks, chopped
- 1 sweet onion, chopped
- 1 tablespoon garlic, minced
- 1 (28-ounce) can low-sodium diced tomatoes
- 1 tablespoon fresh oregano, chopped
- 2 teaspoons fresh basil, chopped
- 8 ounces dry whole-grain linguine
- Freshly ground black pepper

Preparation:
1. In a large saucepan, heat the olive oil over medium-high heat. Brown the turkey until cooked through, about 6 minutes.
2. Add the celery, onion, and garlic and sauté until softened, about 4 minutes.
3. Stir in the tomatoes and their juices, oregano and basil, and bring the mixture to a boil. Reduce the heat to low and simmer for 15 minutes.
4. While the sauce is simmering, bring a large pot of water to a boil and cook the pasta according to package instructions until al dente. Drain.
5. Season the sauce with pepper and serve over the pasta.

Serving Suggestion: Top with mozzarella cheese and basil.
Variation Tip: Add ½ cup of dry red wine for more taste.
Nutritional Information per Serving:
Calories 432 | Fat 11g | Sodium 149mg | Carbs 61g | Fiber 4g | Sugar 9g | Protein 27g

Mozzarella Chicken Bake

Prep Time: 10 Minutes
Cook Time: 30 Minutes
Serves: 4

Ingredients:
- 1½ pounds skinless, boneless thighs, chicken thighs, cubed
- 2 garlic cloves, minced
- 1 tablespoon oregano, chopped
- 2 tablespoons olive oil
- 1 tablespoon red wine vinegar
- ½ cup canned artichokes, drained and chopped
- 1 red onion, sliced
- 1-pound whole-wheat fusilli pasta, cooked
- ½ cup canned white beans, drained and rinsed
- ½ cup parsley, chopped
- 1 cup mozzarella, shredded
- Salt and black pepper, to taste

Preparation:
1. Heat a pan with half of the oil over medium-high heat. Add the meat and brown for 5 minutes.
2. Grease a baking pan with the rest of the oil.
3. Add the browned chicken and the rest of the ingredients to the baking pan except the pasta and the mozzarella. Toss gently.
4. Top with the cooked pasta, sprinkle the mozzarella on top and bake at 425°F for 25 minutes.
5. Divide the bake between plates and serve.

Serving Suggestion: Serve with a simple salad.
Variation Tip: Chicken breasts or tenderloins are both good substitute options.
Nutritional Information per Serving:
Calories 195 | Fat 5.8g | Sodium 167mg | Carbs 12.1g | Fiber 3.4g | Sugar 2g | Protein 11.6g

Cocoa Brownies

Prep Time: 10 Minutes
Cook Time: 20 Minutes
Serves: 8
Ingredients:
- 30 ounces canned lentils, rinsed and drained
- 1 tablespoon honey
- 1 banana, peeled and chopped
- ½ teaspoon baking soda
- 4 tablespoons almond butter
- 2 tablespoons cocoa powder
- Cooking spray

Preparation:
1. Preheat the oven to 375°F.
2. In a food processor, combine the lentils with the honey and the other ingredients except for the cooking spray and pulse well.
3. Pour the mixture into a pan greased with the cooking spray, making sure to spread the mixture out evenly. Bake in the preheated oven for 20 minutes.
4. Cut the brownies and serve cold.
Serving Suggestion: Top with a scoop of your favorite ice cream.
Variation Tip: Use aluminum-free baking powder for a better taste.
Nutritional Information per Serving:
Calories 200 | Fat 4.5g | Sodium 87mg | Carbs 8.7g | Fiber 2.4g | Sugar 6.5g | Protein 4.3g

Peanut Butter Yogurt Bowl

Prep Time: 5 minutes
Serves: 4
Ingredients:
- 4 cups vanilla Greek yogurt
- 2 bananas, sliced
- ¼ cup creamy peanut butter
- ¼ cup flaxseed meal
- 1 teaspoon nutmeg

Preparation:
1. Divide the yogurt into 4 bowls and add the banana slices on top.
2. Microwave the peanut butter for 30 to 40 seconds and add it to the bananas.
3. Sprinkle the flaxseed meal over the top.
Serving Suggestion: Top with nutmeg before serving.
Variation Tip: Banana can be replaced with berries.
Nutritional Information per Serving:
Calories: 370 | Fat: 10.6g | Sat Fat: 2.2g | Carbohydrates: 47.7g | Fiber: 4.7g | Sugar: 35.8g | Protein: 22.7g

Coconut Rice Pudding

Prep Time: 10 Minutes
Cook Time: 3 Minutes
Serves: 4
Ingredients:
- ½ cup rice
- ¼ cup shredded coconut
- 3 tablespoons Swerve
- 1½ cups water
- 14 ounces coconut milk
- Pinch of salt

Preparation:
1. Spray the inside of an Instant Pot with cooking spray.
2. Add all the ingredients to its inner pot and stir well.
3. Seal the pot with the lid and cook on High for 3 minutes.
4. Once done, allow to release the pressure naturally for 10 minutes. Then release the remaining pressure using quick release.
5. Remove the lid.
6. Serve and enjoy.
Serving Suggestion: Serve with a sprinkling of cinnamon powder over the top.
Variation Tip: Add cardamom for more flavor.
Nutritional Information per Serving:
Calories 302 | Fat 23.5g | Sodium 57mg | Carbs 33.3g | Fiber 0.8g | Sugar 11.6g | Protein 3.8g

Strawberry Popsicles

Prep Time: 10 minutes (plus 4 hours for freezing)
Serves: 8
Ingredients:
- 2½ cups strawberries
- ½ cup almond milk

Preparation:
1. Wash the strawberries with cold water and remove their hulls.
2. Blend the strawberries and almond milk in a food processor until smooth.
3. Place the mixture into molds with sticks and let them freeze for 4 hours.

Serving Suggestion: Serve with low-fat yogurt.
Variation Tip: Almond milk can be replaced with any milk.
Nutritional Information per Serving:
Calories: 56 | Fat: 4.6g | Sat Fat: 4g | Carbohydrates: 3.9g | Fiber: 1.2g | Sugar: 2.5g | Protein: 0.7g

Vanilla Custard

Prep Time: 10 Minutes
Cook Time: 20 Minutes
Serves: 4
Ingredients:
- 1 tablespoon corn flour
- ⅓ cup sugar
- 1 vanilla bean
- 1 cup milk
- 4 egg yolks
- 1 cup cream

Preparation:
1. Cook the vanilla, milk, and cream in a saucepan over medium heat, stirring continuously.
2. Whisk the eggs in a large bowl. Add the sugar and corn flour. Mix well.
3. Add the egg mixture to the saucepan.
4. Cook until the required thickness is achieved, stirring continuously.
5. Serve.

Serving Suggestion: Serve with chopped fruits of your choice.
Variation Tip: You can replace corn flour with plain flour.
Nutritional Information per Serving:
Calories 272 | Fat 16g | Sodium 84mg | Carbs 24g | Fiber 0g | Sugar 20.9g | Protein 6g

Chocolate Mousse

Prep Time: 5 minutes (plus 2 hours for chilling)
Serves: 4
Ingredients:
- ¾ cup milk
- 3.5 ounces dark chocolate, grated
- 2 cups Greek yogurt
- 1 tablespoon honey
- ½ teaspoon vanilla extract

Preparation:
1. Put the milk and chocolate into a saucepan and gently heat until the chocolate has melted.
2. Wait for it to start to boil, then add the honey and vanilla extract and stir well.
3. Pour the chocolate mixture over the Greek yogurt in a bowl.
4. Thoroughly combine all the ingredients before transferring to individual bowls or glasses.
5. Refrigerate for at least 2 hours.
6. The chocolate mousse can be stored in the refrigerator for up to 2 days.

Serving Suggestion: Top with Greek yogurt and some raspberries before serving.
Variation Tip: Honey can be replaced with dry berries.
Nutritional Information per Serving:
Calories: 328 | Fat: 18.2g | Sat Fat: 9.8g | Carbohydrates: 25.4g | Fiber: 2g | Sugar: 21.6g | Protein: 15.8g

Peach Sorbet

Prep Time: 10 Minutes
Cook Time: 10 Minutes
Serves: 4
Ingredients:
- 2 pounds peaches, pitted and quartered
- 2 cups apple juice
- 1 cup stevia
- 2 tablespoons lemon zest, grated

Preparation:
1. Heat a pan over medium heat, add the apple juice and the rest of the ingredients, and simmer for 10 minutes.
2. Transfer to a blender and pulse.
3. Divide the mixture into cups and keep in the freezer for 2 hours before serving.
Serving Suggestion: Garnish with peach slices and mint leaves.
Variation Tip: Add a tablespoon of lemon juice for a tangier taste.
Nutritional Information per Serving:
Calories 182 | Fat 5.4g | Sodium 50mg | Carbs 12g | Fiber 3.4g | Sugar 29.2g | Protein 5.4g

Olive Oil Brownies

Prep Time: 7 minutes
Cook Time: 25 minutes
Serves: 9
Ingredients:
- ¼ cup olive oil
- ¼ cup Greek yogurt
- ¾ cup sugar
- 1 teaspoon vanilla extract
- 2 eggs
- ½ cup flour
- ⅓ cup cocoa powder
- ¼ teaspoon baking powder
- ¼ teaspoon salt
- ⅓ cup walnuts, chopped

Preparation:
1. Preheat the oven to 350°F and line a baking pan with parchment paper.
2. Blend the olive oil and sugar in a blender.
3. Add the vanilla extract and mix well.
4. Add the beaten eggs, walnuts, and yogurt and mix well.
5. Blend the flour, cocoa powder, salt, and baking powder in another bowl and add them to the olive oil mixture.
6. Decant the mixture into the baking pan.
7. Bake for 25 minutes. Let it cool and cut in squares.
Serving Suggestion: Top with chocolate chips before serving.
Variation Tip: Walnuts can be replaced with any nuts.
Nutritional Information per Serving:
Calories: 150 | Fat: 8.4g | Sat Fat: 2g | Carbohydrates: 56.5g | Fiber: 3.9g | Sugar: 45.4g | Protein: 54.1g

Cherry Cream

Prep Time: 2 Hours
Cook Time: 0 Minutes
Serves: 4
Ingredients:
- 2 cups cherries, pitted and chopped
- 1 cup almond milk
- ½ cup whipping cream
- 3 eggs, whisked
- ⅓ cup stevia
- 1 teaspoon lemon juice
- ½ teaspoon vanilla extract

Preparation:
1. In a food processor, combine the cherries with the milk and the rest of the ingredients. Pulse well.
2. Divide the mixture into cups and keep them in the fridge for 2 hours before serving.
Serving Suggestion: Serve along with some cherries.
Variation Tip: You can substitute the almond milk with coconut milk.
Nutritional Information per Serving:
Calories 200 | Fat 4.5g | Sodium 61mg | Carbs 5.6g | Fiber 2.6g | Sugar 8.3g | Protein 3.4g

Stuffed Figs

Prep Time: 10 Minutes
Cook Time: 20 Minutes
Serves: 6
Ingredients:
- 20 almonds, chopped
- 2 tablespoons raw honey
- 4 ounces goat's cheese, divided
- 10 fresh figs, halved

Preparation:
1. Preheat the broiler to high.
2. Place the halved figs on a baking sheet with the cut sides up.
3. Top each with ½ teaspoon of goat's cheese and a teaspoon of almonds.
4. Broil for two to three minutes, and then allow them to cool for five minutes before drizzling with honey to serve.

Serving Suggestion: Top with some dates and mint leaves.
Variation Tip: Choose unblemished figs.
Nutritional Information per Serving:
Calories 209 | Fat 9g | Sodium 69mg | Carbs 27g | Fiber 3.6g | Sugar 21.5g | Protein 8g

Cinnamon Honey Apples

Prep Time: 10 minutes
Cook Time: 10 minutes
Serves: 6
Ingredients:
- 6 apples, peeled, cored & diced
- 1 teaspoon cinnamon
- 1 small orange juice
- ⅛ teaspoon nutmeg
- ⅓ cup honey

Directions:

1. Add apples and remaining ingredients into the saucepan and mix well and cook over medium heat.
2. Simmer for 10 minutes.
Serving Suggestion: Stir well and serve warm.
Variation Tip: Add ½ teaspoon of vanilla extract.
Nutritional Information per Serving:
Calories 181 | Fat 0.5g | Sodium 3mg | Carbs 48.1g | Fiber 5.7g | Sugar 39.9g | Protein 0.8g

Mint Strawberry Treat

Prep Time: 10 minutes
Cook Time: 50 minutes
Serves: 6
Ingredients:
- Cooking spray
- ¼ cup stevia
- 1½ cups almond flour
- 1 teaspoon baking powder
- 1 cup almond milk
- 1 egg, whisked
- 2 cups strawberries, sliced
- 1 tablespoon mint, chopped
- 1 teaspoon lime zest, grated
- ½ cup whipping cream

Preparation:
1. Preheat the oven to 350℉.
2. Whisk the egg and almond milk in a bowl.
3. Add the flour, baking powder, stevia, and grated zest. Mix well.
4. Add the whipping cream and stir for 10 more minutes.
5. Add the mint and strawberries, and lightly mix with a spoon.
6. Grease 6 ramekins with the cooking spray and evenly distribute the strawberry mixture between them. Bake for 30 minutes.
7. Let them cool, then serve.
Serving Suggestion: Top with sliced strawberries and mint leaves.
Variation Tip: Substitute stevia with a sweetener of your choice.
Nutritional Information per Serving:
Calories 274 | Fat 9.1g | Sodium 48mg | Carbs 41g | Fiber 0.9g | Sugar 3g | Protein 4.5g

Watermelon Berry Popsicles

Prep Time: 5 minutes
Cook Time: 5 minutes
Serves: 10
Ingredients:
- 3 ½ cups watermelon cubed
- ½ cup Greek yogurt
- ½ cup strawberries, sliced
- 1 ½ teaspoon lemon juice
- ½ cup raspberries

Directions:
1. Add watermelon and remaining ingredients into the blender and blend until smooth.
2. Pour blended mixture into the popsicle molds and place in refrigerator for 6 hours.
Serving Suggestion: Serve chilled and enjoy.
Variation Tip: You can also add lime juice instead of lemon juice.
Nutritional Information per Serving:
Calories 28 | Fat 0.3g | Sodium 4mg | Carbs 5.4g | Fiber 0.7g | Sugar 4g | Protein 1.4g

Strawberry and Yogurt Muffins

Prep Time: 20 minutes
Cook Time: 20 minutes
Serves: 5
Ingredients:
- 1 teaspoon balsamic vinegar
- ¾ cup fresh strawberries, hulled and chopped roughly
- 1 teaspoon white sugar
- ¾ cup whole-wheat flour
- ½ tablespoon baking powder
- ¼ teaspoon salt
- 4 tablespoons olive oil
- ¾ cup low-fat Greek yogurt
- ¼ teaspoon almond extract
- Pinch of black pepper
- ¾ cup all-purpose flour
- ¼ teaspoon baking soda
- ¼ cup brown sugar
- 1 egg
- 1 teaspoon vanilla extract

Preparation:
1. Preheat the oven to 390°F and line a muffin tin.
2. Mix the strawberries, white sugar, vinegar, and black pepper in a glass bowl.
3. Cover the bowl and set it aside for one hour.
4. Add the flours, baking soda, baking powder, and salt to a large bowl and blend well with a wire whisk.
5. In another bowl, mix the brown sugar thoroughly with the olive oil and egg until well combined.
6. Stir in the yogurt, almond extract, and vanilla extract.
7. Blend the yogurt mixture into the flour mixture and then gently fold in the strawberries.
8. Place the mixture evenly into the prepared cups in the muffin tin.
9. Bake for 20 minutes.
10. Allow to slightly cool on a wire rack and then invert the muffins onto a serving platter.
Serving Suggestion: Serve topped with additional strawberries.
Variation Tip: Cinnamon can also be added.
Nutritional Information per Serving:
Calories: 308 | Fat: 13.1g | Sat Fat: 2.4g | Carbohydrates: 40.2g | Fiber: 1.5g | Sugar: 10.3g | Protein: 8.2g

Berry Yogurt

Prep Time: 5 minutes
Cook Time: 5 minutes
Serves: 4
Ingredients:
- 1 ½ cups blueberries
- 1 ½ cups blackberries
- 1 teaspoon lime juice
- 1 cup Greek yogurt
- 1 tablespoon honey
- ⅛ teaspoon salt

Directions:
1. Add berries, yogurt, honey, lime juice and salt into the blender and blend until smooth.
2. Cover and place in refrigerator for 2 hours.
Serving Suggestion: Serve chilled and enjoy.
Variation Tip: Add lemon juice instead of lime juice.
Nutritional Information per Serving:
Calories 111 | Fat 1.5g | Sodium 91mg | Carbs 20.3g | Fiber 4.2g | Sugar 14.6g | Protein 6.3g

Silky Chocolate Mousse

Prep Time: 5 minutes
Cook Time: 5 minutes
Serves: 4
Ingredients:
- 2 avocados, scoop out the flesh
- 1 tablespoon unsweetened almond milk
- ½ teaspoon vanilla
- 3 ½ tablespoons honey
- 3 tablespoons cocoa powder

Directions:
3. Add avocado flesh and remaining ingredients into the blender and blend until smooth.
4. Divide mousse into the four serving bowls and place in refrigerator for 15 minutes.
Serving Suggestion: Serve chilled and enjoy.
Variation tip: You can also add coconut milk instead of almond milk.
Nutritional Information per Serving:
Calories 272 | Fat 20.2g | Sodium 10mg | Carbs 26.1g | Fiber 8g | Sugar 15.7g | Protein 2.7g

Strawberry Crunch

Prep Time: 10 minutes
Cook Time: 55 minutes
Serves: 18
Ingredients:
- 1 cup white sugar
- 3 tablespoons all-purpose flour

- 3 cups fresh strawberries, sliced
- 3 cups rhubarb, cubed

For the crumble
- 1½ cups flour
- 1 cup packed brown sugar
- 1 cup cashew butter
- 1 cup oatmeal

Preparation:
1. Preheat the oven to 375°F
2. Mix the rhubarb, 3 tablespoons of flour, white sugar, and strawberries in a medium bowl. Put the mixture in a baking dish.
3. In another bowl, mix 1½ cups of flour, brown sugar, butter, and oats until a crumbly texture is obtained.
4. Evenly place the mixture over the fruit mixture in the baking dish.
5. Bake for 45 minutes or until crispy and light brown.
Serving Suggestion: Garnish with mint leaves.
Variation Tip: Substitute strawberries with blueberries or raspberries.
Nutritional Information per Serving:
Calories 253 | Fat 10.8g | Sodium 178mg | Carbs 38.1g | Fiber 12g | Sugar 8g | Protein 2.3g

Cinnamon Honey Baby Carrots

Prep Time: 10 minutes
Cook Time: 20 minutes
Serves: 4
Ingredients:
- 1 pound baby carrots
- 1 teaspoon cinnamon
- 1 tablespoon honey
- 1 tablespoon olive oil

Directions:
1. In a bowl, toss carrots with honey, cinnamon and oil.
2. Add carrots into the air fryer basket.
3. Cook at 375° F for 20 minutes. Turn halfway through.
Serving Suggestion: Allow to cool completely then serve.
Variation Tip: You can also add maple syrup instead of honey.
Nutritional Information per Serving:
Calories 87 | Fat 3.7g | Sodium 89mg | Carbs 14.1g | Fiber 3.6g | Sugar 9.7g | Protein 0.8g

Pomegranate Granita

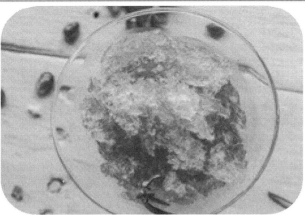

Prep Time: 4 hours 10 minutes
Cook Time: 0 minutes
Serves: 2
Ingredients:
- 4 cups pure pomegranate juice (no sugar added)
- ¼ cup honey
- ¼ teaspoon ground cinnamon
- Pinch of sea salt

Preparation:
1. Whisk the pomegranate juice, honey, cinnamon, and salt in a medium bowl until well blended.
2. Pour the pomegranate mixture into a 9-inch x 13-inch x 3-inch metal baking dish.
3. Freeze the mixture for at least 4 hours, scraping the surface with a fork every 30 minutes or so until the mixture looks like colored snow.
4. Store the granita in the freezer in a sealed container for up to 2 weeks, scraping with a fork when you want to serve it.

Serving Suggestion: Garnish with fresh rosemary.
Variation Tip: You can make granita with almost any type of juice or puréed fruit. Adjust the honey to suit the sweetness of whatever fruit you try in this recipe.
Nutritional Information per Serving:
Calories 205 | Fat 0g | Sodium 119mg | Carbs 56g | Fiber 0g | Sugar 54g | Protein 0g

Minty Coconut Cream

Prep Time: 10 minutes
Cook Time: 0 minutes
Serves: 2
Ingredients:
- 1 banana, peeled
- 1½ cups coconut flesh, shredded
- 2 tablespoons mint, chopped
- 1½ cups coconut water
- 2 tablespoons stevia

- ½ avocado, pitted and chopped

Preparation:
1. In a blender, pulse the coconut with the banana.
2. Add the rest of the ingredients, and pulse well.
3. Divide into cups and serve cold.

Serving Suggestion: Garnish with mint leaves.
Variation Tip: Substitute stevia with a sweetener of your choice.
Nutritional Information per Serving:
Calories 193 | Fat 5.4g | Sodium 121mg | Carbs 7.6g | Fiber 3.4g | Sugar 15.4g | Protein 3g

Nutty Cranberry Biscotti

Prep Time: 10 minutes
Cook Time: 1 hour
Serves: 4
Ingredients:
- ¼ cup olive oil
- ¾ cup white sugar
- 2 teaspoons vanilla extract
- ½ teaspoon almond extract
- 2 eggs
- 1¾ cups all-purpose flour
- ¼ teaspoon salt
- 1 teaspoon baking powder
- ½ cup dried cranberries
- 1½ cups pistachio nuts

Preparation:
1. Preheat the oven to 300℉.
2. Mix the olive oil and sugar thoroughly in a bowl.
3. Add the eggs and extracts, and stir well.
4. Add the baking powder, salt, and flour, and combine well.
5. Add the cranberries and nuts, mixing well to combine.
6. Divide the mixture in half. Form two 12-inch x 2-inch logs and place them on a parchment-lined baking sheet.
7. Put in the oven and bake for 35 minutes or until the blocks are golden brown.
8. Remove from the oven and allow to cool for about 10 minutes.
9. Set the oven to 275℉
10. Cut the blocks into ¾-inch-thick slices and place the slices back on the baking sheet.
11. Bake for 10 minutes or until dry.
12. Serve hot or cold.

Serving Suggestion: Top with your favorite berries.
Variation Tip: Substitute all-purpose flour with almond flour.
Nutritional Information per Serving:
Calories 92 | Fat 4.3g | Sodium 55mg | Carbs 11.7g | Fiber 2g | Sugar 3g | Protein 2.1g

Watermelon Cream

Prep Time: 10 minutes
Cook Time: 0 minutes
Serves: 2

Ingredients:
- 1-pound watermelon, peeled and chopped
- 1 teaspoon vanilla extract
- 1 cup heavy cream
- 1 teaspoon lime juice
- 2 tablespoons stevia

Preparation:
1. In a blender, combine the watermelon with the cream and the rest of the ingredients, pulse well.
2. Divide the mixture into cups and keep them in the refrigerator for 15 minutes before serving.
Serving Suggestion: Garnish with mint leaves.
Variation Tip: Feel free to use a sweetener of your choice.
Nutritional Information per Serving:
Calories 122 | Fat 5.7g | Sodium 26mg | Carbs 5.3g | Fiber 3.2g | Sugar 14.6g | Protein 0.4g

Cheesy Coconut Balls

Prep Time: 10 minutes
Cook Time: 6 minutes
Serves: 4

Ingredients:
- 4 eggs
- ¼ cup olive oil
- ¼ teaspoon salt
- ⅓ cup coconut flour
- ¼ cup coconut flakes
- ½ teaspoon xanthan gum
- ¼ teaspoon baking powder
- 2 teaspoons garlic powder
- ¼ teaspoon onion powder
- ½ cup Gruyère cheese, grated
Preparation:

1. Preheat the oven to 350°F.
2. Line a baking sheet with parchment paper.
3. Pulse the eggs, olive oil, and salt until smooth in a food processor.
4. Add the coconut flour, coconut flakes, xanthan gum, baking, garlic, onion powder, and cheese; continue to pulse until smooth.
5. Mold 12 balls out of the mixture and arrange them on the baking sheet at 2-inch intervals.
6. Bake for 25 minutes or until the balls are golden brown.
Serving Suggestion: Serve with your favorite dip.
Variation Tip: Substitute coconut flour with almond flour.
Nutritional Information per Serving:
Calories 295 | Fat 24g | Sodium 282mg | Carbs 10.4g | Fiber 5.9g | Sugar 1.1g | Protein 11.3g

Avocado Mousse

Prep Time: 10 minutes
Cook Time: 10 minutes
Serves: 7

Ingredients:
- 2 avocados, peeled, cored, and mashed
- 3 tablespoons erythritol
- ⅓ cup heavy cream
- 1 teaspoon almond butter
- 1 teaspoon vanilla extract
- 1 teaspoon cocoa powder

Preparation:
1. Mix up the avocado with erythritol until smooth.
2. Place the butter in a saucepan and allow it to melt.
3. Add the mashed avocado mixture and cocoa powder, then stir well.
4. Sauté the mixture for 3 minutes.
5. Meanwhile, whisk the heavy cream at high speed for 2 minutes. Transfer the cooked avocado mash to the bowl and chill in ice water.
6. Add the whisked heavy cream and vanilla extract when the avocado mash reaches room temperature. Stir gently.
7. Transfer the mousse into small cups and chill for 4 hours in the fridge.
Serving Suggestion: Garnish with mint leaves.
Variation Tip: Use a sweetener of your liking.
Nutritional Information per Serving:
Calories 50 | Fat 4.7g | Sodium 2mg | Carbs 6g | Fiber 0.6g | Sugar 4.5g | Protein 1g

Banana Chocolate Squares

Prep Time: 10 minutes
Cook Time: 30 minutes
Serves: 24

Ingredients:
- ²/₃ cup white sugar
- ¾ cup cashew butter
- ²/₃ cup brown sugar
- 1 egg, beaten
- 1 teaspoon vanilla extract
- 1 cup banana puree
- 1¾ cups flour
- 2 teaspoons baking powder
- ½ teaspoon salt
- 1 cup semi-sweet chocolate chips
- ½ cup almonds, chopped

Preparation:
1. Preheat the oven to 350°F
2. In a bowl, add the sugars and butter and beat until lightly colored.
3. Add the egg, banana puree, and vanilla, then stir well
4. Mix the baking powder, flour, almonds, and salt in another bowl. Add this mixture to the butter mixture.
5. Stir in the chocolate chips.
6. Prepare a baking pan and place the mixture in it.
7. Bake for 20 minutes.
8. Let it cool for 5 minutes before slicing into equal-size squares.

Serving Suggestion: Serve with a hot beverage.
Variation Tip: Substitute almonds with pecans.
Nutritional Information per Serving:
Calories 174 | Fat 8.2g | Sodium 125mg | Carbs 25.2g | Fiber 11g | Sugar 5g | Protein 1.7g

Almond Bites

Prep Time: 10 minutes
Cook Time: 14 minutes
Serves: 5

Ingredients:
- 1 cup almond flour
- ¼ cup almond milk
- 1 egg, whisked
- 2 tablespoons almond butter
- 1 tablespoon coconut flakes
- ½ teaspoon baking powder
- ½ teaspoon apple cider vinegar
- ½ teaspoon vanilla extract

Preparation:
1. Mix the whisked egg, almond milk, apple cider vinegar, baking powder, vanilla extract, and butter.
2. Add the almond flour and coconut flakes, then knead the dough. If the dough is sticky, add more almond flour.
3. Make medium-sized balls from the dough and place them on the rack of an air fryer.
4. Press them gently with the palm of your hand. Lower the air fryer lid and cook the dessert for 12 minutes at 360°F.
5. Check if cooked; cook for 2 minutes more for a crunchier crust.

Serving Suggestion: Serve with a hot beverage of your choice.
Variation Tip: Switch up almond flour with coconut flour.
Nutritional Information per Serving:
Calories 118 | Fat 10.6g | Sodium 19mg | Carbs 3.6g | Fiber 1.6g | Sugar 1.1g | Protein 4.1g

Chia Seed Pudding

Prep Time: 12 hours 5 minutes
Cook Time: 0 minutes
Serves: 4

Ingredients:
- ½ cup chia seeds
- 1½ cups rice milk
- 1 teaspoon vanilla extract
- ¼ teaspoon cinnamon
- ¼ cup maple syrup

Preparation:
1. Add the above-listed ingredients in a bowl or a mason jar and mix well! Make sure the chia seeds don't stick to the container sides.
2. Cover the mixture and refrigerate overnight.

Serving Suggestion: Top with berries and mint leaves.
Variation Tip: You can also add fruit before serving.
Nutritional Information per Serving:
Calories 164 | Fat 6.2g | Sodium 37mg | Carbs 30.2g | Fiber 6.2g | Sugar 11.9g | Protein 3.1g

Sweet Rice Pudding

Prep Time: 10 minutes
Cook Time: 50 minutes
Serves: 5

Ingredients:
- 2 cups water
- ¼ teaspoon salt
- 1 cup Arborio rice (sticky Italian rice), uncooked
- 1 stick cinnamon
- Rind of 1 lemon, in large pieces
- ¼ cup almond butter, divided
- 4¼ cups whole milk and about ¼ extra for egg yolks (if using)
- 3 egg yolks, beaten (optional)
- Vanilla extract (optional)

Preparation:
1. In a saucepan, combine the water and salt. Bring to a boil and then stir in the rice.
2. Reduce the heat to medium-low and simmer, stirring continuously, until the rice has absorbed almost all the water (about 20 minutes). Don't let it dry up completely so as not to burn it.
3. Add the cinnamon, lemon rind, half the butter, and the milk. Adjust the heat to medium-high. With continuous stirring, bring to a boil again and then reduce to a simmer.
4. Check for any rice that may have stuck to the bottom of the pan. Cook for 20 minutes.
5. Add the remaining butter and continue stirring while simmering for 10 more minutes. If using egg yolks (for a richer pudding), beat them well in a small bowl with the extra milk.
6. Pour this into the mixture gradually, mixing well after each addition. Cook a little longer to cook the yolks and thicken the mix further. Stir in vanilla (optional). Remove from the heat.
7. Discard the cinnamon stick and lemon rind. Pour into serving containers.

Serving Suggestion: Sprinkle cinnamon powder on top.

Variation Tip: May be served chilled or at room temperature.

Nutritional Information per Serving:
Calories 392 | Fat 10.5g | Sodium 215mg | Carbs 43.4g | Fiber 2.9g | Sugar 11.9g | Protein 11.5g

Cherry and Mint Sorbet

Prep Time: 3 hours 10 minutes
Cook Time: 0 minutes
Serves: 2

Ingredients:
- ½ cup maple syrup
- 2 cups cherries
- ¼ cup mint leaves
- 2 teaspoons lemon juice
- ¼ cup water
- ¼ cup coconut milk
- ⅛ teaspoon salt

Preparation:
1. Place the above-listed ingredients into a blender.
2. First blend on low and then at high speed to a thick and smooth consistency.
3. Serve immediately or store in your freezer for 2–3 hours to firm up.

Serving Suggestion: Garnish with mint.

Variation Tip: Switch up cherries with strawberries.

Nutritional Information per Serving:
Calories 426 | Fat 15g | Sodium 149mg | Carbs 79g | Fiber 1g | Sugar 73g | Protein 2g

4-Week Diet Plan

Week 1

Day 1:
Breakfast: Tuna Lemon Avocado Salad
Lunch: Brown Rice Pilaf With Raisins
Snack: Veggie Tortilla Wraps
Dinner: Italian Chicken Meatballs
Dessert: Strawberry Popsicles

Day 2:
Breakfast: Olive Scrambled Eggs
Lunch: Simple Sautéed Cauliflower
Snack: Carrot Cake Balls
Dinner: Broiled Blackened Tilapia
Dessert: Chocolate Mousse

Day 3:
Breakfast: Cheesy Potato Frittata
Lunch: Mediterranean Sautéed Kale
Snack: Chicken Skewers
Dinner: Chili Beef Stew
Dessert: Mint Strawberry Treat

Day 4:
Breakfast: Fruity Quinoa Bowl
Lunch:
Snack: Sweet Potato Chips
Dinner: Shrimp Salad
Dessert: Chia Seed Pudding

Day 5:
Breakfast: Pumpkin Pancakes
Lunch: Chickpea Bulgur
Snack: Easy Avocado Hummus
Dinner: Marinated Grill Chicken
Dessert: Pomegranate Granita

Day 6:
Breakfast: Tahini and Feta Toast
Lunch: Baked Black-Eyed Peas
Snack: Butternut Squash Fries
Dinner: Garlic Chicken Thighs
Dessert: Silky Chocolate Mousse

Day 7:
Breakfast: Quinoa Porridge
Lunch: Greek Inspired Rice
Snack: Salmon and Celery Salad Wraps
Dinner: Grilled Squid
Dessert: Cinnamon Honey Baby Carrots

Week 2

Day 1:
Breakfast: Breakfast Chives Frittata
Lunch: Greek Chicken Gyro Salad
Snack: Grilled Veggie Sandwich
Dinner: Zesty Shrimp
Dessert: Peanut Butter Yogurt Bowl

Day 2:
Breakfast: Tuna Lemon Avocado Salad
Lunch: Spicy Zucchini
Snack: Baked Eggplant Fries
Dinner: Grilled Salmon
Dessert: Stuffed Figs

Day 3:
Breakfast: Cheesy Potato Frittata
Lunch: Pesto Brussels Sprouts
Snack: Veggie Tortilla Wraps
Dinner: Greek Tilapia
Dessert: Minty Coconut Cream

Day 4:
Breakfast: Yogurt with Berries and Nuts
Lunch: Ratatouille
Snack: Chicken and Veggie Flatbread Pizza
Dinner: Grilled Squid
Dessert: Almond Bites

Day 5:
Breakfast: Coconut Pumpkin Soup
Lunch: Greek Chicken Gyro Salad
Snack: Chickpeas and Veggie Gazpacho
Dinner: Shrimp Stir Fry
Dessert: Nutty Cranberry Biscotti

Day 6:
Breakfast: Veggies and Egg Scramble
Lunch: Asparagus Stir-Fry
Snack: Chicken Skewers
Dinner: Cod and Brussels Sprouts
Dessert: Watermelon Berry Popsicles

Day 7:
Breakfast: Spinach and Egg Scramble
Lunch: Cucumber and Tomato Salad
Snack: Carrot Cake Balls
Dinner: Herb-Crusted Halibut
Dessert: Banana Chocolate Squares

Week 3

Day 1:
Breakfast: Cheesy Potato Frittata
Lunch: Pumpkin Cauliflower Curry
Snack: Sautéed Apricots
Dinner: Almond-Crusted Tilapia
Dessert: Silky Chocolate Mousse

Day 2:
Breakfast: Shakshuka
Lunch: Zucchini Feta Fritters
Snack: Baked Italian Fries
Dinner: Beef and Prune Stew
Dessert: Mint Strawberry Treat

Day 3:
Breakfast: Cherry Oats Bowl
Lunch: Chickpea Stew
Snack: Spicy Deviled Eggs
Dinner: Feta Turkey Meatballs
Dessert: Sweet Rice Pudding

Day 4:
Breakfast: Oat and Berry Parfait
Lunch: Chickpeas With Garlic and Parsley
Snack: Butternut Squash Fries
Dinner: Grilled Harissa Chicken
Dessert: Minty Coconut Cream

Day 5:
Breakfast: Eggs Florentine
Lunch: Greek Avocado Salad
Snack: Easy Avocado Hummus
Dinner: Clams Toscano
Dessert: Pomegranate Granita

Day 6:
Breakfast: Breakfast Berry Oats
Lunch: Zucchini Avocado Carpaccio
Snack: Parsley Nachos
Dinner: Halibut With Kale
Dessert: Mint Strawberry Treat

Day 7:
Breakfast: Tahini and Feta Toast
Lunch: Spinach Pesto Pasta
Snack: Baked Italian Fries
Dinner: Buttered Thyme Scallops
Dessert: Cinnamon Honey Apples

Week 4

Day 1:
Breakfast: Chicken Spinach Soup
Lunch: Cucumber and Tomato Salad
Snack: Sautéed Apricots
Dinner: Grilled Swordfish
Dessert: Peanut Butter Yogurt Bowl

Day 2:
Breakfast: Veggies and Egg Scramble
Lunch: Zucchini Feta Fritters
Snack: Cauliflower Fritters
Dinner: Shrimp Salad
Dessert: Vanilla Custard

Day 3:
Breakfast: Artichoke Casserole
Lunch: Mediterranean White Beans
Snack: Salmon and Celery Salad Wraps
Dinner: Easy Beef Bourguignon
Dessert: Pomegranate Granita

Day 4:
Breakfast: Quinoa Porridge
Lunch: Tomato Lentil Bowl
Snack: Peanut Butter Balls
Dinner: Garlic Chicken Thighs
Dessert: Coconut Rice Pudding

Day 5:
Breakfast: Yogurt with Berries and Nuts
Lunch: Cauliflower Rice
Snack: Parsley Nachos
Dinner: Almond-Crusted Tilapia
Dessert: Peach Sorbet

Day 6:
Breakfast: Broccoli Tart
Lunch: Pumpkin Cauliflower Curry
Snack: Carrot Cake Balls
Dinner: Grill Lemon Chicken
Dessert: Mint Strawberry Treat

Day 7:
Breakfast: Creamy Millet
Lunch: Mashed Fava Beans
Snack: Zucchini Fritters
Dinner: Grilled Harissa Chicken
Dessert: Minty Coconut Cream

Conclusion

The Mediterranean diet is one of the famous and healthiest diets. This diet is pretty simple. Few foods are restricted in this diet. You can enjoy most types of foods in this diet. A lot of researchers and health experts recommend this diet. In this diet, you should follow the principles of the Mediterranean diet. There are a lot of health benefits of this diet. In this diet, you should eat a lot of vegetables, fruits, nuts, seeds, whole grains, a moderate amount of seafood, poultry, cheese, yogurt, and consume red meat in very few amounts. In this cookbook, you will get delicious, healthy, and satisfying Mediterranean diet ideas and recipes. This diet consists of healthy nutrients such as fats, proteins, vitamins, carbohydrates, and many more. This diet consists of healthy foods only. I am sure you will love this cookbook. Thank you for purchasing it.

Appendix 1 Measurement Conversion Chart

VOLUME EQUIVALENTS(DRY)

US STANDARD	METRIC (APPROXIMATE)
1/8 teaspoon	0.5 mL
1/4 teaspoon	1 mL
1/2 teaspoon	2 mL
3/4 teaspoon	4 mL
1 teaspoon	5 mL
1 tablespoon	15 mL
1/4 cup	59 mL
1/2 cup	118 mL
3/4 cup	177 mL
1 cup	235 mL
2 cups	475 mL
3 cups	700 mL
4 cups	1 L

WEIGHT EQUIVALENTS

US STANDARD	METRIC (APPROXIMATE)
1 ounce	28 g
2 ounces	57 g
5 ounces	142 g
10 ounces	284 g
15 ounces	425 g
16 ounces (1 pound)	455 g
1.5 pounds	680 g
2 pounds	907 g

VOLUME EQUIVALENTS(LIQUID)

US STANDARD	US STANDARD (OUNCES)	METRIC (APPROXIMATE)
2 tablespoons	1 fl.oz.	30 mL
1/4 cup	2 fl.oz.	60 mL
1/2 cup	4 fl.oz.	120 mL
1 cup	8 fl.oz.	240 mL
1 1/2 cup	12 fl.oz.	355 mL
2 cups or 1 pint	16 fl.oz.	475 mL
4 cups or 1 quart	32 fl.oz.	1 L
1 gallon	128 fl.oz.	4 L

TEMPERATURES EQUIVALENTS

FAHRENHEIT(F)	CELSIUS(C) (APPROXIMATE)
225 °F	107 °C
250 °F	120 °C
275 °F	135 °C
300 °F	150 °C
325 °F	160 °C
350 °F	180 °C
375 °F	190 °C
400 °F	205 °C
425 °F	220 °C
450 °F	235 °C
475 °F	245 °C
500 °F	260 °C

Appendix 2 Recipes Index

Made in the USA
Coppell, TX
10 March 2022

74790544R00092